D1512127

YOUR CREATIVE POWER

YOUR
CREATIVE POWER

How to Use Imagination

BY

ALEX OSBORN

CHARLES SCRIBNER'S SONS, NEW YORK
CHARLES SCRIBNER'S SONS, Ltd., LONDON

1949

COPYRIGHT, 1948, BY
ALEX F. OSBORN

Printed in the United States of America

*All rights reserved. No part of this book
may be reproduced in any form without
the permission of Charles Scribner's Sons.*

*Since this page cannot accommodate all
the copyright notices, the opposite page
constitutes an extension of the copyright
page.*

COPYRIGHT SOURCES QUOTED

Bennett, Arnold, *How to Live on Twenty-four Hours a Day,* Doubleday & Co., New York, 1939.

Boraas, Julius, *Teaching to Think,* The Macmillan Co., New York, 1922.

Brande, Dorothea, *Wake Up and Live,* Simon and Schuster, New York, 1936.

Carnegie, Dale, *Biographical Roundup,* Greenberg Inc., New York, 1944.

Carrel, Alexis, *Man, the Unknown,* Harper & Bros., New York, 1935.

Chase, Stuart, *The Tyranny of Words,* Harcourt, Brace & Co., New York, 1938.

Conant, James B., *On Understanding Science,* Yale University Press, New Haven, 1947.

Cowling, Donald, and Carter Davidson, *Colleges for Freedom,* Harper & Bros., New York, 1947.

Crawford, Robert P., *Think for Yourself,* McGraw-Hill Inc., New York, 1937.

Curtis and Greenslet, *Practical Cogitator,* Houghton Mifflin Co., New York, 1945.

de Kruif, Paul, *The Microbe Hunters,* Harcourt, Brace & Co., New York, 1926.

Dewey, John, *How We Think,* D. C. Heath Co., Boston, 1910.

Dimnet, Ernest, *The Art of Thinking,* Simon and Schuster, New York, 1929.

Ferber, Edna, *A Peculiar Treasure,* Doubleday & Co., New York, 1939.

Fosdick, Harry Emerson, *On Being a Real Person,* Harper & Bros., New York, 1943.

Fryer and Henry, *An Outline of General Psychology,* Barnes and Noble, New York, 1936.

iv

Greenslet, Ferris, *The Lowells and Their Seven Worlds*, Houghton Mifflin Co., Boston, 1946.

Hahn, Arnold, *Use Your Mind*, Henry Holt & Co., New York, 1931.

Hammond, John Winthrop, *Men and Volts*, J. P. Lippincott Co., New York, 1941.

Hepner, Harry W., *Psychology Applied to Life and Work*, Prentice-Hall, Inc., New York, 1941.

Jackson, Josephine A., and Helen M. Salisbury, *Outwitting Our Nerves*, Garden City Press, Garden City, 1944.

Jastrow, Joseph, *Managing Your Mind*, Greenberg Inc., New York, 1935.

Maugham, W. Somerset, *Strictly Personal*, Doubleday & Co., New York, 1941.

McClure, Matthew Thompson, *How to Think in Business*, McGraw-Hill Inc., New York, 1923.

Musselman, Morris McNeil, *Wheels in His Head*, McGraw-Hill Inc., New York, 1945.

O'Connor, Johnson, *Ideaphoria*, Human Engineering Laboratory, Boston, 1945.

Overstreet, Harry Allen, *Let Me Think*, The Macmillan Co., New York, 1940.

Peale, Norman Vincent, *A Guide to Confident Living*, Prentice-Hall Inc., New York, 1948.

Roberts, Richard, *The Spirit of God and the Faith of Today*, Willett Clark & Co., Chicago, 1930.

Robinson, James Harvey, *Mind in the Making*, Harper & Bros., New York, 1939.

Sadleir, Michael, *Trollope, A Commentary*, Houghton Mifflin Co., Boston, 1927.

Schnackel, H. G., *The Art of Business Thinking*, J. Wiley & Sons Inc., New York, 1930.

Spearman, C., *Creative Mind*, D. Appleton & Co., New York, 1931.

Thomas, Lowell, *How to Keep Mentally Fit*, Howell, Soskin Inc., New York, 1940.

Vaughan, Wayland, *General Psychology*, Odyssey Press, New York, 1936.

Wallas, Graham, *The Art of Thought*, Harcourt, Brace & Co., New York, 1926.

Wiggam, Albert Edward, *The Marks of an Educated Man*, Bobbs-Merrill Co., New York, 1930.

Woollcott, Alexander, *The Story of Irving Berlin*, G. P. Putnam's Sons, New York, 1925.

This book is dedicated to
BRUCE BARTON
in appreciation of our 30 years
as partners and friends . . . A. F. O.

ABOUT THE AUTHOR . . . *by Samuel Hopkins Adams*

Hamilton College graduates have the habit of keeping an attentive eye upon their fellow alumni. Thus, although he graduated eighteen years after me, I knew of Alex Osborn long before he had any inkling of my interest.

There was another Alex in that able class of 1909, Alexander Woollcott, whom I had sponsored into a newspaper job upon his graduation. Only a few years thereafter he was a notable in the newspaper and theatre worlds. About the time of his early success, we met at the home of Laurette Taylor, where one met everybody. Aleck buttonholed me:

"What do you know about my classmate Alex Osborn?"

"Nothing," I answered.

"Well, you'd better."

"Why? What am I supposed to do about this Osborn?"

"Nothing. Nobody has to do anything about him. He'll do it, himself."

"All right," I said. "I'm open to conviction. What is he doing?"

Aleck was a bit vague about that. His friend and classmate had been teacher, reporter, had taken a shot at magazine writing, had touched upon banking and a few other lines, and was something in factory management. "It isn't what he's doing; it's what he *is*," Woollcott insisted.

When the subject next came up between us, Alex Osborn was well on his way to becoming head of the great advertising firm of Batten, Barton, Durstine and Osborn, and I had come to know and admire him personally as one of the most versatile, vigorous, and provocative minds among my wide range of acquaintances. His classmate recalled to me our conversation of years before.

"What do you think of Osborn now?" he demanded with rather the air of having patented, or, at least, invented him.

"You were right," I admitted.

"I am always right," said Aleck Woollcott blandly.

Whether or not that statement is debatable, there is no question as to Alex Osborn. In his chosen profession of advertising, as financier, as educator (he has served for seven years as a trustee of his alma mater), as leader in charitable and civic movements, as author of several books, as amateur artist, and, more than all else, as what may be termed an applied thinker, he has more than justified not only the Woollcott prophecy, but the hopes and expectations of an army of friends.

SAMUEL HOPKINS ADAMS

ABOUT THE BOOK . . . *by Alex Osborn*

Ten years ago, the editor of a leading magazine invited me to lunch. I had been one of his contributors, but we had never met. He broke the ice by asking, "What is your hobby, Mr. Osborn?"

"Imagination," I replied. He paused, then wrote on the back of an envelope, "MY HOBBY IS IMAGINATION."

"Mr. Osborn," he said, "you must do a book on that. It's a job that has been waiting to be done all these years. There is no subject of greater importance. You must give it the time and energy and thoroughness it deserves." That remark started this book.

Although I earned my master's degree in practical psychology and have devoted most of my life to the psychology of advertising, I cannot claim to be a psychologist. Nor have I tried to write as a psychologist. I have felt free to take figurative liberties with academic concepts. For instance, I realize that imagination is an integral part of man's mind-body function; and yet, for the sake of clarity and readability, I refer to imagination as if it were an entity of itself.

My frequent use of the term "brainstorm" may bother the reader at first. Although Chapter 33 will fully explain, an inkling of its meaning may be helpful here: "Brainstorm" is used mainly to label the kind of conference where a few people sit down together for an hour or so solely to use their creative imaginations—solely to suggest ideas on a specific subject, right then and there.

During the past ten years, in quest of material and insight, I have interviewed hundreds of people and have read hundreds of books, speeches and articles. I am indebted to all who talked with me and to all whose writings I read. Many of their names will be found in the index.

My especial thanks go to those whose books were most

helpful, and this list includes: Julius Boraas (*Teaching to Think*), Alexis Carrel (*Man the Unknown*), James B. Conant (*On Understanding Science*), Robert P. Crawford (*Think for Yourself*), Paul de Kruif (*The Microbe Hunters*), John Dewey (*How We Think*), Ernest Dimnet (*The Art of Thinking*), William H. Easton (*Creative Thinking*), Joseph Jastrow (*Effective Thinking*), T. Sharper Knowlson (*Originality*), Matthew Thompson McClure (*How to Think in Business*), Johnson O'Connor (*Ideaphoria*), Harry Allen Overstreet (*Let Me Think*), James Harvey Robinson (*Mind in the Making*), C. Spearman (*Creative Mind*), Graham Wallas (*The Art of Thought*), and almost all authors of psychology text-books, especially: J. F. Dashiell, Floyd C. Dockeray, Fryer and Henry, A. T. Poffenberger and F. Wayland Vaughan.

ALEX F. OSBORN

CONTENTS

xiv

YOUR CREATIVE POWER

Chapter I

THE LAMP THAT LIT THE WORLD
CAN LIGHT YOUR LIFE

"I'M SORRY KID—YOU'RE FIRED!" Thus the ax fell on my neck one Saturday at midnight.

Jimmy Starks, managing editor of the Buffalo *Times*, had proclaimed my doom. Being a kindly man he had added, "It's a rotten break, but Norman Mack has just come back from Europe, and he says our city-room payroll is too high. So he ordered me to fire the last three men I hired."

I gulped and left for my lodging in the slums where I earned my room-rent at a settlement-house by teaching on weekday evenings. It seems a century ago, but I can still recall almost every step of my heavy-hearted trek through lonely streets lined with ghosts of warehouses and factories. To get through college, I had worked during my vacations. Even with my summer earnings, my folks had had to scrape to help me through. My pangs of shame did more to keep me from sleep that night than did the screeches of the switch-engines beneath my window. When I did doze off, I could hear the locomotives blaring at me: "What a failure!"

As I look back at that dismissal, I realize it was a normal and helpful experience, even though my 21-year-old eyes magnified it as a tragedy. Anyway, the next morning I filled a scrapbook with clippings from the Sunday *Times*. At noon I went to the Buffalo *Express* and asked the city editor for

1

a job. He wanted to know how much experience I had had. "Only three months," I said, "but won't you please look over these clippings?" He did so, for he, too, was a kindly man—Steve Evans by name.

"They are pretty amateurish," was his comment, "but Johnny Whiston, our police reporter, is sick and I will take a chance on you as his substitute for a few weeks. It's a big gamble, and I am taking it only because in each of these articles there seems to be an *idea*."

That remark of Steve Evans put an idea into my head; and that idea has grown on me ever since. No one in college or elsewhere had ever told me about the value of ideas. But here I had found that ideas were diamonds. "If ideas are that valuable," I said to myself that evening, "why don't I try to turn out more of them? If a Boy Scout can think up one good turn to do each day, why can't I think up a new idea each day?" Well, that's how I got started on making imagination my hobby.

Since my newspaper days, my work has been in advertising; and that means in ideas. Starting from scratch I became the head of an organization of about 1,000 people, many of whom were blessed with more inborn *talent* than I. Whatever creative success I gained was due to my belief that creative power can be stepped up by *effort*, and that there are ways in which we can guide our creative thinking.

Although my associates might attest that by such means I have steadily stepped up my own creative power, my claim to any right of authorship is *not* based on my creative record —but rather on my record as a *creative coach*. More than a few will testify as to how I helped them to make *more* of their imaginations. It is this experience which gives me hope that this book may be of aid to others.

2.

My faith has often been shaken during the 35 years in which I have made imagination my hobby. Too often have

I heard intelligent people sneer at would-be creators as "nutty" or "wacky"—as "crackpots," as "guys with wheels in their heads," or with "bees in their bonnets." Scholars have scoffed at ideas as being worth "a dime a dozen."

Colleges have slighted the creative mind. They have taught as much about animal psychology as about human imagination. Hardly any textbooks give creative thought more than a lick-and-a-promise. A few other books, and good books, *have* covered creative thinking. But, compared to any other subject, the literature is scant. A trained librarian, after weeks of work for me on this subject, expressed her amazement thus: "I have been in library work for 20 years. I never knew until now that less has been written about ideas than about any other subject."

The *thinking* mind is man's exclusive gift. All animals are endowed with memory, instincts and emotions, but *lack* man's *thinking* power.

Our thinking mind is mainly two-fold: (1) A *Judicial Mind* which analyzes, compares and chooses. (2) A *Creative Mind* which visualizes, foresees, and generates ideas. These two minds work best together. Judgment keeps imagination on the track. Imagination not only opens ways to action, but also can enlighten judgment.

You do much to improve your *judicial* mind. You go to school. You read history. You study logic. You learn mathematics. You debate. You deliberate. You weigh pros and cons. *But what steps do you take consciously to improve your creative mind?* Isn't it a fact that, except when forced by circumstances, most of us don't even *try* to use our creative minds? This book may well be worth your while even if all it does is to make you *more conscious of the creative power within your reach.*

3.

My faith in ideas has been bolstered in recent years by the fact that there is an ever greater recognition of imagination as mankind's greatest gift. Although this book will try mainly to show how to step up creative power to enrich one's own life, we might take a glance at what ideas have meant in the forward march of mankind. John Masefield summed this up by saying: "Man's body is faulty, his mind untrustworthy, but his imagination has made him remarkable. In some centuries, his imagination has made life on this planet an intense practice of all the lovelier energies."

"Were it not for slow, painful, and constantly discouraged *creative effort*," said J. H. Robinson, "man would be no more than a species of primate living on seeds, fruit, roots, and uncooked flesh." No one will ever know to whom we should erect monuments for such of our indispensable innovations as the use of fire. That and another creative triumph, the wheel, both came out of the Stone Age.

The main use of the wheel up until 1000 A.D. was for war chariots. Then someone had the idea of using it as a backsaver in the form of a water wheel. By the time William the Conqueror took over England, over 5,000 mills in that tiny country were driven by water power.

"It was imagination," said Victor Wagner, "that enabled man to extend his thumb by inventing the vise—to strengthen his fist and arm by inventing the hammer. Step by step, man's imagination lured, led and often pushed him to the astonishing heights of power he now so apprehensively occupies."

It was only about 500 years ago that Europe began to rate the power of thinking, and especially creative thinking, on a par with the power of brute force. This new attitude was the essence of the Renaissance.

Uncle Sam's great luck was to be the beneficiary of the world's creative upsurge. As the *New Yorker* has said, "Ideas are what this country is made of." Without doubt, our new heights in standards of living have been reached through ideas.

One new idea inherited by America from England was a new way to use fire by means of internal combustion en-

gines. This was hooked up with wheels to form the backbone of our automotive industry. Without this industry,
America's standard of living would be far lower. It, alone,
gives gainful occupation to over 7,000,000 of us. Farming
employs only 9,875,000, even including farm families as
well as hired hands.

Agricultural ideas have made far richer the rich soil of
our country. The creative genius poured into farm machinery by the McCormicks and the Deeres has helped make it
so that each farmhand can now turn out far more food than
formerly. When America was young, it took 19 farmers to
feed one city-dweller. Today 19 farmers produce enough
food for themselves and for 66 other people.

And yet, it is only recently that the *value* of imagination
has been fully recognized even in America. A few years ago,
the Chrysler Corporation started to hail imagination as "the
directing force" which "lights tomorrow's roads, explores
today for clues to tomorrow, hunts better ways for you to
live and travel." And the Aluminum Company has recently
adopted a newly coined word, "imagineering," which means,
says Alcoa, that "you let your imagination soar and then
engineer it down to earth. You think about the things you
used to make, and decide that if you don't find out some
way to make them immeasurably better, you may never be
asked by your customers to make them again."

Yes, competition has forced American business to recognize the importance of conscious creative effort. So much
so that, more and more, the heart and center of almost
every successful manufacturing company is now its creative
research. Industrial research used to do but little more than
take things apart in order to find out what caused what
and why. The new research adds to such fact-finding a
definite and conscious creative function aimed to discover
new facts, arrive at *new* combinations, find *new* applications. Thanks to thinkers like Dr. James B. Conant, imagination's importance to science is now recognized as never
before.

But, alas, the newest and most pressing problems of our nation are not so much the improvement of *things* as the solution of *people*-problems. Overshadowing all such, is our international impasse. We are applying plenty of research to this, but in the ineffective form of merely finding facts and making diagnoses. To arrive at new and good ideas which might solve the world's *people*-problems, there is *no conscious creative effort at all comparable to what industrialists are doing to better the things they make.*

Later we will show how General Eisenhower was the first to recognize the need to organize creative thinking as a distinct and separate function in our national affairs. We will see how this same principle can be applied to our international problems, and to our acute domestic problems such as labor.

4.

How true it is that, in our own private lives, Micawber-like we wait for things to turn out well, and meanwhile fail to make conscious use of our imagination—despite the fact that, in most cases, with enough creative effort, each of us could find the ideas that would smooth our rocky roads!

The Arabian Nights shows how creative thinking can turn a woman's life from tragedy to joy. King Shahriar had gone so sour on women that he married one wife after another solely to cut off her head. A Miss Scheherazade was among those forced to become the King's bride. To put off the day of her death, she thought up the scheme of telling a story to the monarch every night for 1001 nights. Her tales so fascinated the despot that he kept postponing her killing. Finally, after spinning a new yarn every night for nearly three years, Scheherazade won his love, saved her own life, and gained his kingdom for her three children.

One story Scheherazade told was about "Aladdin and His Lamp." *Our* Aladdin's lamp is the creative power which is within the reach of every man and woman.

That lamp could light the way through many a marital labyrinth. Divorce has become so common that, when forms were sent out to Harvard's Class of '32 in order to gather biographical data, lines were left to insert *two* marriages and one *divorce*. There are now about 500,000 divorces a year in the U. S. A.—twice as many as 10 years ago. In how many of these cases has the man or woman or relative or friend consciously applied *imagination* in search of ways to avoid the rocks? Psychiatrists have attempted diagnoses in many cases. Lawyers have given lots of advice, but mainly by way of judicial or critical judgment. In hardly one case out of ten has there been any conscious effort to think up the new ideas which might keep the family together.

"What's the matter with Sonny?" "I am worried about Sissy." How often we hear parents spouting like that. But how often do parents try to spout ideas that might cure the fault? Children may be pearls, as Cornelia said, but ideas can be diamonds in the hands of parents. Here's an example that might be helpful to those who seek more peace at home, with fewer brawls among the little ones. . . .

A mother, about to gather the clan for Christmas week, feared that her eight-year-old daughter and her five-year-old nephew would be in constant clash. She said to her husband, "We could ward off this bedlam if we could think up the right idea." She buckled down and came up with a plan. She closeted her daughter and her nephew. Before their wide eyes she poured 50 golden pennies into each of two glasses, saying, "This glass, Cynthia, is yours. This glass, Jackie, is yours." She explained that, for each breach of peace, a penny would be taken out of either glass or both. She promised that on New Year's Day, each might have whatever pennies were left. Then she placed the glasses on a shelf where both could watch them. Cynthia and Jackie acted like angels the whole week. A year later, when Jackie arrived for another Christmas at the old homestead, he actually asked his aunt to "put up those pennies again."

Most parents do try and try hard. Often they use their

heads to try to figure out the cause. Seldom do they put their heads together and say to each other, "Now that we know pretty well what the trouble is, let's sit down and think up what we can do to put the child back on the right track. Let's take a pad and make a list of at least 25 ideas that might work."

Isn't it too bad that most parents would feel *embarrassed* to attempt any such deliberate effort? But, here again, what we need most is a conscious appreciation of the fact that ideas have been, and can be, the solution of almost every human problem. And, here again, we all need to realize this truth: Each of us *does* have an Aladdin's lamp, and if we rub it hard enough, it can light our way to better living—just as that same lamp lit up the march of civilization.

Chapter II

CREATIVE EFFORT PAYS IN MORE
COINS THAN CASH

"THAT LITTLE IDEA OF YOURS will bring in $5,000,000 a year." Sanford Cluett would have laughed at any such forecast when he first found a way to stop cloth from shrinking. But as it turned out, the Cluett Peabody Company actually did make as much as $5,000,000 a year from royalties on Mr. Cluett's "Sanforizing" process.

Some people sneered at Henry Ford as having had "only *one* idea in all his life." Yes, but that was a big idea—how to make cars cheap enough for the millions. From that idea he gained more riches than any man, not excepting Midas. But such fabulous rewards from imagination are exceptions. They are not held out as hopes to those who read this book.

The rich rewards of writers are likewise cited solely by way of passing interest. Robert Fuoss, managing editor of the *Saturday Evening Post,* says that it is harder than ever "to find enough good fiction *at any price."* One novel can now bring in far more gold than Charles Dickens received in his whole life. It is not unusual for a one-time radio script to bring a dollar a word.

When the movies want your printed words, the extra rewards are high. Although only $50,000 was paid for the picture rights to *Gone With the Wind,* Paramount offered $450,000 for *Dear Ruth.* Even the bare plot of an unwritten novel may bring big money. Charlie Chaplin paid Konrad Bercovici $95,000 for his skeleton outline of *The Dictator*.

There is more chance than ever for the fictioneer to reap rich rewards from his ideas; but there is less and less chance for the gadgeteer to do so. The reason for this is that industries now have such highly creative resources of their own. Only once in a blue moon does an outsider now hit the jackpot as happened a while ago to Dr. Charles Fuller, a Yonkers dentist. He thought of shaping a toothbrush like a dentist's mirror; and Squibb developed that hunch into the big-selling Angle Tooth Brush.

Of course there are still opportunities for inventive effort. Raymond Yates has recently listed 2,100 inventions urgently needed. And countless others are still open to the free-lance gadgeteer. But the average new invention yields but a pittance. In my own attempts in this field, my gross income per patent has been less than $500. The chances are that most free-lance inventors could reap more reward in other fields, or as full-time members of a manufacturer's staff.

2.

A more likely monetary reward for stepped-up creative power is in getting ahead in an organization. As a shrewd Cape Codder, George Moses, has said: "In the long run, it is the employee with the most and best ideas who gets paid off." Physiologist R. W. Gerard gave the same fact this twist: "Imagination accounts for the *arrival* of the fittest."

That seems obvious enough, but "lamentably enough," said Victor Wagner, "every day, several million young men resign themselves to sterile drudgery by thoughtlessly ignoring, or blandly defaulting, the marvelous faculty of imagination. The most valuable motto these should have is: 'Use your imagination.'"

Creative power can bring progress in any phase of business, especially in salesmanship. A salesman is like a football player. He has to take his signals as given, and follow them out stride by stride. But once he gets the ball up to the line, the rest is up to his ingenuity.

My first territory as a salesman included Dunkirk, N. Y., where no retailers carried the beds and mattresses I was supposed to sell. The one outlet my boss wanted was Lang's. But Mr. Lang had never liked our line and had bought nothing during the 12 years my predecessor had solicited him. So, with fear and trembling I went into Mr. Lang's store one June afternoon. He was not there. I told the bookkeeper that I would wait.

A 'teen-age girl came in. I heard her crying on the shoulder of the bookkeeper: "I have to write an essay on women's suffrage, and I just can't do it!" I butted in. Right then and there, I wrote the essay for little Miss Lang. A little later her father returned to the store. I did not try to sell him any goods that day. But I came back the next week, and from then on we had a good outlet in Dunkirk.

The best selling is *helpful* selling; and this kind calls for *ideas*. A salesman has to use his imagination, deliberately and consciously, to think up just what little thing he can do to be helpful to each customer. Every case calls for a different strategy. Resourcefulness can turn a peddler into a star.

A salesman's creative power is promptly reflected in his pay. In other phases of business there are too few *immediate* incentives for ideas—except by way of suggestions systems which are now at work in 6000 organizations. These devices will be discussed more fully later on; but here's a quick example. The National Biscuit Company offers money prizes to its 28,000 employees for their ideas. Two shop workers, Arnold Facklam and Robert Diehl, recently were paid $2,500 extra for the best suggestions of the year.

But the real reward of creative effort is not the occasional prize, but the steady climb—the greater likelihood of advancement. More and more, promotions are based on demonstrated creativeness. The head of a big firm decided to retire. He had seven able assistants. When I asked him how he had picked his successor, he replied: "Year after year, one of my aides had sent me frequent memos which usually began, 'This may sound screwy but . . . !' or 'Maybe you've thought of this, but . . . !' Even though many of his ideas were trivial, I finally decided that he was the man to succeed me because this business would dry up without a leader who *believes* in ideas, and has the gumption to spout plenty of his *own*."

George Morrison, president of the General Baking Company, had to select an executive vice-president. He picked 60-year-old Thomas Olsen, an accountant. I asked Mr. Morrison why. "Because he *thinks* young. He always has an idea," replied Mr. Morrison.

3.

And, of course, if you are in search of a job, your creativity can reward you richly. You need your imagination to help you decide the kind of a job you want and where you are most likely to land it. To get your foot in the door, your imagination can be an open-sesame. In actually landing a job, your creative thinking can do much to turn the trick. If you can show proof of your capacity for ideas, you are more wanted by a prospective employer. "Managers of big and little enterprises are constantly and eagerly on the lookout for imaginative men," said Victor Wagner.

One young friend of mine came back from war eager to get into a different line. Thanks to the G. I. Bill of Rights, his old job was open, but a certain new pasture looked greener. He knew almost nothing about the field he wanted to enter. He did know what firm he wanted to join. He feared that his first interview would spell success or failure. So, instead of applying in the routine way, he spent a week calling on customers of his prospective employer.

At the end of the week he had dug up 10 pretty good ideas. Then he got his interview, during which he modestly brought up his 10 ideas in the form of tentative questions.

His new boss has since told me that my young veteran friend is getting along famously. "I am mighty glad he didn't just ask me for a job in the usual way," said his employer. "I had already made up my mind not to take on any more men. So I would have turned him down if he hadn't shown in our first meeting that he was a man who knew how to get ideas. And I'm glad to say that the same ingenuity he used in getting the job is showing up in his work."

4.

Happier living is one fruit of increased creativity within the reach of all of us. Later chapters will suggest ways to use our imaginations to brighten our lives. But let's first take a glance at the premise, and do so through the eyes of my associate Robley Feland. He started his career as editorial assistant to Elbert Hubbard, author of *A Message to Garcia*. All through Mr. Feland's successful business life, he has applied his power of imagination not only to writing, but to personnel work and even to finance.

"The sources of happiness," said he, "include health, friends, a family of deep loyalties, wealth, religion, love. The one thing all these sources have in common is the sense of resourcefulness—the feeling that, above and beyond the requirements of daily living, we possess extra powers with which to cope with unforeseeable needs or mischances. The need may be for something as material as a warm blanket, or as spiritual as a kind thought. But, unsupplied, it leaves us uncomfortable or unhappy."

"High up in our resources for happiness," he continued, "we can place the proved knowledge that we have, in our thinkery, a well-exercised power to think ourselves out of trials and difficulties. Although it is impossible to lift ourselves over a fence by our bootstraps, it is possible—*it can be easy*—to lift ourselves over life's obstacles by the force of our applied imagination."

Isn't it axiomatic that the more ideas we can think up, the more satisfying our lives are likely to be?

5.

Arnold Bennett urged the use of creative effort as an antidote for worry. Worry is essentially a *mis*use of imagination. By driving our imagination into healthful lanes, we can do much to drive away worry and arrive at better health.

Dr. Henry Link and other eminent psychologists agree that lack of creative effort is often at the bottom of mental unrest and nervous upsets. The prime purpose of occupational therapy is to steer the patient's mind into creative channels. Isn't it obvious that when nerves need calming, activated creative effort is a most likely remedy? Isn't it obvious that when a mind gets twisted with an inferiority complex, one way to help untangle it is to make the patient do something creative, and thus induce a curative sense of self-respect?

Even when *bodies* go out of whack, heightened creative effort may be as helpful as surgery or drugs. Betsey Barton is one source for this statement. You have probably read her writings in leading magazines. Her first book, *And Now To Live Again,* impressed Bernard Baruch so deeply that he ordered copies sent to all institutions which practice mechanical therapy. I watched Miss Barton grow up. Through her early years, she was lighthearted, lightfooted, and full of fun. Then in her early teens, riding home with her brother one evening, her car overturned and she was maimed. After several operations by the world's best surgeons, she was told that her spinal cord had been severed and could not be respliced.

It was almost as hard for her to walk as if she had no legs, but by exercise and courage she at last made herself walk well enough to demonstrate to returning legless veterans how they, too, could walk again.

Today she is a charming, cheerful doer of great and good

deeds. Apart from exercise, it was creative activity, above all else, which enabled her to remake her life. She heroically fanned her creative spark until it flamed with a health-giving heat. For one who had never thought she could write, she became a truly great writer, as her new novel has so eloquently proved. For one who had done no art except little-girl scribbles, she learned to paint like a professional.

Betsey Barton has pointed out that many a creative great has been diseased or handicapped. "Keats," she said, "is the most famous. But Thomas Mann and Noel Coward have never been fully well. Katherine Mansfield, Emerson, Thoreau, were all sickly. Housman said he did his best work when he felt ill."

"But," I asked, "instead of being any richer in *talent* while unwell, could it be that those writers instinctively sought to forget their ills by losing themselves in supreme *effort*? Couldn't they actually make themselves feel better by acquiring the glow that comes from thinking up something worthwhile?"

"Yes," said Miss Barton, "we all know the sense of well-being that flows from just having an idea and putting it into words or action. Even by writing an amusing letter, we can add a spark to our daily life. The thing for us to do is to expand such moments into quarter-hours, then into half-hours, then into hours—until, finally, our creative mood becomes a constant part of us.

"There is no question but that the more we try to create, the better we feel. And this holds true with both the well and the unwell."

6.

To most people work and fun can never be synonymous. But the fact is that creative work can be fun. By and large, no people enjoy their toil as much as those who deal in ideas. Movie-makers, authors, artists, advertising men, reporters, stylists, and creative researchers are prone to gripe that stomach-ulcers are the wound-stripes of their professions. At heart they know that although necessity is often the mother of creative effort, fun is often the father. This fact was illuminated by Joseph Rossman, of the United States Patent Office. He analyzed the incentives of 710 inventors with 2,400 patents to their credit. "The fun of inventing led all other motives," was his conclusion.

People can get more fun out of life by making more of their imaginations, but creative effort offers still another compensation: A person can make himself *grow* by making his creative spark *glow*. Building one's own stature by heightening one's creative energy is, as Feland said, "like lifting yourself up by your bootstraps." But, as Joseph Jastrow has written, strange as this seems, there is plenty of proof that it is really so.

Yes, the more creative you are, the more of a person you become. The more you rub your creative lamp, the more alive you feel. The cash rewards of creative effort are plenty; but the more frequent and more fruitful rewards come in the coin of happier living.

Chapter III

ALL OF US, ESPECIALLY WOMEN,
POSSESS THIS TALENT

"WHO *ME?* Why I couldn't think up an idea if I tried."
Only a moron could truthfully say that; for there is overwhelming proof that "all God's chillun got wings"—creative
wings.

"There is not a man so deprived of imagination," said
Mangin, "as not to have felt that momentary vertigo of the
heart and thought which I call the *poetic state.*" But Charles
Mangin was a Frenchman and a scholar of long ago. What
say the fact-bitten scientists of today?

Chauncey Guy Suits became head of all General Electric
research when only 40. "*Everyone* has hunches," said Dr.
Suits. "No one is wholly without some spark. And that spark,
however small, is capable of being blown on until it burns
more brightly."

And here's what two educators say in *Colleges for Freedom*: "*All* of us have within us some of the divine creative
urge." Scientific tests for aptitudes support that joint statement by President Carter Davidson of Union College and
President Donald Cowling of Carleton College. The Human
Engineering Laboratories analyzed the talents of large
groups of rank-and-file *mechanics* and found that two-thirds
of these rated *above* average in creative talent. An analysis
of almost all the psychological tests ever made points to the

conclusion that creative talent is normally distributed—that *all* of us possess this talent. The difference is only in degree; and that degree is largely influenced by effort.

2.

Scientific findings are borne out by the countless cases in which ordinary people have shown extraordinary creative power. Stuart Chase has gone so far as to say that most of our best ideas are originated by amateurs. The war furnished overwhelming proof that the rank and file can shine creatively when stirred by a patriotic urge. Literally millions of ideas were brought forward by people who never thought of themselves as in any way creative.

"During the war," said President John Collyer of B. F. Goodrich, "suggestions came in from our employees at the rate of 3,000 per year. And we found that about one-third of these were good enough to deserve cash awards." From 1941 to 1945, the National Inventors' Council in Washington, D. C., received over 200,000 ideas. The Ordnance Department saved over $50,000,000 in 1943 alone, as a result of ideas thought up by rank-and-file employees.

Yes, spurred by war, many, many people thought up many good ideas. What stronger proof could there be that nearly all of us are gifted with creative talent?

3.

"But," you may say, "although those points prove that I have creative *talent*, they don't prove that I have creative *ability*." Yes, there *is* a difference. Most of us have more imagination than we ever put to use. It is too often latent— brought out only by internal drive or by force of circumstances.

Suppose that you were sitting here with me on the sixteenth floor of this building, and I were to say to you, "Here's a pad and pencil. Please write down, within one

minute, just what you would do if you knew that this building would immediately tumble to the ground as the result
of an earthquake." Your answer might be, "I'm sorry but
I wouldn't have an idea."

On the other hand, suppose I were to stage that same
scene so as to seem *real* to you—by having a good enough
actor rush into my office and shout: *"This building is going
to fall down within two minutes!"* If you believed him,
wouldn't you spout not *one* idea but *many* ideas? Isn't it
your *drive*, rather than your degree of *talent*, that determines
your creative *ability*?

4.

And yet, the degree of creative talent does vary. Some
believe that its intensity depends largely on heredity. Professor Ellsworth Huntington of Yale studied the inventiveness of descendants of Pilgrims. He compared the number of their patents with the number granted to sons of
later immigrants. His findings showed that the presence
of colonial blood seems likely to insure a higher degree of
talent.

But might it not be—as Arnold Toynbee has indicated—
that the ingenuity of native New Englanders has been due
to *effort* rather than to inborn talent alone? Their forefathers
had to fight the Indians, the cold, the forests, and the rocks
in the soil. This habit of effort was either handed down
through bloodstreams, or by example. In the latter case, environment rather than heredity could account for superior
creativeness.

In the opinion of Dr. Alexis Carrel, "Imagination and
boldness are never entirely due to environment—neither can
they be repressed by it." It's the old question of the hen and
the egg. To my mind, the truth seems to be that imaginative
talent stems more from environment than from heredity—and
that its *conscious use* is a far greater factor than either.

As Brooks Atkinson has said, it is "the *driving force* of

creation" which is so "remarkably unequal"—not the degree of native *talent*.

5.

There are some geniuses whose lamps *seem* to need no rubbing. Alexander Woollcott and I were college mates. His native brilliance dazzled and perplexed me. I had to rub hard to get any rays at all from my little lamp, while his seemed so big that all he seemed to need to do was to brush his sleeve against it. But the more I saw of him throughout his later life, the more I realized that his abounding mental energy was what made him so creatively productive.

A. J. Musselman is another who apparently could not help but spark almost all the time. He invented the coaster brake and hundreds of other new things. After he had made millions out of his ideas, he built a private golf-course in Kentucky. To put his links into the public eye, he thought up a weird annual event— a *club-throwing* contest. But my friend Paul Hyde knew Musselman as a boy in Wichita, and he told me that Musselman, above all else, was a bundle of energy.

Another seeming exception is Clarence Budington Kelland, who, in our century, has turned out more fiction than even Dumas did in his. Those who do not know Kelland might well think that he is just a bubbling spring—that his creations just flow, with less effort than is needed to turn a faucet. But, on a vacation with Kelland, I was constantly with him except in the morning. While the rest of us dozed or dawdled, Kelland arose from an early breakfast, chained himself to his typewriter, and forced his creative wheels to spin. "How did you get along this morning?" I would ask him. "I got a lot done," was his usual reply. But now and then he would growl, "I wrote and wrote, but nothing I wrote was any good." Yes, Bud Kelland has made his success by living up to the law laid down by Elbert Hubbard some 40 years ago—"the way to write is to write and write and write."

Brains like those may require less motive power. But it is a matter of degree. We who are blessed with less talent have to crank-up our idea-motors more often, and we have to fuel them with more mental sweat. *But no talent is brilliant enough to create without conscious drive.*

6.

Is it true, as commonly believed, that the female is less creative than the male? Psychologists, in their scientific testing, have found no such difference between sexes. In all the aptitudes so far found measurable, Jane is just as bright as Joe. Even more so, according to the Johnson O'Connor Foundation, which found from 702 tests of women that their average *creative* talent is definitely higher than the average man's. Based on these tests, the female is as much as 25 per cent ahead of the male in relative creativity.

Most housewives work their imaginations far more than most husbands do. The man's job is usually routined, while the woman is on her own almost every hour of the day. Few women realize how much creative power they have to use. When a wife is successful in handling her husband, how else does she do it but by continually thinking up the right idea to turn the trick? And what ingenuity a woman must use in shopping, in thinking up meals, in prettying up the garden, in rearranging the furniture, in getting her youngsters to do this and not to do that!

When the wartime workers were thinking up so many ideas, women won the limelight. Bernice Palmer was featured in *Life* for having thought up eight devices to speed up production of engine parts. "One of her most useful inspirations," said *Life,* "came when she remembered the way her mother had made doughnuts."

No woman would deny that she "racks her brains" for Christmas gifts. This means that she *does* have imagination, and *works* it when driven by duty or affection. During the whole year, few men do more creative work than she does at Christmas—in thinking up new and different presents for her husband, her children, Aunt Julia, Cousin Tillie, and all the others on her Christmas list. In most cases she also has to think up all those gifts which are tagged: "Merry Christmas from *Daddy*."

You can't be a good mother without using imagination. When baby won't eat, you don't give up at the first howl of protest. You think up a way to get her to eat. Sheer instinct pushes parents into the habit of thinking up whatever will benefit their offspring.

But it is so easy to let our creative thinking slide into low gear. That's why home menus so often tend to become monotonous. With a little self-spurring, a woman can win a grateful grin from her husband as he savors a meal made festive by a new touch.

Miss Florence Gray is a math teacher and an in-law of mine. She was chosen to write a tribute to her principal on his golden anniversary. "I can't do it," she said to me in despair. "I never have any ideas." I told her that psychological tests showed schoolteachers as a class to have a high degree of creative imagination—that as a successful schoolteacher she undoubtedly had plenty of talent—and that all she had to do was to try and to keep trying.

Later she told me that her tribute "To Our Beloved Principal" had made a hit. I asked her how she had gone about it. "After I saw you, that night," she said, "I tried to think up ideas before I retired. I jotted some down and then went to bed. During the night I kept jumping up and jotting down more ideas. In the morning, to my amazement, I had plenty of good ideas to work on. My tribute almost wrote itself the next day." Miss Gray no longer underestimates her creative power.

My own wife, too, claims to possess no creative power. She proved otherwise when recently a new grandson arrived. She bought a plain basket and trimmed it with a skirt made from her graduation dress. The baby's father makes his living in creative research but he was so thrilled at his infant's new bassinet that he marveled at the ingenuity of his "non"-creative mother-in-law.

Beyond doubt, women are most creative when the need moves them. But most women hesitate to try beyond that point. Whereas most men are held back by *laziness*, what blocks most women is *lack of confidence*—failure to realize that they *have* Aladdin lamps and that by rubbing them, they can light their way toward brighter lives.

Chapter IV

EDUCATED OR SELF-EDUCATED— OLD OR YOUNG

"IF I'D ONLY GONE TO COLLEGE, what a person I could have been." How often that alibi is secretly harbored or openly whined! And yet there is no evidence that higher education induces creative power. For one thing, colleges almost ignore the subject of imagination.

Then, too, those who go to work in their 'teens tend to pack into their memories the *first-hand* experience which forms the richest fuel for creative lamps. More than that, these youngsters are forced to acquire the *habit of effort* on which creative power so largely depends.

According to scientific tests for creative aptitude, there is little or no difference between college or non-college people of like ages. Dr. William H. Easton, a man of many degrees, remarked: "Education is not a vital factor. Many highly trained persons are sterile creatively, while others accomplish outstanding results in spite of an almost total lack of formal instruction."

In centuries to come the world will probably remember a man who flunked at college, and yet became a great writer, a competent painter, and the creator of plans which helped win the greatest war in history. Yes, Winston Churchill was the poorest scholar in his class at prep school. He did badly in all subjects, especially mathematics. Despite this, he was put in charge of the finances of Great Britain as Chancellor of the Exchequer. In his most recent writings he hit a new creative high.

Some who never reached high school have gone far in creative achievement. Lena Himmelstein came here as a Russian immigrant of 16. She built the Lane Bryant business out of her idea that expectant mothers would like to dress so as to look less expectant. Likewise, the Wildroot Company is a monument to men without schooling. The business was founded by Robert Kideney and Morrel Howe—two barbers who presided over adjoining chairs at the old Iroquois Hotel in Buffalo. This company attained national leadership in its line under the creative guidance of Harry James Lehman, who was driving a junk-wagon for his uncle while his friends were at high school.

2.

History records that many great ideas have come from those devoid of specialized training in the problem involved. The telegraph was worked out by Morse, a professional painter of portraits. The steamboat was thought up by Fulton, likewise an artist. A schoolteacher, Eli Whitney, devised the cotton gin.

Early in the war, a new shell-fragment detector was thought up by an unscientific employee of New York City's transit system. From Pearl Harbor on, that device saved many a life. There were many such cases where untrained people out-thought the highly trained—so many that a federal official was led to comment: "The guy who doesn't know the difference between a torch-welder and a torch-singer has outdone himself in suggesting solutions to technical problems of war production."

There are scientists who have learned their technology without benefit of college. Their creative power sometimes makes up for their lack of technical schooling. Such a man is Charles McCuen, recently chosen to succeed Charles Kettering as head of General Motors research—despite the fact that Mr. McCuen never graduated from college.

Except for Oliver Goldsmith's going to Holland to teach English when he couldn't speak Dutch, what could be more preposterous than writing music without musical training? Irving Berlin spent his boyhood as a waiter in Chinatown. He never learned to play, except by ear and only in the key of F-sharp. Many a lass of 12 reads music better than the man who wrote the only American piece which John Alden Carpenter has included in the world's greatest music. Alexander Woollcott knew Berlin well. He denied that Irving could play with only one finger. But he loved to tell about Chico Marx who, on hearing that Berlin had sliced his thumb, observed in withering accents, "Well, that won't interfere with his piano playing." Woollcott's highest tribute to Berlin was this: "He can neither read music nor transcribe it—*he can only give birth to it.*"

3.

Many writers have reached the heights without the help of diplomas. Mark Twain left school when he was 12. Later he received an honorary degree from Yale, and likewise from Oxford. His genius was built out of exciting experiences in life. His travels filled his mental storehouse with creative treasure which his pen could draw out at will.

According to Larry White, Dashiell Hammett was thrown into creative work with no literary training at all. After his army-hitch in the first World War, Ex-Corporal Hammett got himself a job in San Francisco with the Pinkerton Detective Agency. He didn't like the plodding nature of his daily work; but, with two new babies in two years, the Hammetts had to have a regular pay check. So he wearily kept sleuthing until one day his boss called him in and proclaimed: "Hammett, you will never make the grade as a detective. You are fired! My advice is to take up writing. Your *detective* work has been punk, but your *reports* have been colossal."

Thus, with only experience to save him, Dashiell Hammett was plunged into the creative sea and swam to the top as a mystery-writer.

Please don't get me wrong. I favor higher education. Otherwise I would not have sent my children to college. Otherwise I would not have accepted election as a trustee of Hamilton College. Higher education gives us a greater grasp on life, a more orderly way of thinking, a clearer judgment. These gains are vital to good living. And the longer we live, the more they count.

The point is that the degree of one's creative power does not depend upon a degree. This point is stressed because self-confidence is one of the keys to increased creativity. Those who missed out on college should feel no fear that they were thereby handicapped creatively.

4.

Another enemy of self-confidence is a common notion first expressed by Plato. "Experience takes away more than it adds," he wrote. "Young people are nearer ideas than old people." With due respect to Plato, how could he say that while still listening to the 60-year-old Socrates as he spouted ideas so new that they led to his death 10 years later?

"What you want is ideas, and I can think up more of them because I'm young." That was as big a lie as I ever implied, but I thought it was the truth at the time I said it to William Deininger when I solicited his appointment as advertising agent. I was then 27.

Despite his years, that old-time baker had just thought up the biggest idea of his life—and that was to make a loaf so good that it would be preferred by women who baked at home, as most women did in those days. He had named it Bond Bread because all ingredients were listed on the wrapper and guaranteed by a bond.

He was the new head of the General Baking Company, a combination of individually owned baking plants in about 20 eastern cities. The merger had not worked. The finances had slid precariously. Mr. Deininger had been called upon to avert disaster. The new loaf was his last hope. He took a great risk in giving so grave an advertising responsibility to so young a man

The first idea I hit upon was to introduce Bond Bread in each town by holding a city-wide baking contest. Altogether, 43,040 housewives baked loaves at home and submitted them to show just how they would like their bakers' bread to look and taste. Bond Bread was so good that success came unexpectedly fast. When we started in Philadelphia, I said to Colonel Louis J. Kolb, whose bakeries had been merged into General Baking, "Well, that's how Bond Bread is selling in each of the cities where it's been started. How many loaves per week do you think we might sell in Philadelphia after we get going?"

"Oh, about 150,000," said the Colonel. But before a year was over, Philadelphia alone was buying Bond Bread at the rate of over 1,000,000 loaves a week. The brand is going stronger than ever wherever it is baked and sold. Although these territories cover only about one-third of the country, about 8,000,000 loaves are now bought by housewives each week.

A young man thought up the little ideas that went into the advertising; but it was an old man who thought up the *big* idea of Bond Bread.

5.

"The joy of succeeding while still young," was a phrase penned by Bruce Barton. But if success comes too soon, it may mean tragedy. Such was the lot of Alexander the Great whose career might seemingly reinforce Plato's contention, but weakens it instead. A study of Alexander's life shows that before he conquered Persia at the age of 25, he had been highly creative in many ways other than military. After 25, his creativity was paralyzed by vanity. From then on, his only new idea was beardlessness—to shave his face so that he might again look as young as when winning the world. How could such creative talent dim down and die out so soon? The answer is that his *effort* died first, and as a result, his talent dried up.

Plato's opinion might also seem to be confirmed by the life of Robert Louis Stevenson. But he was still writing brilliantly when he died at the age of 44. Had he been of normal health instead of consumptive, and had he lived his three-score-and-ten, Stevenson would undoubtedly have written as well, or better, after 60 as before 40.

In some cases, abnormal talent does flame early in life and then burns out. Hence the term "infant prodigies." But it could not have been such precocity that prompted Plato's remark. Nor could such be the basis of a similar opinion voiced by Oliver Wendell Holmes when he said: "If you haven't cut your name on the door of fame by the time you reach 40, you might as well put up your jackknife."

Holmes' own life belied that statement. Until he was 48, he was an unknown physician and professor. His literary fame started with his *Autocrat of the Breakfast Table*, which he wrote when nearing 50. His most creative period was between then and when he wrote his *Ralph Waldo Emerson* at the age of 75. The career of Holmes' own son likewise refutes the theory that creative power wanes with youth. Chief Justice Holmes wrote his first great book, *The Common Law*, when he was 72. During the panic of 1933, when he was over 90, he was leaned upon by the President of the United States for suggestions on how to pull the nation through its crisis.

Dr. Charles Dorland's analysis of 400 outstanding careers showed that, on the average, creative peaks were reached around 50. But he also found many instances of brilliant creative achievement in the 60s and 70s. The truth is that imagination lasts longer than memory, and that we can keep up our creative power, regardless of age, as long as we keep our inner drive in high gear.

6.

In college at the age of 17 it was my good fortune to see much of a 60-year-old grad who lived across the campus. Long after that, he was still recognized as one of the world's most creative thinkers. At 76, as U. S. Commissioner Plenipotentiary to the Conference on Limitation of Armaments, the record shows he was then more fertile with suggestions than any man of half his age. That was Elihu Root.

Thomas Jefferson retired to his homestead in Virginia when he was 66. Visitors at Monticello are amazed at the many innovations he thought up from then on. In his 70s and 80s, he was still originating. Benjamin Franklin was likewise both a statesman and an inventor. He was also a creative writer. One of his masterpieces was his appeal to Congress for the abolition of slavery. He wrote that in 1790, when he was 84.

Among creative scientists, Dr. George Washington Carver, at 80, was still turning out new ideas—so many that more than ever he merited the tribute paid him by the New York *Times* as "the man who has done more than any other man for agriculture in the South." An earlier scientist, Alexander Graham Bell, perfected his telephone when 58, and when past 70 solved the problem of stabilizing the balance in airplanes.

"Writers die young," they say. But this, too, is untrue. Milton lost his sight when 44, wrote *Paradise Lost* when 57, and wrote *Paradise Regained* when 62. David Belasco still wrote successful plays when he was over 70. Mark Twain, at 71, turned out two books—*Eve's Diary* and *The $30,000 Bequest*.

Julia Ward Howe wrote the *Battle Hymn of the Republic* when she was 43. But Alexander Woollcott once told me the best writing she ever did was *At Sunset*, which she penned at 91. The first time George Bernard Shaw won a Nobel Prize was when he was nearing 70.

Carl Sandburg is still clicking. He has been a writer

mainly of non-fiction. Fiction takes more creative power than fact. A few months ago, at 70, he finished a new novel for which the movies paid him $100,000.

Even if our native *talent* should stop growing when our body stops growing, it would still be true that our creative *ability* can keep growing year after year in pace with the *effort* we put into it. W. Somerset Maugham has put his seal on that truth. "Imagination grows by exercise," said he, "and, contrary to common belief, is more powerful in the mature than in the young." In discussing this with a lawyer who holds that creative effort is vital to legal success, he offered this analogy: "There is a principle in the law that you lose that with which you are endowed unless you make *use* of it. The same principle applies to our gift of imagination. It seeps out of our possession if we put it to no use. It grows ever more valuable if we make it work."

Psychologist George Lawton has stated that the mind does not stop growing at 50, but keeps on growing until 60. From then on, according to Lawton, mental ability ebbs so slowly that, at 80, we can still be almost as good mentally as at 30. And specifically, when it comes to creative talent, Lawton tells us that although older people are apt to lose some of their memory power, "creative imagination is ageless."

Most of us know older people who spark more ideas than our younger friends. One instance that drove this home to me was something that happened to my mother. At 80, she fell and broke her shoulder. Her crony of about the same age, a Mrs. Frank Mulfeld, was heartbroken to learn that Mother's right arm could never be used again. They had loved to play cards together; but how could Mother play with only one hand? Mrs. Mulfeld shopped the big stores in New York searching for a device for one-armed card playing. Failing, she took on the task of creating one herself. Her son worked out her idea and fashioned the rack which my mother used until she died at 94 .

7.

There are child prodigies whose creative flame dies out early; and there are also slow-burners who seem dull in early years but brilliant in later life. One whose career I have watched with pleasure was a student in my night-school class. A bashful boy, slow of speech, he was the last lad in the world you would expect ever to show outstanding ingenuity. He became a reporter, conscientious but far from sparkling. Slowly he grew until finally he became a Washington correspondent. There, among men marked by creativity more brilliant than in almost any other group, he won their admiration to the point that he became president of the National Press Club. The President of the United States sought him out for his suggestions as to the course the Administration should steer. That man's name is Alfred Kirchhofer. He is managing editor of a great daily newspaper, and also directs a great radio station. He grew more and more creative year by year during his 40s. On his record it seems certain that during his 50s and 60s he will keep on increasing his creative power.

And why not? Psychologist Lawton, in speaking of the agelessness of imagination, made the point that the older we grow, the more we should know. Apart from native talent and inner drive, the essential ingredient in creativity is that which we have stored up in our minds. "When our minds are filled with rich and varied experiences," said Dr. Harry Hepner, "we discover concepts that would not occur to us when our contacts with life were more limited."

Of course, if we let ourselves get in a rut, lose our zest for life, quit being curious, and just plain stop trying—then we cannot help but be less creative as we amble down the hill. Otherwise we can count on the fact that we don't have to be youthful to be mentally fruitful, despite what the immortal Plato once said.

Chapter V

CREATIVE POWER NEEDS NO
IVORY TOWER

"LET'S ASK ALEX to climb up into his ivory tower and bring down some ideas." On that note, Bruce Barton joshingly ended a meeting where a group of us had tried in vain to think up a way out of a jam. The next day we met again, and my associates combined two of my new ideas into one which filled the bill. Did I get those ideas in an ivory tower? No—partly while eating lunch all alone, and deliberately alone—partly by walking alone for two miles that evening— and partly by rubbing my lamp while scraping my chin in my bathroom.

America's architecture is being enriched with more and more temples of research. These laboratories are the ivory towers of science. They provide not only equipment but also a climate ideal for concentrated contemplation. And yet, creative scientists would fall short if they created only while in their ivory towers. For example, Dr. Suits of General Electric has stated that he gets some of his best ideas in bed, while flying from plant to plant, or "while staring out of a Pullman window." A. J. Musselman claimed that he gave birth to his coaster-brake idea while speeding down a Rocky Mountain steep—not in a limousine but on a runaway bicycle.

33

2.

Artists need ivory towers. Even amateur painters have studios. W. T. Grant, founder of the chain of stores bearing his name, retired and became an accomplished painter of flowers. He built a studio in an upper story of his home and made it an ivory tower which could be reached solely through a private staircase, especially constructed for his exclusive use. The world's leading manufacturer of overalls, Stanley Sweet, has a similar studio in his Manhattan home. His hobby is painting portraits of friends.

Grant Wood had a studio too, although not quite so fancy. And yet Grant Wood claimed that his studio was mainly for *execution*—that his real *creative* work was done out on the farm. One of his sayings was this: "All the good ideas I have ever had came to me while I was milking a cow."

Most writers, too, need ivory towers. At dinner one night with Henry Morton Robinson, he told me how he was turning out his new novel. He had a large home in the country, but even by going from one room to another he found he could not change his atmosphere enough to bring out his creative best. So he built a little hut on a nearby hill. Then, each morning after breakfast, he forced himself to walk through the woods and lose himself in that tower with the characters he was creating.

And yet most authors will admit that they pick up their ideas here, there and everywhere. Edgar Lustgarten, fast-coming English author of mysteries, works without time-table and without ivory tower. According to his publisher, "He never stops. He writes anywhere and everywhere—in pubs, on buses, even walking down the street."

Samuel Johnson may not have been entirely right when he said that any man could write anywhere, if he would only set himself to it "doggedly enough." But it is true that although artists and writers may require ivory towers, ideas can be created almost everywhere.

3.

One virtue of an ivory tower has to do with time rather than place. If we set aside a definite period for creative thinking we can best lure the muse. This rule should govern those of us in business. We should "take time out for thinking up ideas—*nothing else*," said Don Sampson. Too many business men tackle routine first, usually because it is easier. Sampson rightly recommends mornings for thinking, afternoons for routine.

At home, a bed is a good place to take time out for ideas. We might well devote a half-hour each week pondering creatively over family problems. Set aside a definite period, say on Sunday afternoon. Go to your room, close the door, kick off your shoes, lie down. Pick yourself a creative chore.

In such ways we can go to bed, not to nap, but to awaken our imaginations. But bed is also a good place for creative thinking even when we go to bed to try to sleep or to get well. One use of sleep is to let ideas simmer. By sleeping on ideas, we often hatch out better ones. This can be far more productive if, before we turn out the lights, we actually jot down the best thoughts we have been able to dream up while awake. The very making of these notes tends to free our minds and thus enable us to fall asleep the sooner. But those notes also tend to engrave our minds with thoughts on which our subconscious can work better while we sleep.

In the dark hours when our army first landed in North Africa, a great help was the series of emergency landing fields which our men were able to set up almost overnight— magic carpets smooth enough for planes to take off and to land. These landing-field mats were the brain-child of Walter E. Irving. When I asked him how, when and where he got his best ideas, he paid tribute to beds as creative cradles.

"The bed, the bedside pad and pencil," said Mr. Irving, "are great aids to ideas and schemes. Only last night I scrawled over four sheets of paper in the pitch dark. But my notes were easily deciphered this morning, and they contain possible solutions to a current problem. A few months ago in a Washington hotel I awakened from a dream about 2:30 A.M. Then and there I sketched a simple idea that I believe will soon start an important new product. Had I just turned over and gone to sleep I am sure I never would have thought of it again." Another who believes that bed can be a hot-house for ideas is Alfred Hull. The creator of more new types of electron tubes than any other inventor, Hull has said that most of his best ideas have crept up on him "in the middle of the night."

Insomnia is a vicious circle. When we find we cannot get to sleep, we begin to worry over our wakefulness. We try harder to get to sleep, and new fears flit through our squirrel-cage. If we could realize that the usual reason we cannot sleep is that we do not need sleep, we could turn insomnia into opportunity. Instead of counting sheep, we can pick on something for which we want ideas, and then roam our minds around that hunting-ground. It can be fun. It may be profitable. It may bring sleep.

One evening I boarded a sleeper just after I had learned that a friend had expressed ingratitude toward me. Long after I had crawled into my berth, I still could not sleep. My mind insisted on debating with my estranged friend. The more I mentally argued, the more my emotions boiled and my body tossed. A hard day was coming up and I needed sleep. Knowing that my "peeve" would keep me awake, I sought something creative to think over. I picked out a business problem with which we had been wrestling the day before. I wrapped my mind around that with two-fold result. For one thing, I landed an idea which the next morning developed into a full-fledged plan. For another thing, I finally got to sleep.

Not only can insomnia sometimes be overcome by creative thinking, but, strangely enough, insomnia may even awaken creativity. According to Ernest Dimnet, unless insomnia saps us to the point of exhaustion, it can sometimes make our imaginations more than normally lucid.

4.

Next to the bedroom there is a tiled tower called the bathroom where our creative minds likewise like to work. A good long shower or a hot tub often induce ideas. One reason is that while we bathe we are shut off from distracting influences.

Beards are about the only advantage men have over women in the field of creativity. You often hear idea-workers confess: "That came to me while I was shaving." Dr. Suits recently told of one of his associates who had made two important discoveries. The basic idea for each of these came to the man while removing his morning beard. Shaving, like bathing, provides the same solitude, the same soothing sound of running water, and the same sense of well being. Still another reason why shaving and creative thinking often go together is that the mind is usually more creative in the early hours. "The Muses love the Morning," said Erasmus.

5.

The exercise that seems to go best with creativity is just plain walking. Since the days of Thoreau, hiking in lonely places has been a favorite way to court ideas. I asked an M.I.T. graduate, "Who was the most creative of all your professors?" He said Dr. Warren K. Lewis. I asked if he knew whether Dr. Lewis consciously did things to make himself more creative. "I don't really know," said my cautious friend, "but he is a great man for hiking through the woods. It is common belief that he does this partly for exercise, but mainly as a help to his creative thinking."

If you know what ideas you are hunting, a lonely walk may help a lot. But if you have no set creative aim, and want only to expose your mind to ideas, a walk through busy marts may likewise help. I asked a friend of mine why he wore a cane when visiting New York. "I come to New York to get ideas," said he. "I don't want to think about my own business while here, so I carry a cane to make me feel that I am not working. My grindstone back home tends to close my mind. Here, with wide-open mind, I can walk along Fifth Avenue and Broadway and can pick up ideas which will help me when I discard my cane and become a manufacturer again."

Nothing could be more distracting than a stroll along the Atlantic City boardwalk on an Easter Sunday. And yet, a retailer friend of mine goes there every Easter, with no set aim as to what he is looking for, but with the confidence that if he keeps his mind open while there he will drink in ideas which will suggest other ideas. He regards that Sunday as one of his most valuable business days.

6.

Chores are good coaxers of creativity. Elbert Hubbard was an advocate of wood-chopping for this purpose. Recently a creative researcher said that the best idea he ever had came to him while chopping ice from his front steps.

While at work on a creative quest, an atmosphere of reverie may intensify the creative flame. Many find that some of their best ideas come to them while in church. Others claim that attending concerts kindles their creativity. Some think the ideal ivory tower is the stern of a boat. There is something about sailing that lends itself to continuous contemplation. Dr. E. F. W. Alexanderson, the inventor, has testified that some of his best ideas have been plucked out of the blue while placidly sailing his sloop.

Jefferson lived 100 miles from Washington. At Monticello you can still see the buggy he drove back and forth between his plantation and the Capital when he did not go on horseback. With a horse that needed no guidance, with a pace that made for tranquility, with no stop-signs to interrupt—what an ivory tower his horse Wildair, or his one-man buggy must have been!

How seldom you see anybody really working on a plane

or train! You occasionally catch someone reading a report, or studying figures. And a few of those who just sit and stare may also be working their minds for all we know. But it is only once in a blue moon that you see anybody active at creative work. And yet one of the classics of creative writing was put together on a train—Lincoln's Gettysburg speech. And General George Marshall wrote his best speech in longhand, high above the Atlantic, while flying back from Moscow.

Something about a plane's whir and a train's rhythm tends to make creative juice flow. During the most hectic period of my business life I found more time than ever to indulge in literary work because my duties called for long jumps around the country and I found that while on train or plane I could relax best by trying to write something in no way connected with my business. So when a young writer asked me how I found time to do so many short pieces for magazines, I told him: "If I have any secret it is to write as you ride. I have to travel about 1000 miles a week. On trips or in between, I make notes of whatever sounds as if it might make a story. Then on the train or plane I pull out my yellow pad, moisten my pencil, and just scribble. I dash off a loose draft just to rough out the idea. This is later typed in triple space. When I next find a spare hour, I work it over and over. In that way I do the creative part of my writing while traveling and the critical part—the editing—at home."

7.

My best idea was born on the subway. For months I had tried to think up a plan to mutualize the ownership of our company. One night I dined uptown at my brother's home. On the way back to the subway, I was about to buy a paper when it occurred to me that I might use those 20 minutes to get nearer to the idea I had been seeking. I found a seat and began to make notes. Pretty soon the car was crowded. The chatter was babel, and the noise of the train was bedlam. In the midst of all that I hit on *the* idea for which I had strained for so long. I wouldn't have landed it then if I had bought a newspaper or if I had forgotten my pencil.

"Hold on," you may say, "do you mean to claim that if we want to create more we should seek out a setting where concentration is difficult?" No. But we do mean that with proper concentration it is possible to track down ideas anywhere, at any time. Concentration is nothing but attention, sharply focused and steadily sustained. It is an acquired habit rather than a native gift. When concentration becomes a part of one's nature, it can be carried on almost anywhere, under almost any circumstances. Fatigue and apathy do more to kill concentration than noise or crowds.

The cultivation of concentration is not easy, as Arnold Bennett has pointed out. "When you leave your house," said he, "concentrate your mind on a subject—no matter what, to begin with. You will not have gone ten yards before your mind has skipped away from under your very eyes and is larking around the corner with another subject. Bring it back by the scruff of the neck."

A good way to court concentration is to rub a pencil against paper. For pads and pencils are keys to the kind of concentration which enables us to think, with or without an ivory tower, while sitting still or on the move, in quiet or amid noise. And such concentration is in turn a key to creativity.

Chapter VI

IMAGINATION TAKES MANY FORMS,
INCLUDING NON-CREATIVE

THE LAST FEW CHAPTERS have aimed to instill self-confidence in those who, for some reason, might have thought *they* could not step up *their* creative power. Later we will cover specific ways to guide our minds in quest of ideas. Let us now look at our equipment, of which imagination is the basic part.

"What do you mean by imagination?" was the question flung at me after speaking at a banquet. It's a tough question because that word is wider than a three-ring-circus tent and covers wild beasts as well as tame. Sylvester Mawson's streamlined thesaurus lists over 50 synonyms. The textbooks seem unable to agree on any definition. But, since all of us *have* imagination, each of us has a first-hand knowledge of what it is and does. According to Gilbert Chesterton, none of us should belittle such self-understanding. "A man can understand astronomy," he said, "only by being an astronomer. He can understand entomology only by being an entomologist—or, perhaps, an insect. *But,* he can understand a great deal of anthropology merely by being a man. He is himself the animal which he studies." By the same token, it is your own imagination which you now study.

The terminology of psychology tends to muddy rather than clarify our understanding. It is too bad that psychol-

ogists do not take a leaf out of the book of St. Paul, who said,
"Unless ye utter by the tongue speech easy to be understood,
how shall it be known what is spoken?" If you study the
masterful outline of psychology by Fryer and Henry, you
cannot help noting how many different names have been
given to the very same thing by so many different psychologists—not only recently but over the past 300 years.

In *The Tyranny of Words,* Stuart Chase wrote that if a
pure research scientist should announce, "Chlorophyll makes
food by photosynthesis," these words would float over the
head of even a practical engineer. "But," said Chase, "if the
same fact were stated in the words 'Green leaves build up
food with the help of light,' laymen as well as experts would
get the point." Charles Kettering deplored the lingual barriers between different groups of experts and suggested: "The
first thing to do is to get them to speak the same language."
Ralph Coghlan of the St. Louis *Post Dispatch* remarked that
scientists "have developed a lingo impossible for anybody
but themselves to understand."

Dean George Russell Harrison of M. I. T. pointed up the
need for clarity by telling a story about a plumber of foreign
birth who wrote the National Bureau of Standards to the
effect that he had found hydrochloric acid could work wonders in clogged drains, but wanted to know whether its use
would do any harm. A technical member of the staff replied: "The efficiency of hydrochloric acid is indisputable,
but the corrosive residue is incompatible with metallic permanence." The plumber wrote back and thanked the Bureau
for telling him that his method was okay. This upset the
federal scientist. So he consulted his superior, who then
wrote the plumber: "We cannot assume responsibility for the
production of toxic and noxious residue with hydrochloric
acid and suggest you use an alternative procedure." But even
that did not close the file.

The plumber replied how glad he was that the Bureau
was crazy about hydrochloric acid for use in drains. In
despair the two scientists appealed to the head of the Bureau.

He closed the file by dictating this: *"Don't use hydrochloric acid. It eats hell out of the pipes."* The plumber found that statement both understandable and quotable.

We will abide by the moral of Dr. Harrison's tale and strive to throw light on imagination in terms we all can understand—even though, by doing so, we may stray from the terminology of psychology.

2.

The many forms of imagination fall into two broad classes. One consists essentially of the kinds which *run themselves* and sometimes run away with us. The other class is made up of the kinds we can run—which we can *drive,* if and when we will. The first group is the non-creative. The second is the creative.

The non-creative includes uncontrollable and unhealthy forms such as hallucinations, delusions of grandeur, persecution complexes, and similar maladies. Delirium is a less chronic phase of the same form. Nightmares are akin to delirium.

Inferiority complexes are another form. Until recently, such ills were seemingly beyond control. But psychiatry has found ways to correct this perverse form of imagination, and Dr. Harry Fosdick and Dr. Henry Link have helped by buttressing with *religion,* the therapy of the psychiatrists. Still another form of twisted imagination is the martyr complex, sometimes called the "wounded-hero" complex. This consists of imagining hurts to one's feelings and exaggerating such hurts to the point of morbid self-pity. Hypochondria is a similar form; but it makes the victim "enjoy" his imaginary ills.

A basic cause of such complexes, according to Dr. Josephine A. Jackson, is the "desire to run away from difficulty—to *misuse* one's imagination as a way to flee from reality." This concurs with Freud's theory that "every neurosis has the result—and therefore probably the purpose—of forcing the patient out of real life, of alienating him from actuality."

3.

The non-creative class includes forms that are normal and, except for dreams, are largely controllable. The dream is one of the most mystic phases of imagination, according to Heraclitus. In the fifth century before Christ, he wrote: "The waking have one and the same world; the sleeping turn aside, each into a world of his own."

The *speed* of our dreams is most mystifying. As a little boy, I had the flu and after my temperature had gone down, my folks bundled me up and sat me at the dinner table. I tried to eat my broth, but felt too weak. I heard my father start to tell something about a trolley-car and the next thing I knew, I was lying on the floor. I had fallen off my chair in a faint. My father had jumped up, had emptied a glass of water into his napkin, and had swabbed my face. Only a few seconds elapsed between fainting and waking, but in that moment I had dreamed so much—as I could later recall in detail—that it would take *hours* to live what I had dreamed. There were more words as well as action in that dream than in a half-hour of drama on the radio. What power of magic our imaginations must possess when, in two seconds, we can dream the equivalent of 2,000 words!

Day-dreaming is the most common use of non-creative imagination. Sometimes called reverie, this is for some of us the usual form of our so-called thinking. It takes less than no effort. We merely let our imaginations join hands with our memories and run here and there and everywhere—without design and without direction, except as set by our prejudices, our desires, or our fears.

Dr. Josephine Jackson warns that day-dreaming may become unhealthy when, "instead of turning a telescope on the world of reality—as positive imagination does—this negative variety refuses even to look with the naked eye." Victor

Wagner has called day-dreams "the rat-holes of escape from the stubborn realities of the workaday world." But with children, day-dreaming is natural and is less harmful than with grownups. The young gain innocent pleasure from merely imagining their desires to be gratified. But when this habit carries on into later life, such reverie is almost sure to grow into vicious phantasy.

4.

Worry is a non-creative form of imagination, all too normal and too often accepted as uncontrollable. Dr. Harry Fosdick has labeled it "anxious fear." It is a bane of human beings from which animals are immune, and he regards this as "a tribute to one of man's supreme endowments—imagination." He likens worry to running reels of morbid movies through our minds. "But," he says, "we can *change* those reels. We can substitute for destructive and fearful imaginings, positive and constructive pictures of life, its meaning and its possibilities. Thus we can prove at last that 'as man thinketh so is he.' "

When based on imaginary troubles, worry is a fussy phase of fear. Real fear is a deeper emotion. When founded on facts or probabilities, fear is a form of anticipative imagination which can bring out the best in us, mentally and physically. It can stir us "to prepare for the worst while hoping for the best."

And then there are the *blues*. Sometimes these are due to untoward events or other external causes. Often they come out of one's own chemistry, as during the aftermath of influenza. But no matter what the source, isn't it a fact that when we are in the dumps, it is because our imagination is putting *us* over the jumps—instead of *our riding our imagination with a strong enough rein?*

Chapter VII

CREATIVE IMAGINATION
IS MANIFOLD AND INTER-ACTING

"JUST IMAGINE!" When you hear people say that, what do they mean? Something that is truly creative? No. They are probably referring to forms which are *almost* creative, quite controllable, and generally enjoyable. Let's scan some of these before we tackle the truly creative.

First there is *visual imagery,* the power to see things in the "mind's eye." Through this talent, any of us can create a mental picture of almost anything whenever we wish. It is a photographic type of imagination which takes several forms. The one in which memory plays but little part might be termed the *speculative imagery.* You may never have visited Niagara Falls, but you could lay down this book, look at the ceiling and make yourself "see" the great cataract.

On the other hand, with nothing to go on, speculative imagination may project an untrue picture. I found that out as a lad of 12, about to go to a farm in the foot-hills of the Catskills. I had heard about the brook on that farm. I pictured it as a placid stream, about three feet deep and 10 feet wide; and I pictured myself canoeing on its smooth surface. Accordingly, I began to save pieces of canvas and strips of metal, with the hope of making myself a canoe when I got to the country.

Let's interrupt here and look at another phase of imagery

called *reproductive imagination.* Speculative imagination may work in any tense, but reproductive imagination works only in the past. It enables us deliberately to bring pictures *back* into our minds. Through this power I can now visualize that brook where I was going to ply my canoe. I can see it as it *was*—a mere rocky rill, only a few feet wide, with not enough water on which to ply a toy boat, let alone a canoe.

My first actual view of the brook so upset me that I "sublimated," by deciding to build a bridge instead of a canoe. Through reproductive imagination, I can now bring back to the screen of my mind a fairly clear picture of that bridge. Wait! Instead of a *still* picture, I can make it a *motion* picture. Yes, there I am, a little boy with hair parted in the middle, kneeling in the hot sun, dipping a brush into a pail of whitewash, then spreading it over the rough boards of the bridge.

Although reproductive and speculative imageries tend to flash on and off at their own whim, we nevertheless can control these photographic powers at will. This is likewise true of the third phase of visual imagination called *structural visualization.* Scientific tests of talents give great weight to this form of imagination. Johnson O'Connor described it as "an inherent sense for three-dimensional forms, an instinctive ability to construct in the mind's eye from a flat blueprint a clear picture of a solid object." This skill is important to physicists and other scientists, and, says Mr. O'Connor, "aviators probably use it in bringing a plane to the ground—certainly in blind flying."

All three visual forms of imagination—whether fairly photographic or almost mathematically exact—are highly controllable, as we all know from the way we can operate our own mental cameras at will.

2.

A more nearly creative form serves as a *bridge* by which we can put ourselves into another's place. We all use this *vicarious* imagination most of the time. Sympathy is one of its facets. Without vicarious imagination we could not "feel for others."

That same form is often used to pretend we are someone else, as in a child's play-acting. Little Teddy makes believe he is a railroad engineer. Barby loves to dress up in her mother's dinner-dress. All through life this passive form enables us pleasurably to change places—a fact which largely explains why over 100 million movie tickets are bought each week in America. For, as Walt Disney has said, people go to theaters mainly to lose themselves in the lives of those whom they see and hear.

The same brand of imagination accounts for the fact that every week 45 million American women listen to at least one soap-opera. Why do they tune in except in order to transport themselves into the characters and experiences they hear over the air? Sponsors, producers and script-writers never lose sight of this fact.

How passive this form of imagination can be! For movies and comics, it is even more passive than for reading fiction, since reading does take a little effort—no matter how light the literature may be. Vicarious imagination has a lot to say about what to choose to read. One day the newspapers blared out an announcement by President Truman that the national deficit would be $7,000,000,000 less than expected. Hidden on the same page of one newspaper was a little story about three local boys putting a dog's broken leg into splints. The average woman could put herself into the boys' place more easily than into Truman's shoes. A survey showed that only 8 per cent of the women readers remembered the President's announcement, whereas 44 per cent recalled the dog story.

The Golden Rule embodies the noblest use of vicarious imagination. To "do unto others," we have to imagine how *they* would like to be treated, as well as know how *we* would like to be treated. A similar call for imagination marks every act of kindness, such as the selection of gifts. This not only calls for putting oneself into another's shoes, but also for thinking up long lists of alternatives. To a degree, this calls for *creativity*, since we seldom pick the right gift without creative *effort*.

The key to tact is likewise to put yourself in the other's place; and tact has to do with what you do—or do not do—as well as what you say, or do not say. Environment and training make tact more or less instinctive. But this use of our vicarious imagination does call for an intent-to-please, and should even call for effort. The greater our imaginative talent, the more tactful we should be expected to be—even to the point of making people feel at their ease when otherwise they might feel like fish out of water.

3.

That brings us within a short step of creativity, but let's first look at one way in which our Aladdin's lamp serves somewhat as a light. Let's call this form *anticipative imagination*. In its most passive phase it is the instinct which stops little boys from touching live coals. If you said to a baseball pitcher, "Go out there and use your imagination," he would probably say, "Huh?" Although he may be bankrupt in creativity, he may be rich in anticipative imagination. He has to think ahead for every pitch. With the catcher's help, he must outguess the batter or "to the showers he must go."

All guessing calls for anticipative imagination. Most of us have an idea as to which way the cat will jump. The enjoyment of this form of imagination is what makes horseraces. It must be more than the lure of money that takes so many millions to the track. Otherwise the richer patrons would not bet their two bucks with such gusto.

Carried to extreme, anticipative imagination can be more than passive—it can be so active as to border on the creative. One instance of this was related by a man who had worked on a newspaper when its owner was running for mayor of his city. A few days before election the publisher wrote two alternative headlines and had them set in big type for the front page of the election-night extra. One headline announced his election. The other read: FRAUD AT THE POLLS.

A good mother puts her power of anticipation to admirable use in watching out for her toddling child. "Look out, he's going to pull that piano-cover down on his fingers!" . . . "Look out, he'll pull that lamp over!" . . . "Look out, he'll put his hand in that hot coffee!" . . . Be quiet, father! Mother is 'way ahead of you. She needs no such warnings. She can outguess her baby son; and she will.

Frank Grebe told me how anticipative imagination can be used deliberately to brighten each day. "When you awaken," he said, "pick out the most pleasant parts of the day ahead and think about them. If you concentrate hard enough you can make a dark morning seem sunny." He recommends the same self-medication for fatigue.

The highest form of anticipative imagination is *creative expectancy*. "When we look forward to something we want to come true, and strongly believe that it will come true, we can often make ourselves *make* it come true." That is the nub of creative expectancy as stated by Dr. Albert Butzer. It is a faculty that characterizes the champion, whether he be a Babe Ruth, a Henry Ward Beecher, or an Abraham Lincoln.

4.

Now for truly *creative imagination*. Its functions are mainly two-fold. One is to *hunt*, the other to *change* what is found.

In its hunting function, our Aladdin's lamp can serve us as a searchlight with which we can find that which is not really new, but is new to us. When we thus explore it is well to throw our beam into dark corners. Thus men like Newton lighted up unknown but existent truths such as the law of gravity. This is *discovery* rather than *invention*. But, for invention *or* discovery, we should always swing our searchlight

here, there and everywhere. The more alternatives we uncover, the more likely we are to find what we seek—and this
is often found in the obvious.

A pencil will make any such hunt more fruitful. If we jot
down one alternative after another, the very jotting-down
steps up our creative power; and each alternative we list is
likely to light up another alternative, as we will see later
when we get into *association of ideas*.

When beaten by personal problems we are apt to wail,
"Oh why, oh why, didn't I think of *that*?" We rue the failure
of creative imagination to light our way; whereas we should
face the fact that *we* failed to *work* our creative lamp hard
enough to light up *enough* alternatives.

The *hunting* function should not be too sharply set apart
from the *changing* function. But let's look at this *changing*
function by itself for a moment. Just as our Aladdin's Lamp
can be used for *light,* so it can also be used for *heat.* As a
cooker, imagination can bring together those things or
thoughts which are not new of themselves, but can be cooked
up into that which *is* new. In this way, we can do more
than *discover*—we can *invent*—we can produce ideas that
never before existed.

On leaving home one morning I passed through the
kitchen. My wife and daughter were busy with pencil and
pad, pondering the problem of that day's meals. They were
swinging their mental searchlights over all types of meat,
fish and groceries. In their hunt, they discovered the materials they wanted. Later, they cut them, mixed them, cooked
them, and added this and that seasoning. Flour became pop-
overs. Chicken, bean-sprouts and noodles became chow
mein. Thus their imaginations used both hunting power
and mixing power. Their final technique was *combination*—
often called the essence of creative imagination. But combining is only one of *many* techniques.

Creative imagination has been called a *catalyst*; but this,
too, misses the point. As used in chemistry, a catalyst speeds
up or slows down, whereas acceleration or deceleration is

not a vital part of the creative process. The oft-used term of *synthesis* is likewise inadequate. Even the act of bringing things together into new combinations may take more than synthesis alone. Often it calls for breaking up into separate parts and then regrouping them. Analysis, hunting, combining and otherwise changing—these are all parts of creative research. Scientific experimentation calls into play all of these activities and more.

At home, in the office or in the lab, our hunting power finds for us the things that are. Our changing power makes things over in one way or another. Together they become "the power that enables a creative thinker to arrive at new ideas."

5.

Unlike other forms of imagination, creativity is seldom automatic. Even when it seems to work without our bidding, it is usually because we have been *trying* to make it work. Thus, creativity is more than mere imagination. It is imagination inseparably coupled with both intent and effort. Our Aladdin's lamp must not only be pointed but rubbed.

Physiologist R. W. Gerard described creative imagination as the "action of the mind which produces a new idea or insight." The key-word in that statement is *action*. And when Joseph Jastrow termed creative effort "the imagination that looks forward, foresees, supplies, completes, plans, invents, solves, advances, originates," it is significant that there is not a single passive verb in his whole list.

Although we can understand much of *how* imagination works, and *how* to work it better—the *mysticism* of the creative spark cannot help but grow on anyone who contemplates imagination year after year, as I have done in preparation for this book. The question is: "What sparks the spark?" Mortal man may never know the answer. It is a deeper secret than life itself; and we have not yet learned what makes the heart tick. Henry Morton Robinson described its activating force as "a kind of electrical-timing apparatus called the 'pace-maker.'" But—what activates the activator?

Creative imagination is just as mystic or more so. It is understandable only as another evidence of divinity, according to Richard Roberts. "There is at work in the world," said he, "an influence which may be described as creative, wherever it operates. It is capable of reinforcing life and enhancing natural faculty. For this there is impressive evidence."

Chapter VIII

THE CREATIVE FUEL WE STORE—
IS IT RICH OR THIN?

"MANY A MAN FAILS to become a good thinker for the sole reason that his *memory* is too good." When Friedrich Wilhelm Nietzsche wrote that, did he mean memory as mental *storage*—or as an ability to *recall* figures, facts, and names? If he meant the latter, Nietzsche may have been right. Mnemonics wastes mental energy that could better go into creative thinking. No memory expert can have at hand any greater "knowledge" than a moron armed with a *World's Almanac*. Some dumb animals stand higher than some of us in the ability to remember. "A dog," according to Albert Payson Terhune, "can be taught anything within the grasp of the canine mind, in half the time and with twice the thoroughness—and will remember it much longer."

An over-active power of recall may even block creative thinking. When too prone to bring back the past, we tend to work our minds in the wrong direction. Creativity calls for *forward* thinking. Julius Boraas pointed out that although creative imagination uses the materials of previous experience, "the chief aim will not be to reproduce the past—on the contrary, it will be to *avoid* reproducing the past."

Nietzsche was wrong in decrying memory if, by memory, he meant our mental storehouse. A well-furnished mind is a vital part of creative power. The knowledge and impressions we have tucked away are, in fact, indispensable, according to Professor Charles Grandgent of Harvard, who wrote: "Imagination, like reason, cannot run without the gasoline of knowledge." And H. G. Schnackel said, "Any *addition* to the individual's store of usable experience is potential material for the exercise of the imagination."

2.

First-hand experience provides the richest fuel for creative power. It is more apt to stay with us and to well up when needed. Second-hand experience—such as superficial reading, listening, or spectating—gives us far thinner fuel.

Having been born and brought up in the Bronx, I can't claim to be a country boy. But first-hand observation has convinced me that those raised on farms gain richer material for creative use than those reared in the city. This should be true, for surely we gain more from milking a cow than from seeing milkbottles on window-sills. While the Park Avenue boys went to shows and concerts, the Main Street boys were running errands, doing chores, working in stores and harvesting on neighboring farms. Thus they mentally stored first-hand material with which later to enrich their judgment and their creative power—as *Who's Who* so repeatedly reveals!

Edna Ferber laid great stress on creative gold gathered in youth. In her *Showboat*, she had to describe the Mississippi at flood-time. Says she, in her autobiography, *A Peculiar Treasure:* "I found I did not need to consult books or ask old-timers to relate their river experiences. I just took my childhood memories of the Mississippi and the Des Moines at flood-time out the back of my head where they had been neatly stored for so many years and pinned them down on paper." And concerning her novel, *Come and Get It*, she says: "I again made use, as always, of the old yellow-trunk method by fishing up out of my memory the paper-mill lore and knowledge acquired in girlhood years spent in the Fox River Valley."

Would the name of Thomas Alva Edison be written across the creative sky if he had been raised in the Loop? Think of the first-hand experience he put under his belt at the age of twelve as candy-butcher on Grand Trunk trains. Think of the creative fuel he must have stored by publishing a newspaper when still under fourteen. Between times, he bought and sold fruit and vegetables, and, while still in his teens, he dashed-and-dotted in a telegraph office. So much did he learn first-hand that, by the time he was 22, he had perfected the Universal Stock Ticker and had sold it to Western Union for $40,000.

Hardship can force the city-boy to gain riches by way of first-hand experience. Horatio Alger should have known about Ely Culbertson. His story is unusual in that he chose city hardship on purpose. Culbertson's father was a Scotsman who developed oil in Russia and, appropriately enough, sent Ely to Yale. The son quit, turned his money over to his brother, and spent three years in the slums of New York in order to prepare himself as a writer, which he then planned to become.

In that neighborhood around the Bowery, another young man profited by hardship, but not because he chose. This was Irving Berlin, whose four sisters did needlework in sweatshops, whose father scraped up his few dollars by chanting in synagogues and inspecting meat to make sure it was Kosher. As a singing waiter, Berlin grew rich in first-hand experience which he later recognized as a creative asset. "You can't write a song out of thin air," he once said. "You have to know and feel what you are writing about." The creative spark with which he was born was undoubtedly brighter than bright. The effort he put into flaming that spark was boosted by adversity. But oh, how rich was the fuel with which he had early filled his lamp!

Yes, prosperity tends to impoverish us creatively, whereas hard going tends to enrich us.

3.

Travel is another rich source. Lowell Thomas proved what this can mean to a man's creative capacity. As a boy, his fancy was stirred by books which took him into the far corners of the earth. As soon as he grew up, he set off to see the world first-hand. He covered India, Australia, Asia and Alaska, as well as Europe. He was the first American ever to take pictures in Afghanistan. His more than 40 books, his lectures to thousands of audiences, his sparkling broadcasts —all this creative output stems from the first-hand experience he gained from his travels.

On May 9, 1942, I was working with Lowell Thomas in his apartment on West 59th Street, New York. His office called him to the phone to report a flash that had come in— our Navy had joined battle with the Japs in the Coral Sea. Lowell was due to go on the air within less than two hours. The American public was hungry for news. A mere statement of the start of the struggle would be far from enough. Into that phone, Lowell snapped suggestion after suggestion to his editorial assistant—where to look for background—whom to interview for sidelights. He was able thus to make his imagination work like wildfire mainly because he had had so much first-hand experience. He had even sailed through the Coral Sea in his travels up and down the world.

Eugene O'Neill combined travel with adversity to fill his lamp. Like Culbertson, he had a well-to-do father. Busting out of Princeton, he became an office-secretary in New York, a gold-hunter in the Honduras jungle, a seaman on a Scandinavian wind-jammer, a sewing-machine repairman in Buenos Aires, a hide-sorter in La Plata, a loafer on the New York waterfront, a patient in a tuberculosis sanitarium. Thus, before his first play was published when he was 24, he had stored up the first-hand experience of a dozen lives.

Another source is reading. Many examples show how material thus stored up in early years can make for creative power in later life. Bernard Shaw was absorbing Shakespeare when seven, and by twelve was reading Byron. In his 'teens he soaked up Dickens, Dumas, Herbert Spencer, and many others. It was many years later before he first succeeded as an author and years after that before he won recognition as a creative giant.

In a lesser way, Alexander Woollcott was another such. When I was first thrown in with him as a 16-year-old Freshman at college, I was dumbfounded at how much he had already read. He had absorbed so much literature and drama that, at the age of 15, he had served as a professional critic for the *Philadelphia North American.*

Likewise, in later life, the fuel on which imagination feeds can be enriched through reading. General Marshall's friends say that his chauffeur is frequently seen going to the library and borrowing a dozen or more books at a time. The General reads a lot before he goes to sleep. If he awakens, instead of wrestling with insomnia he snaps a switch and reads and reads until sleep comes.

Above all else, reading can supply that which imagination needs in a specific creative pursuit. I asked Clarence Budington Kelland how he could be so versatile as to write romances, factual articles, humorous stories, western adventures, and then turn out a historical novel like his one on Giovanni's heroic exploits during the sixteenth century. "That's easy," said Kelland. "I long since learned how to write a story and the epic of Giovanni de Medici is just another story."

"But," I said, "how could you know enough about Giovanni and his times?" "That's simple, too," said Bud. "For 30 years I read about the Renaissance—all the history I could lay my hands on—almost all the fiction covering that period. Then after 30 years, when I decided to novelize Giovanni, I did all the new research I could. By the time I started the novel, I knew Giovanni as well as I know my best friends in the Dutch Treat Club." Kelland then told me that while writing Giovanni, much of what he put on paper was so strange to him that he could not recognize it either as anything he had known about, or had consciously thought up.

4.

Taking in the movies, watching sports, listening to the radio—these are second-hand experiences which provide fuel less rich than that stored by reading. As readers we put in at least a little effort. As supine spectators or idle listeners we put in none. For that reason, what we thus take in is too dilute.

Contacts are likely to be richer sources; but the richness depends on how we conduct our conversations. Ben Duffy was our company's office-boy in 1919 and is now our president. He never went beyond high school, and yet is now the peer of the 481 college graduates on our staff. Although born and brought up in midtown Manhattan, he has a width and depth of knowledge you would expect of a boy reared in the backwoods like Abraham Lincoln. Where and how does Duffy get so much and such rich material as is stored in his mind? The answer is largely from his contacts. Most of us are superficial in conversation, but Ben goes deep by always asking fruitful questions. He is non-subjective. He listens hard. *Effort* enriches the fuel he siphons into his memory.

That sort of self-education certainly steps up creative power. Eddie Rickenbacker's first claim to fame was as a racing driver. From there he became the ace of aces in America's first air-force. As a thinker, he won his wings through study and more study. He did not even go to high school, but on his own he put himself through many courses including mechanical engineering.

Alexander Graham Bell laid down a *Rule of Three* for self-education: (1) *Observe* as many worthwhile facts as possible, (2) *Remember* what has been observed, (3) *Compare* the facts so as to come to conclusions, which Dr. Bell called "real knowledge." "That," said Dr. Bell, "was what made John Burroughs a great naturalist, Morgan a great financier, Napoleon a great general. It is the foundation of all education. And the wonderful thing about it is that gaining an education in this way is not a penance, but a delight."

William H. Easton likewise stressed self-education. "As the scope of our creative work depends upon our store of knowledge," said Dr. Easton, "we should be constantly engaged in enlarging this store by study, experiment, and observation. We must therefore have a high capacity for self-instruction." But the richness of what we store is not the only value. The *effort* we have to put into self-education also pays off in added creative power. To most of us, reading is a pastime; with a few of us reading is self-education. It depends on how we read as well as what we read. The more energy we put into it, the more we get out of it—especially if our energy takes the form of note-making.

Bruce Barton's books such as *The Man Nobody Knows* have caused some of my friends to ask me how his mind came to be so filled with such rich fuel. His secret is no secret to those of us who have traveled with him on business trips. Bruce always takes with him a few biographies or other serious works. Almost before the train starts, he opens his bag, and takes out a book. Then, with pencil in hand, he settles down to read—or rather to *study*. His office book-shelves are filled with over 1,000 volumes, all annotated for his own self-education. I picked one of these at random to see what Bruce had scribbled on the fly-leaf. Here is the list, exactly as I found it in his copy of *The Autobiography of a Mind* by W. J. Dawson:

> Page
> 16—are we murdering wonder
> 17—our old neighbor, God
> 20—common joys
> 25—we are no longer horrified
> 41—only hard religions succeed
> 43—farewell sermons
> 53—worn out preachers

Page

Some men build standby tanks by way of special files, and fill them with creative fuel. Charlie Upson, head of the Upson Company at Lockport, has pioneered many new developments in fibreboard. Among his treasures are file upon file of references to countless ideas created by Ben Franklin.

Chapter IX

THE POWER OF ASSOCIATION JOINS
MEMORY WITH IMAGINATION

"THAT REMINDS ME." These three words sum up most of what is known about that part of our creative power called *association of ideas*—a faculty which gears imagination to memory, and causes one thought to lead to another.

The ancient Greeks made much of this phenomenon. Plato played it up in his writings, and Aristotle stressed it as the very keystone of human psychology. They violently disagreed as to *how* this power works. Just so, psychologists and philosophers have battled ever since—with new and longer words like *associationism* and *re-integration*. But let's skip these and call it *association*, or some simpler term like *chain-thinking* or *link-thinking*.

Association works harder for those whose imaginative talent is more intense and whose mental storage is lusher. In the main, it works automatically but can be sped up by effort. Its power may partially depend on *vividness* of experience. The identical incident may click with me, but not with you. I recently said to the wife of a life-long friend, "Remember that Sunday supper at your house when Richard Washburn Child told us what Woodrow Wilson had privately said to him about the Versailles treaty?" That clicked nothing whatsoever in her mind. She had forgotten. Having entertained so many famous people, Mr. Child had been just another guest to her. But I had never before broken bread with an Ambassador, and to do so had so thrilled me that the whole event was fresh in my mind after 30 years.

Association plays a big part in the *accidental* factor of creativity. While pondering the workings of chain-thinking, I went to the dentist's. His drilling hurt but slightly. Instead of squirming, I let my left hand rove around and touched the little tube that carries gas to the Bunsen burner. "What smooth delicate rubber," I thought. "It feels like a baby's cheek."

That touch of rubber reminded me of how my friend Ed Germain had used rubber to help fool the Nazis just before the Normandy invasion. His factory had turned out balloons in the shape of full-size ships, tanks and big guns. Our boys in England inflated these dummies and set them where Nazi patrols could see them from the air. Thus the Nazis were kept in doubt as to where our real armada was being mobilized. This association of ideas between these full-sized decoys in Europe and the little tube in my hand flashed across my mind in less than a second flat.

A few days before, I had gone to a shop specializing in models for window-displays and had bought a man's head to demonstrate a talk I was about to give. That same morning I had been in an apparel shop where I ran across Clem Kieffer, the store's display manager. Thus quite naturally, as the dentist drilled, there flashed across my mind: "babies . . . rubber . . . giant toys . . . clothing models . . . Clem Kieffer." All this made me then ask myself: "Instead of making manikins out of heavy plaster, so costly to ship and so easy to break, why not make them out of rubber to be shipped flat, stored flat, and then inflated for use in a window?"

Even as my mind worked in that somewhat creative way, I analyzed my own mental gyrations and, within the next half hour, started to write down the above report. My son, just home from college, dropped in. "What are you working on?" he asked. I told him. A few minutes later he said, "Say, dad, weren't those inflated figures that we saw in Macy's parade on Thanksgiving Day 10 years ago?" Of course they were. Thus, that which I had thought might be a "new" idea had come out of the sub-soil of my mind—from a seed planted 10 years before.

2.

The ancient Greeks laid down as the three laws of association: contiguity, similarity, and contrast. By *contiguity* they meant nearness, as when a baby's shoe reminds you of the infant. By *similarity* they merely meant that a picture of a lion will remind you of your cat. By *contrast* they meant that a midget might remind you of a giant. In the next 19 centuries, only one other law was added. This was Hume's law of "cause and effect," which meant that a yawn may remind you that it's time to retire.

Association can work in many ways. Our figures of speech provide a parallel that may throw light on its diverse actions. Similarity, of course, is the prime law of association, and a simile is the simplest of the figures based on similarity. A graceful lily might remind you of your little daughter. As a simile, you might say, "Helen is like a flower."

The metaphor *implies* similarity. You see a play where everything happens from birth to death, and it reminds you of the world. "The world is a stage," might be your metaphor. You see a wizened old man who reminds you of death. We add a scythe and, by personification, we call death "the grim reaper." Allegories, fables and parables are likewise founded on similarity. These hit home mainly by causing us to bring other thoughts to mind either directly or by way of moral.

Association works through partial identity and this likewise is the basis of at least two figures of speech. When a part suggests the whole, as in "the hand that rocks the cradle rules the world," it's synecdoche. When we see a cradle and think of a mother, this is association by partial identity. When one word suggests another as in "the pen is mightier than the sword," that's metonymy. When we hear the word bugle and it makes us think of "Taps," that's association.

Association likewise works through sounds rather than words, and in this way parallels onomatopoeia. You hear a melody your wife played during your courtship, and you think of your wedding-day. Not that there is any connection, but you hear the whir of a vacuum-cleaner and think of a dentist's drill.

A silly story may help illustrate how association works by sound. Police officers traced a thief to a junk-yard. They decided to hunt for him among the bags of broken glass piled up against the back fence. The thief fooled them, for when they shook the bag in which he was hiding, he gurgled, "Tinkle, tinkle, tinkle." How did that whacky anecdote occur to me? I was thinking of suggestive sounds and "Jingle Bells" came to my mind. Jingle reminded me of tingle, and tingle suggested tinkle. Hence the inanity. Please pardon.

Other figures of speech are founded on contrast, listed by Aristotle as the third law of association. In irony we use the opposite of what we mean to convey, such as "a loud-mouth is never wrong." By the same token, association works by contrast as when I meet a noisy lout, and am reminded of my nice quiet brother. Antithesis, another contrasting figure, couples opposite words, such as: "What's mine is yours, and what's yours is mine." In the same way, a snow-storm in the Laurentian Mountains may remind me of a drought in the Arizona desert.

Hyperbole calls for deliberate exaggeration. The biographer of Baron Munchausen sought to picture a snow-fall ludicrously deep. "Snow-banks as high as a church-spire," he may have thought to himself. "But where, then, could the Baron tie his horse?" And his answer was, "To the top of a steeple of course." Thus, through exaggeration, the author's chain-thinking led him to a delightfully preposterous word-picture.

"The tyranny of words" stems from association of ideas. "Communism" meant Christian living in the days of the old

Oneida community, whereas now the European version of the same word spells Godlessness. On the other hand, when 645 students were asked to put down the greatest word in our language, the majority chose "mother." Nearly all the rest chose "home." No two other words can click so many memories.

Even smells can invoke chains of thoughts. The aroma of boiling coffee can take some of us back to a camp in the woods, even though the odor may come from a mammoth urn in a downtown cafeteria. As an exaggerated illustration of why laws of association cannot be pinned down, here's a weird passage my daughter loved to quote while at college: "What is a double petunia? A petunia is a flower like a begonia. A begonia is a meat like a sausage. A sausage-and-battery is a crime. Monkeys crime trees. Tree's a crowd. A crow crowd in the morning and made a noise. A noise is on your face between your eyes. Eyes is opposite from nays. A colt nays. You go to bed with a colt. And wake up in the morning with a case of double petunia."

3.

Many students of imagination have stressed *combination* as the essence of creativity. "A creative thinker," said Dr. Easton, "evolves no new ideas. He actually evolves new combinations of ideas that are already in his mind." Chain-thinking naturally contributes much to the creation of combinations. For most combinations are based on groupings of like things and thoughts; and similarity is the basic law of association.

When I was sales-manager of a bed-factory, we had a chance to bid on a large hospital order. But the legs of the beds had to be fitted with sliding glass casters, and the only ones we could buy were too high-priced. So I put my mind to trying to think up a way to meet that specification at less cost. The next noon, at the desk of my boss, we were talking about other matters when my elbow touched his water bottle. I looked at it and saw its glass-stopper. That started me on the idea of casting glass into plugs with spirally grooved stems. A nick at the bottom of the bed-post provided a bayonet-catch. The result was a tight-fitting sliding glass-caster at a cost of about $1.00 per bed less. Thus did association of ideas play into my hands by showing me how to turn a glass-stopper into a bed-caster.

The power of association can also lead us into creative undertakings. Wilbur and Orville Wright were wild about flying kites. They were in the bicycle business and had no thought of airplanes. One day they read about a German meeting his death in an attempt to glide off a mountain with giant wings fastened to his arms and a tail fastened to his back. That led the Wright brothers to construct a glider with nothing but sport in mind. One thing led to another, and the history made by the Wrights at Kitty Hawk was directly due to that chain of ideas.

When I see a dog, I am pleasantly reminded of my boyhood—the hut I built up in a tree for me and my dog, Zip—the old swimming-hole in the Harlem River where Zip and I had such fun splashing around together. But the sight of a dog always terrified Louis Pasteur. Even a distant bark would agonize his mind with memories of neighbors driven crazy and poisoned to death by bites of a mad wolf which raged through his boyhood village. "I have always been haunted by the cries of those victims," he said time and again.

Pasteur had just startled the world with his man-guarding vaccines. Dozens of deadly diseases were crying for his genius. But, suddenly he gave up everything else and started on a mad hunt for the secret of rabies. Thus did a childhood memory push Pasteur into a new field, a field in which relatively few human lives had ever been lost. That was in 1882 when he was past 60.

For three long years he risked his life living with mad dogs. At last he came through with a vaccine to cure the victims of rabies. On a July night in 1885 he tried the first injection on a little boy whose life seemed doomed. The boy lived. That was Pasteur's last work, and probably the triumph which gave him his greatest thrill—so closely was it linked to those heart-rending cries which had haunted him for over 50 years.

What made Cecil de Mille soar above his fellow-producers and put out pictures like *The King of Kings*? "I have no doubt," said he, "that my father's vivid reading of Biblical stories planted in my impressionable mind a reverence and respect for the Bible, perhaps even a sense of its dramatic values, which in subsequent years was to turn me to the Great Book for themes to thrill motion picture audiences."

Especially when thinking creatively in groups, association is a powerful factor. We bat ideas around the table and one idea bumps another into existence. I say, "How about this—?" The next man to me listens and suddenly exclaims, "That gives me an idea." Then he sets forth a suggestion based on my first thought. And so it goes, one idea suggesting another and still another.

4.

Calvin Coolidge believed in letting nature take its course, but added that he "liked to *nudge* nature." We can nudge association, too. It's like growing dates. Ancient Egypt and modern Arizona are much alike and both are lush with dates. But without man's toil, Arizona dates would be mostly stones. The meat comes from a mating between the male palms and the female. In Africa, this fertilization is done by nature. In Arizona, human effort has to transfer the pollen from the male trees to the female trees each and every spring.

Thus it is with cross-fertilization of ideas. We should nudge nature with purposiveness, according to Aristotle, who recommended that we "hunt for the next in the series, starting our train of thought from what is now present or from something else, and from something similar or contrary or contiguous to it." And in recent years, James Ward, English psychologist and philosopher, stressed how association can be enriched by *selective attention*. The more persistent our interest is, said he, the more we can profit from association. In other words, although association normally runs through our mental hose hither-and-yon, and willy-nilly—if we keep our nozzle trained on the creative task at hand, we can make our flow of association sprout more seeds for us.

While working on this book, my mind increasingly dwelt on the mystery of imagination. One morning I went to the cellar and noticed an old kiddy-car which reminded me of my son. I thought how glad I was that he was back at college, and had escaped the fate of so many of his mates while crossing the Rhine with the 17th Airborne. That reminded me of planes. And that reminded me of jet planes. "I wonder who thought up the first jet plane and how he came to do so." That was my next thought. And it came to me because my mind was saturated with my interest in the subject of creative thinking.

Daymond Aiken maintained that our power of association will produce more ideas if we keep a notebook and jot down our hunches, our observations, and our conclusions. "Ideas are flighty things," said Aiken. "That which now seems perfectly clear may later get away from you. Make a habit of jotting down ideas as they occur to you. Although many of them will not work out, they may *suggest other thoughts*."

The use of check-lists can help make chain-thinking yield more creative dividends. A would-be writer of articles, for instance, could well look over index after index of many magazines. In a few hours he could probably bring to his mind at least 50 ideas for possible subjects, none exactly the same as covered by the indices. And there are scores of other such check-lists by which we can consciously add amperage to the power of chain-thinking.

Clement Kieffer operates a strange kind of check-list in the form of a grab-bag. In charge of window displays for Kleinhans' store in Buffalo, he has won more prizes for ideas than any man in his line. In addition to cash awards, he has garnered about 350 medals and cups. He has 33 windows to fill each week. It is his stint to come up with at least one new idea every day of the month including Sundays.

For his check-list he uses a big box into which he throws clippings and pieces of paper with notes or sketches of ideas he has thought up. His grab-bag bulges with over 3,000 such idea-starters. I asked him why he did not organize them in orderly files. "If I did that," he replied, "I would then go to just one place and pick up only one or two thoughts. I have found from experience that by pawing through hundreds of random ideas, I not only am more likely to get one that seems to fit my need—but, far more than that, I find that one idea suggests another, and after doing a lot of pawing, am apt to come up with something new and different from any in my grab-bag."

Yes, grab-bags, check-lists, note-pads, purposiveness, stick-to-it-iveness—with these we can cause our power of association to well up more ideas for us out of the storage-tanks called memory.

Chapter X

EMOTIONAL DRIVE AS A SOURCE
OF CREATIVE POWER

IN THE MAIN, the action of association is like momentum and is usually a by-product of the energy we generate to empower our imagination. This force stems from two sources—our *emotions* and our *will*. Nearly all driving-power is a mixture of both.

Emotional drive is self-starting and largely automatic, whether based on hunger, fear, love or ambition. The other kind of energy depends upon determination rather than feelings, and has to be cranked and cranked hard. The next chapter will describe specific ways to do this cranking.

According to Dr. William Easton, even scientists must be motivated by "enthusiasm, devotions, passions, for creative thinking is not a purely intellectual process; on the contrary, the thinker is dominated by his emotions from the start to the finish of his work."

Brain surgeons are now linking emotions with imagination. Their knives are proving that every brain has a section that can create ideas. It is called the "silent area" since it controls no body-movement, and has naught to do with what we see or hear or physically feel. Back of this area is a lump of tissue called the thalamus. In this lobe, our basic emotions are centered. We have always known that ideas flow faster under emotional stress. Now we know that our

71

emotional lobe is wired by nerves to the frontal area in such a way as to affect creative thinking. In the new surgery for insanity, the nerves are severed between the emotional lobe and the "silent area." This new technique has been successful in over 1000 cases. It is too early to know to what extent the creative faculty may be set back by thus being cut off from the basic emotions. But this development in psychosurgery certainly provides further evidence that the creative part of us is not a thing apart—that it is hooked up with, and can be driven by, emotions.

2.

When in a jam our imaginations often soar. But this does not mean that a crisis makes our creative talent any greater; it merely means that exigency can throw our emotional drive into high gear. Napoleon laid great stress on this human trait. He held that mental excitement fuses acquired knowledge with imagination and thus produces, right then and there, the winning strategies and tactics.

That may have been true of Napoleon, and is often true with average men. But far safer and better is the steady plodding and planning of the Eisenhowers. For passion often works imagination too wildly in a life-and-death dilemma. Normally, it is good creative policy to make our imagination shoot wild—as long as we have time later to choose our good ideas from our bad. But when a passion of panic overruns us, our imagination is too prone to go haywire.

That fact has been proven in many ways, and especially in fires. When the Winecoff Hotel in Atlanta burst into flames, desperate people thought up ideas that led to their death. To save her small son, a woman on the seventh floor threw him out of the window. A girl made a rope out of her sheet and tried to let herself down to an aerial ladder which was just about to reach her. She lost her grip and met her death on the marquee. Fright is too treacherous a drive—because it's an animal urge that throws us back to where we were before our intellects developed. As Dr. Harry Fosdick has said, "it works without benefit of brain."

Akin to fright is fear of punishment. This spur may make us work hard physically, but how can a man focus his creative mind when obsessed by fear of punishment? Even the slightest degree of coercion tends to cramp imagination. Dr. Howard E. Fritz, research-head of the B. F. Goodrich Company, has pointed this out. "To induce creative thinking," he said, "we cannot dominate or threaten. Such methods will not and cannot inspire."

"Inspiration is and can be the product only of free men," added Dr. Fritz. If this is so then democracy provides the healthiest climate for creativity. Fortunately in America, creative minds are not paralyzed by fear of what their political beliefs might bring down upon their houses. Totalitarian rulers have to keep fear alive in every heart lest their regimes may tumble.

After the last war, our government sent to Germany my friend Dr. Max E. Bretschger, one of America's most creative chemists. His mission was to determine how far German scientists might have gone ahead of us in creation of new chemicals for advanced warfare. German chemists had always been great chemists. Wouldn't you think that, under the Nazi whip, they would have been driven far beyond what our chemists had achieved?

"No," said Dr. Bretschger. "To our surprise we found that we had out-thought them." Because they were so concerned about their personal lives in the hands of Hitler, they could not drive their minds to get the most out of their imaginations.

3.

Love is a steadier and better driving-power. Love of country inspired hundreds of thousands of our people to think up ideas that helped win the last war. Their spur of patriotism was intensified by their love of sons, husbands, brothers and sweethearts far away on the fighting front. An outstanding war-time creator was Mrs. Frances Herman, mother and grandmother. She thought up a way to speed up production of war instruments by over 33 per cent. She accounted for what she did on the grounds that her own son was in uniform, and also that her extra efforts made her feel "as though we were a second front right here."

Love makes the average woman unceasingly think up things for her family. The overpowering drive of maternal instinct has been scientifically proved beyond doubt. Among others, a group of Columbia scientists has demonstrated that, even with animals, the *maternal* drive generates far more ingenious effort than thirst or hunger or sex.

Grief sometimes intensifies the spur of love and steps up creative drive. This was true of the young Toronto girl who, in her first attempt at song-writing, composed a smash hit. Ruth Lowe later told her story of how she did this. Her husband, a handsome young pianist, had died shortly after they were married. She was left to face the future alone, with a piano that remained closed. One night her father urged her to try to forget herself by playing a piece. She said she never wanted to play the piano again—it reminded her too poignantly of her lost husband. Her father urged her to quit giving way to emotion—"to take it out on the piano."

"But Dad," she said, "I don't know any of the songs people are playing now." To which her father replied: "Well, then make something up." That was what led her to try to write a song. And the song she wrote was *I'll Never Smile Again*.

4.

Love when turned to hate can likewise lift a "non"-creative person to creative heights. Remember the story about the camera-gun that shot the leg off a girl in the New York subway? According to Bellevue Hospital, A. Rocco was a man of "average intelligence." He had been a good-for-nothing floater. His first wife threw him out. His hatred led him to invent a machine to kill her. *Time* described this device as "a package-camera ingeniously devised of cream cheese boxes, wire, and an empty tin can with an innocent baked bean label. This casing concealed a 12-gauge Stevens single shot, sawed-off shotgun."

With fiendish ingenuity, Rocco picked up a girl and led her to hunt his first wife so as to "snap a picture of her" with that lethal camera. He gave her the story that her quarry was a jewel thief and he a detective. The empty-headed girl did the dirty-work for Rocco not knowing she was shooting a woman's leg off with her "camera."

What imagination! To what heights Rocco could have risen if his talent had been steadily empowered with decent emotions and reasonable will-power!

5.

"I address myself only to those among you who have ambition to become millionaires." Andrew Carnegie thus greeted a student-body. Greed for gold does provide an emotional drive in all pursuits including the creative. "But," said W. B. Wiegand, "the motive power which stokes the fires of creative thought is far more subtle, and indeed far more potent, than the lure of gold. It is ofttimes a spirit of intellectual adventure which will supply this magic touch of motivation." Yes, adventure—and let's own up to it—vanity, too, in the guise of self-realization.

The fear of poverty is even a stronger urge than the hope of riches, and this fact makes adversity an ally of creative effort. Many of our most creative people came from forebears who had long faced starvation or persecution, or both. From them, their Americanized children inherited the urges that go with adversity.

Even a generation ago, the shadow of the poorhouse made native Americans strive so hard as to induce the habit of effort on which imagination feeds. I know that in my own case, my chronic drive goes back to a childhood of insecurity,

My sharpest memory of early years is the night I was awakened from my sleep by voices in the next room. I was only about six, but I can almost recall the very words my father said to my mother, in their double-bed: "I can't help it, Kitty. I am going to lose my job and we are going to have to scratch to make ends meet. We haven't enough saved to live on for more than a few months, and I am worried about you and the kids." Eventually they went to sleep, but I stayed awake. An hour later, about four o'clock in the morning, I went in and woke them up. "I heard you and mama talking," said I, "and I couldn't get back to sleep. Don't worry about money. Remember that box of pencils you gave me last Christmas? I still have them, and I'll go down on the corner and sell them for five cents apiece—so we will be all right." Undoubtedly I over-dramatized this crisis at the time; but it did serve to spur me into an incurable habit of effort.

It is often true, as George Moore remarked, that "the muse was with us when we were poor, but when we were rich she deserted us." When economic pressure is lifted, a man has to pump back into himself some of that feeling of *must*. Gerald Carson, a successful idea-man in New York, replied when asked how he forces his imagination: "I just make myself think of baby needing new shoes." His baby has had no cause for any such worry, but prosperous Carson prods his imagination by using it to re-create the motivation of his struggling days.

Hard going induces hard effort in the nation as well as the individual. As F. Wayland Vaughan has pointed out, "Creative effort in times of prosperity has tended to ebb, whereas depressions have brought about extra efforts that have resulted in many of the advancements which have put America ahead of the rest of the world."

6.

The drive we need to make the most of our imagination is usually a mixture of inner urges and self-imposed spurs.

And even these may change from time to time. In Michael Sadleir's analysis of Anthony Trollope's life, speaking of the writings of Anthony's mother, Sadleir said: "Her novels were *first* written from stark necessity—*later* from congenial and profitable habit." Thus it is that a person may first be forced by economic compulsion or some other strong emotion, and then be driven by habit. Even habit may wane and public acclaim may then step in as the main urge.

But the habit of effort is the surest standby, according to Edna Ferber, who wrote as follows in her autobiography: "With millions of others I have been a work worshipper. Work and more work. Work was a sedative, a stimulant, an escape, an exercise, a diversion, a passion. When friends failed or fun palled or spirits flagged, there was my typewriter and there was the world, my oyster. I've worked daily for over a quarter of a century, and loved it. I've worked while ill in bed, while traveling in Europe, riding on trains. I've written in woodsheds, bathrooms, cabins, compartments, bedrooms, living-rooms, gardens, porches, decks, hotels, newspaper offices, theatres, kitchens. Nothing in my world was so satisfactory, so lasting and sustaining as work."

Very few will admit it, but just plain fun ultimately becomes one of the urges after a habit of creative effort has been formed. Even those who have to rub their lamps for a living often rub them for diversion. The editor of a great magazine, with two hours to spend on a train, amused himself by imagining himself to be a struggling publisher of a one-man weekly newspaper. Before he reached his destination, he had thought up about 50 things he would do if his circulation were in the hundreds instead of in the millions.

And so we run the gamut of emotional drives. With some, these are far more powerful than with others. But, in the long run, our feelings are too unsteady as forces on which any of us can wholly rely for our creative power. We still have to do a lot of tugging on our bootstraps.

Chapter XI

WHERE THERE'S A WILL
THERE ARE WAYS TO THINK UP

IN SPORTS, even strenuous sports, we can relax insofar as we don't have to exert our minds. Likewise, we can with ease control our minds in other non-creative ways. We can easily make ourselves say the Lord's Prayer—we could even do this standing on the corner of Fifth Avenue and Forty-Second Street despite all the noises and sights. Yes, we "can tyrannize over the mind every hour of the day and in no matter what place," as Arnold Bennett said; but not without lots of effort can we drive our imaginations.

Most of us agree that the average person must and can try hard to make imagination work; but a few still seem to feel that a genius just gushes ideas. The geniuses themselves say otherwise. Dr. Willard Henry Dow, who helped win the last war by wringing magnesium out of the ocean, has openly resented his being hailed as an automaton of alchemy. According to him his "genius" is nothing but hard work. Ideas have not come easy even to men like E. M. Statler. His personal secretary, Bert Stanbro, told me: "Although the hotel-world thought of E.M. as a genius, I know that every one of his great ideas came from sweating and sweating hard."

The electrical industry is a monument to man's imagination and the General Electric Company has had many so-called geniuses. If you look closely into their beliefs, you will find agreement with a remark recently made by Charles E. Wilson, General Electric president: "There just ain't no golden chariot that will take you there."

2.

"Mankind," said Battista Grassi, "is composed of those who work, those who pretend to work, and those who do neither. Unless you are in the first class, you will probably fail to summon up the energy to make yourself do the things that you have to do to get the most out of your imagination." And wrote Pasteur to his family: "To will is a great thing, dear sisters, for action and work usually follow will, and will opens the door to success"—and being Pasteur, he naturally meant success in a creative sense.

But we are no Pasteurs. So again comes the question as to whether average persons are up to such captaining of their minds. In answer, William James wrote, "The *normal* opener of deeper and deeper levels of energy is the will." And Brooks Atkinson attested: "*Every man* can achieve a great deal . . . according to the burning intensity of his will and the keenness of his imagination."

Many young men have come to me for creative jobs and I have been amazed to find how few have ever called on their wills to work their imaginations. One of my test questions has been, "What did you ever try to think up on your own accord?" In nine out of ten cases the answer has been, "Nothing." How can they hope for creative responsibility when they have never learned the first lesson?

3.

Some *hows* may help. One way to "put your mind to it" is to make a date with yourself—to set a time and place, as when you go to your room on a Sunday afternoon to play idea-solitaire. Most writers use this device. In Phoenix, after

a meeting at which we both spoke, I asked Clarence Budington Kelland how he went to it. He confessed that he never
would turn out a thing if he did not schedule himself—that
each morning after breakfast he had to gird himself to start
tapping his typewriter, and had to force himself to keep
pounding hour after hour. He admitted that his genius is
about 30 per cent knack and 70 per cent sweat.

Alan Ward, one of our most creative men, makes a date
with himself to think up while washing dishes on Saturday
mornings after breakfast. Would you believe that I sometimes make a date with myself to attack a creative task while
driving? One morning I woke up to the fact that a certain
problem needed immediate solution. I made a date with
myself to brainstorm that problem during my hour's drive
to work. On the way I saw a lad signaling for a hitchhike.
I hesitated, but stopped; he got in and I said: "If you don't
mind, please don't talk because I have to think." Since the
road was straight and the traffic sparse, I could concentrate
as well as if in my office. At about half way, I suddenly got
the wanted idea, pulled off the road, took out a pad and
wrote an outline. Starting off again, I said to my young passenger: "Now you can talk, but first, don't you think I'm
kinda crazy?" "No," he replied. Our talk then revealed that
he was just finishing high school at the top of his class and
planned to become a newspaper reporter while, at the same
time, studying law at night. That helped me understand why
he had not thought me "nuts."

Pick a place. As a rule, offices are less good for creative
thinking than for judicial functioning. One man I know has
found he can ponder creative problems far better by staying
home in the morning. Once when I faced a hard creative
task, I went to an inn over 100 miles away. Not only was I
uninterrupted—not only did I get away from routine—but,
because I had made such effort to go so far solely to engage
in creative effort, my imagination seemed to work far
better. The very taking of that trip tended to sharpen my
imagination.

4.

Set a deadline. Give your I.O.U. Write a letter promising that you will have a certain number of ideas to offer at such-and-such a time. Your will is apt to kow-tow to a definite commitment. When you fix a deadline, you add an emotional power in the form of fear lest you may fall down.

Many creative people are driven by automatic deadlines. A columnist faces one such whip each day. A minister's weekly deadline badgers him into creative action. Our family listens each Sunday to Dr. Albert Butzer. At Sunday dinner one of us is likely to say: "Wasn't that a wonderful sermon this morning?" We seldom stop to think how tremendous was the creative effort that went into that sermon. The basic idea of each sermon—just that alone—requires more creative juice each week than most of us turn on in a month. And, beyond the theme, some fifty other ideas have to be thought up to give power and sparkle to each sermon.

Deadlines thrust upon us in business are often the spurs which win our spurs for us. Such was the turning-point in Walter Chrysler's career. As a boy apprentice in the Union Pacific shops, he loved locomotives, and learned the purpose of every bolt and nut. One day an engine pulled in with a cracked cylinder-head. The superintendent of motor-power called young Chrysler into his office. "Boy," he said, "we haven't any other locomotive to take the place of this one. This has got to be fixed in two hours. Can you do it?" After he had it fixed, Chrysler remarked: "Believe me that was some whale of a job. If I *hadn't* said I could do it in two hours, I wouldn't have put in so much mental sweat, and would have *failed*. I got myself in a spot where I had to finish it on time. And I did."

5.

Team up. Make a date with somebody else. That's the way Irving Berlin got started on song-writing. A neighbor of his in Chinatown had a knack of inventing tunes. Irving had thought up the first line for a new song. So he went to neighbor Nick and said, "See if you can write some music about a girl from sunny Italy." Nick wrote the tune and Berlin wrote the words. Alexander Woollcott described this first effort of Berlin's and its arduous teamwork. "*My Sweet Marie from Sunny Italy,*" wrote Woollcott, "was wrought with great groanings and infinite travail. Much of it had to be doctored by Nick, with considerable experimenting at the piano and a consequent displeasure felt by the patrons at Nigger Mike's who would express their feelings by hurling the damp beer-cloths at the singer's head. Truly it might be said that Berlin's first lyrics were wrought while he dodged the clouts of his outraged neighbors."

There have been famous man-and-wife teams in the history of creativeness. But the average man and wife—although they face many problems which call for ideas—how rare it is for them deliberately to team up in order to think up together. When I was about to be married, an old friend of mine, De-Forest Porter, gave me this advice: "Mrs. Porter and I have gotten along better than most couples, and it's mainly because we have never gone to sleep with a quarrel on our minds. Whenever we had a disagreement we talked together to find a way to wash it out—no matter how late at night we had to stay up to do it." How many couples have teamed up like that to melt the misunderstandings that might turn into icy barriers? It may seem cynical, but isn't it true that many couples team up their creative minds only when a baby is about to come, and they feel forced to buckle down to picking a name?

6.

To move the will into imaginative action, *pencils* can serve as crowbars. Although it's almost axiomatic that the more notes we make, the more ideas we are likely to produce, how few of us take advantage of this device. One week

I went through six conferences in which, all-told, about 100 men "took part." Only three of them put down any notes.

Note-taking helps in several ways. It empowers association, it piles up alternatives, it stores rich fuel that otherwise would trickle out through our forgettery. But, above all, note-taking of itself induces a spirit of effort.

As recently as 50 years ago, office buildings displayed signs saying: "Peddlers, Advertising Agents, and Dogs Not Allowed." The advertising agency business had its great rise between 1900 and 1930, and its main builders during that period were Stanley Resor of J. Walter Thompson, Harry K. McCann of McCann-Erickson, Albert Lasker of Lord and Thomas, and William H. Johns of the George Batten Company. An 8-year-old upstart, Barton, Durstine and Osborn, merged with the 30-year-old Batten Company in 1928; and Mr. Johns became Chairman of our Board. About then, when I complimented him on his record, he said this: "I never could have made the grade except that I *tried harder*, for Resor, McCann and Lasker are far brighter men than I." Robert Updegraff wrote a book about Mr. Johns, called *Obvious Adams*. Although our "chief" was never regarded as "brilliant," the ideas he laboriously brought to American business made his creative record shine.

Mr. Johns' secret weapons were pencils; and they were so important to him that he went to great ends to choose them. I inherited his desk, and with it some pencils he had personally imported from Germany. Their black lead was as thick as a cigarette. I found other pencils of his just as soft, but easier to keep sharp. He had had these made solely for him by the American Pencil Company.

To Mr. Johns, the usual memo-book seemed too hard to pull out and too cumbersome to use. Likewise, the usual 3 x 5 cards were not reachable enough. So he designed a form 8″ long and only 2½″ wide, made of cardboard stiff enough to stand up and almost stick out of his inside pocket. Several of us adopted the note-cards and, for further "come-on," we had these red-letter words printed on the top of each side: "For Notes and *Ideas*."

My own habits of note-taking might easily mark me as a "nut." Even while listening to a sermon, I sometimes sneak out my narrow card and make a note. Sitting in the dark on a veranda, I have often pulled out my card and scribbled without seeing what I wrote. While playing golf I carry no note-cards, but, whenever I hear or think of something that might lead to an idea, I put it down on my score-card. Once, when without a score-card, I caught and saved an idea on the inside cover of a match-folder.

<h1 style="text-align:center">7.</h1>

Imaginations are not like Ouija boards, which work better when we work our will not at all. But even to play Ouija, we have to *make a start*. To shove off on a mental voyage is not so easy—our brains are so prone to drift. As William James pointed out, "In the dim background of our mind we know what we ought to be doing . . . but somehow we cannot start . . . every moment we expect the spell to break . . . but it continues, pulse after pulse, and we float with it."

A handy-man learned that I, when well over 50, had started to paint in oils, and he showed me some of his pencil-sketches which, to my eye, revealed real talent. He was a widower and lived alone. I felt that painting could brighten his life, so I gave him a complete equipment, plus a book on how to get started. He was delighted. A few months later I asked him, "How are you getting along with your painting, Frank?" He replied that he had not "started yet." When I asked why, he answered: "Because I'm afraid I can't do it good." A year later I queried him again. And even two years later, I found he had yet to squeeze a tube or pick up a brush.

Perhaps, if I had bought him a scholarship at an art school, he might have become a John Falter. For "taking a course" is sometimes a good way of making a start.

As Gertrude Samuels has said, "the favorite method of

melody-men is 'cold bloodedly' to make a start—to pick a tune, any tune, out of the piano." George Meyer, when asked how he turned out *For Me and My Gal*, snapped back: "I just sat down and went to work." And remember the tune, *There Are Such Things*, written by Stanley Adams? He wanted to sing cheer in the midst of war. "So," said he, "I started with a peaceful sky." The point is—he started.

8.

A good way to get going is to *give yourself a quota*. Suppose you first set for yourself a stint of only five ideas. In thinking up those five, others will occur; and the first thing you know you will be on your way to 25. And the more ideas, the more likely it will be that one of them will hit the bull's-eye.

In starting yourself by giving yourself a quota, it is best to make the aim specific. If an employee, you might pick out something as simple as, "What can I do to get ahead in my job?" With pad and pencil, you could sit down at any time and write down five ideas. But don't stop there. Give yourself a new quota of 10 more ideas, and so on until you have listed at least 25. This same technique can work well when it comes to family problems. For example, if a father is worrying about his boy being out too much, he could narrow the aim to: "What can I do to make my boy want to stay home more?" Starting with five ideas, he could easily think up 25—some of which would be *don'ts* as well as *dos*.

Or suppose you were chairwoman of a church supper. Alone, in your boudoir, you could write down at least 10 suggestions to make the event more successful. You could then say to your committee: "Let's think up everything we can to liven up this supper. Here are 10 ideas of mine. Gertrude, I want you to come to our next meeting with a list of 10 ideas for the entertainment part. Adele, I am going to ask you to do the same thing on food. And Maude, there must be lots of ways to better the service—you bring in 10 ideas on that. And Kay, you have a taste for making things look attractive—will you take the subject of decorations and bring in 10 ideas on that? Lighting can do a lot to liven up a supper, so I am going to ask you, Joan, to bring in 10 ideas on that." Together with your own 10 ideas, you would probably end up with 60 or 70 from which your committee could choose the most usable.

9.

Creativity also calls for *keeping going*. We too often give up too easily and too early, mainly because we tend to overrate the power of inspiration and wait for lightning to strike us. Why don't we realize that the way to start is to start, and that there is no truth stronger than the old maxim of "try and try again"? The renowned rowing coach Ten Eyck used to nag his crews with this: "If you hang on two strokes longer than your opponents, you will lick 'em." That would be a good motto to put on the desk of anyone who wants to pull ahead in the creative race.

Because a man named Lester Pfister kept going for five years straight, there is more likelihood that the world can eat well. For America's corn would be less plentiful if Pfister hadn't kept going and going and going to make it hardier. In a chance conversation, he got the idea of inbreeding stalks of corn in order to kill off weaker strains and build up a hardier species. He started with 50,000 stalks, and tied a bag around each tassel. When this was full of pollen, he inverted it over the silk of an ear on the same stalk. Then the tassel was snapped off.

The whole process had to be done painstakingly by hand, season after season. Five years later, Pfister was left with four ears out of his original 50,000 stalks. By that time he was destitute, but had a fortune in hand. For those four ears, unmarred by disease after five generations, represented the source of a perfected seed for which farmers ever since have gladly paid a premium.

Few of us can hope to keep at it as hard as Edison, Chrysler, Pfister or others who have made history by creative doggedness. Or as Abraham Lincoln, who said: "When I got on a hunt for an idea, I could not sleep until I had caught it." And yet can't all of us—by keeping our imaginations on the grindstone just a little longer—spark more ideas and step up our creative power?

Chapter XII

JUDGMENT MAY CHOKE IDEAS—
LET'S KEEP IT IN ITS PLACE

"GOOD JUDGMENT is the test of a trained mind." So said Matthew Thompson McClure, who thus joined John Dewey and other thinkers in putting the judicial mind on a pedestal. But in creative effort, judgment is good only when *properly timed.*

Judicial effort and creative effort are alike in that both call for analysis and synthesis. The judicial mind breaks facts down, weighs them, compares them, rejects some, keeps others—and then puts together the resultant elements to form a conclusion. The creative mind does much the same, except that the end-product is an idea instead of a verdict. Then, too, whereas judgment tends to confine itself to facts in hand, imagination has to reach out for the unknown—almost to the point of making two and two make something more than four.

Of course judgment is important. But if man had had nothing but a judicial faculty where would we be? Without imagination the world would probably still be in a primitive stage—with everything so simple, so judged and re-judged over the centuries, that even judgment would be unimportant.

Compared to creative effort, judicial effort is far easier. Pros and cons "come" to us without strain. Even analysis is relatively easy. Otherwise millions of race-goers would not indulge in all-out efforts along that line in order to win a few dollars on a horse. They study ancestry, the weight each steed must carry, the records of the jockeys. Most of them even analyze what each horse did in previous races, what its post position is to be, and whether track conditions are thus or so. A new $10 gadget called the "Ponymeter" was recently introduced to make all that "work" even easier.

2.

Basically there are two kinds of judgment—critical judgment and constructive judgment. The critical calls mainly for knowledge, whereas the constructive may need help from imagination. Is Nylon better than silk? This calls for a simple process of critical analysis. "Should we do this or that?" Here we have to think up all possible alternatives, and foresee results. We have to ask ourselves questions such as, "What are the consequences?" . . . "What if others did that?" "What if conditions change?" And in each case we have to tap imagination for the answer.

In the average person, judgment grows automatically with years, while creativity dwindles unless consciously kept up. Circumstances force us to use our judicial mind every waking hour. When we arise in the morning, the first questions are: "What will I wear?" . . . "How cold is it outside?" We have to decide a dozen such matters before breakfast. "What will I eat?" . . . "Some bacon, or an egg?" . . . "If I have an egg, would I rather have it fried or boiled?" And so on, from rising to retiring—from childhood to the end—we exercise our judgment. And by exercise it grows, or should grow, better and stronger.

Then, too, education makes our judgment grow. We study mathematics, we study logic, we learn to debate, we read history, we discuss pros and cons. Over 90 per cent of our education tends to train and strengthen our judicial faculties. Still another influence tends to do the same—it's stylish to be an unerring judge. "He's a wonderful man—he never makes any mistakes." You hear that 10 times as often as you hear, "He has imagination *and* he makes it *work*." Instead, our friends are more likely to call us "nuts." Oh, what overweening pride most of us have in our own power of choice. "I would rather be right than President," applies not only to morality, but also to errorlessness.

How few of us ever stop to think that our judgment may be no better than the other fellow's. This is why we are so quick to offer our opinion; and it is this tendency to criticize *too soon* that makes judgment so great a threat to creative effort. A good slogan for all of us would be, "Judge wisely but at the right time."

An overgrown judgment makes our creative minds muscle-bound. Just as weeds choke out flowers in a garden, too much judgment tends to choke out the imaginative talent with which we were born. That's what so often happens to the imagination of little children. While thinking about this chapter I was sitting on the lawn trying to add life to a canvas I had painted of a rainbow over the bay. Four little children came to watch me. Within 10 minutes they made one suggestion after another, and I quickly brushed in their ideas with the result that the painting became livelier than a battle-royal.

The next day, two of those little girls dreamed up the cause of thunder. Molly Millonzi, aged four, was the daughter of a kindergarten teacher and of a brilliant lawyer. Her friend Sarah, aged five, was the youngest of a brood. "What makes thunder?" Molly had asked her mother while being put to bed. "I'll tell you tomorrow," was the cautious reply.

That evening Molly's parents went into conference. With the help of the *Encyclopædia Britannica*, they arrived at a scientific explanation of thunder, and worked out the way to tell Molly in line with the best teachings of child psychology. The next morning, Molly's mother took plenty of time to make sure her child would never again wonder about thunder. Afternoon came. Molly and Sarah were playing on the beach. Black clouds loomed over the bay. Then came the rumble of thunder. Molly rushed up to her mother on the veranda and breathlessly shouted: "Do you know, Mom, what really causes thunder? It's the black angels in the North Pole throwing *thunder-mugs* at each other—Sarah just told me!" No judgment, but what imagination!

3.

The fact that moods won't mix largely explains why the judicial and the creative tend to clash. Unless properly coordinated, each may mar the working of the other. The right mood for judicial thinking is largely negative. "What's wrong with this?" . . . "What's the out about that?" . . . "No, that won't work." Such reflexes are right and proper when trying to judge. And we need a negative attitude for caution such as: "Beware of it—it's too new." . . . "Are we sure this won't be a mistake?"

In contrast, our creative thinking calls for a positive attitude. We have to be hopeful. We need enthusiasm. We have to encourage ourselves to the point of self-confidence. We have to beware of perfectionism lest it be abortive. Edison's first lamp was a crude affair. He must have realized that— must have known that it would certainly be improved—if not by him, by somebody else. He could have hung onto his imperfect model while he tried and tried to make it better. Or he could have junked the whole idea. He didn't do either. His first electric lamps were better than candles, kerosene lamps, or gaslights—so he introduced them. Then he went to work on improvements.

Dr. Suits of G-E has declared the positive attitude "a characteristic of creative people." He urges: "Form the habit of reacting *Yes* to a new idea. First, think of all the reasons why it's good; there will be plenty of people around to tell you why it won't work."

Judgment and imagination can help each other if kept apart when they should be kept apart. In creative effort we have to be a Jekyll-and-Hyde. From time to time, we must

turn off our judicial mind and light up our creative mind.
And we must wait long enough before turning up our judicial
light again. Otherwise, premature judgment may douse our
creative flames, and even wash away ideas already generated.

4.

Creative success is usually in ratio to the *number* of alternatives thought up. Thus, if we conceive 100 alternatives,
our chances of landing the right idea are *more* than 10
times greater than if we stop at 10 alternatives. When we let
judgment start to throw cold water too soon, our imagination
whines, "Oh well, what's the use of trying to think up more
alternatives?" Premature judgment may thus stop us from
keeping going.

Especially in approaching a creative problem, we should
give imagination priority over judgment and let it roam
around our objective. We might even make a conscious effort
to think up the wildest ideas that could possibly apply. For
at this point, we are just warming up our think-up apparatus
—limbering up our imagining muscles. Instead of laughing at
such preliminary flashes—fantastic as they might seem to Old
Man Judgment—we should put them down on paper. One of
them might turn out to be as sensible as a doorkey.

Some of our greatest medical men realize the need to keep
their minds free to pile up alternatives when diagnosing and
thinking up treatment. A friend of mine had an ailment so
mysterious that his own doctor finally gave up in despair, and
took him to Johns Hopkins. A specialist welcomed the local
physician with these remarks: "If you don't mind, I would
rather you wouldn't tell me what your patient's symptoms
are. Let me start from scratch. My reason is that if you tell
me what *you* think, I may find it too easy to agree—and, if
so, may be unable to make my mind reach out and arrive at
a possible cure."

Actually, he did come finally to the same diagnosis as the
local doctor; but, on the way he hit upon a treatment—a treat-

ment so radical that he might not have thought of it if his mind had been blocked by second-hand judgment. That was 15 years ago. The patient is now well over 70 and still working as hard as any other lawyer in the country. In *Who's Who* he is listed as John Lord O'Brian.

One creative friend of mine makes it a rule to exclude outside judgment until he has thought up all possible ideas. To those who prematurely try to pick flaws he says: "I don't want your judgment—not yet. Just now I want more and better ideas. What have you to suggest?" Even in the larger scope of world progress, judgment, in the form of common convictions, can block scientific advance. For, as stated by Harvard President Conant, "a well-established concept may prove a barrier to the acceptance of a new one."

5.

Of the ways to prevent judgment from cramping creativeness, we have already touched on the main method; and that is to *delay* judgment—not only suspend it, but *postpone* it until our ingenuity has piled up all possible ideas. Even at that point we should make no effort to exercise judgment. We should first let our minds coast a while. Mental loafing at the right time induces inspiration which may either add other ideas—or may combine into a better idea two or more of the many we have already thought up.

Some creative writers realize that they should not put on their judicial robes until they have written "30." Others change places with a partner so that neither needs to create and criticize at the same time. Augustus Goetz and his wife, Ruth Goodman, are successful playwrights who, working as a team, have an advantage over a lone-wolf in that respect. Mr. Goetz has given this further advice: "Don't talk about your new play to anybody—use that fresh creative drive to get it down on paper. Don't let anyone read it and counsel you on it until you have completed it to your satisfaction. . . . Your play will lose its emotional and intellectual unity if others do carpentry on it before it is finished. After it is finished, of course, a competent producer, director, and cast, can make valuable contributions."

When working as a team as the Goetzes do, a mutually sympathetic attitude cuts down the danger of killing ideas too soon. But suppose Thomas Edison and George Westinghouse had tried to work in partnership on alternating current. If this problem had not been solved, and if Tesla had not created the A.C. motor, "relatively few homes would have electricity," in the opinion of Harland Manchester. But how could an Edison-Westinghouse team have gotten anywhere, with Edison's judgment so out of sympathy? "There is no plea," said he, "which will justify the use of alternating currents, either in a scientific or commercial sense; and my personal desire would be to prohibit their use." To which Westinghouse cracked back: "Alternating current will kill people, of course. So will dynamite, and whiskey, and lots of other things; but we can perfect ways whereby the deadly electricity of the alternating current can do no harm."

A point to be kept in mind is that in most creative efforts there is no need for any decision as to relative merits of our ideas *until* we come to the question of which one, if any, is to be used. At this time we should be as cold in our criticism as we have been warm in our enthusiasm during the creative process. And when it comes to judging, if we can test, rather than opine, so much the better. Personal judgment can't help but be tinged with environmental prejudices. Seldom can it help but be subjective. Often it leads to debate in which one almost loses one's mind, with no gain except to win an argument. Since opinion can always be wrong—even expert opinion—we can truly regard the technique of testing as one of our great advances in recent years.

It used to be that when picking a title for a movie, directors, executives, and everybody else would wrangle all over the lot. "I think it should be named so-and-so." . . . "That's lousy—I think it should be called so-and-so." Thus the battle would go on until the writers—their creative talent discouraged to the sulking point—would try less hard to suggest titles for the next new picture.

Thanks to George Gallup and Raymond Rubicam, titles are now tested. The best ones among all those suggested for a movie are exposed to theater-goers by investigators. They record the many Tom-Dick-and-Harry reactions, which are then scientifically boiled down to a final judgment—a judgment far keener than that of any man because, as Talleyrand remarked: "There is only one person who knows more than anybody, and that is everybody."

When ideas, instead of being tested, are subjected to personal judgment, a powerful debater can kill the better ones and enable the less fit to survive. Not only that—but, in the very process of testing ideas, new ideas are more likely to crop up, or at least, to stand up. Henry Weaver of General Motors conducts a vast jury to gather consumer judgment as to features already on G-M automobiles, as well as to new ideas under consideration. Recently I asked him about this research of his and among other things he said: "We have far fewer arguments among our engineers as a result, and we are far less fearful of submitting radical ideas for consideration."

Let's not let judgment throttle imagination. Instead, let's check our ideas through tests. If we can't test and have to rely on somebody's judgment, let's not allow our critic to sap our creative energy. Let's judge such judgment. If it's adverse—and we're convinced it's right—we should then get busy, do a backtrack and turn up *more* alternative ideas. If unconvinced, we should "damn the torpedoes" and go "full speed ahead."

Chapter XIII

LET'S TRY NOT TO UNDERMINE
OUR OWN CREATIVE POWER

LONG EXPERIENCE AS A CREATIVE COACH has opened my eyes to the way so many of us *undermine* our own creative power. Creative effort will always breed discouragement by *others* as long as nearly everyone likes to throw cold water. But *self*-discouragement—what a stifler of creativity this so often is, and how uncalled for! We should remember that even the Edisons fumbled and stumbled. And we should bear in mind that we are not aiming to become Edisons, but merely to step up our creative power somewhat—just enough to brighten our lives and help us get ahead. To do even that, we need some degree of self-encouragement.

Self-confidence used to be an American virtue. So much so that our English cousins regarded our early ancestors as swashbuckling and boastful. Even up to the first World War, Americans looked up to the D'Artagnan type. Men were expected to stick out their necks. Mysteriously, the style changed and modesty became the mark of the model American. We have glorified self-effacement to the point that many young Americans are almost ashamed to advance an idea. All this has led to a widespread fallacy that a fellow can get ahead in his job by "keeping his nose clean"—and faster than he can by spouting ideas.

As a result of that attitude, the mortality of good ideas

in infancy is appalling. And most of them are strangled by their own parents before anyone ever hears about them. Why? Not only because sticking out the neck has become a forgotten kind of courage—not only because we cherish our dignity—but often because we're so stuck up over our judicial ability, as outlined in the last chapter.

2.

During the last war, about 11 million Americans had to *make* themselves do *what* they should, *when* they should. You would think, therefore, that our veterans would be the ones most fed up with discipline. On the contrary, college professors tell me that G. I.s show far more self-discipline than the rest of us. The stay-at-homes are more open to Arnold Bennett's criticism that "we have so far allowed ourselves to soften, to abandon our *ingenuity,* that we have grown to abhor the very word 'discipline.'" And yet, how can we *work* our creative minds unless we are willing to accept a little discipline from ourselves?

Another tendency that militates against creativity is our yen to "conform." This carries the curse of conventionalism and "convention is a great discourager of originality." To be more creative, we have to take ourselves by the scruff of the neck and warn ourselves against being copy-cats.

"For fear I'll look foolish" goes with wanting not to seem different. This fear has stood in the way of many whom I have tried to coach. At the risk of sermonizing, I have reasoned with them: "Which is worse—to look foolish to others, or to look foolish to yourself? Granted that others may think some of your ideas are silly. But what could be more silly than for you to throttle your own creative mind on so foolish an excuse?"

And I have tried to point out to them that truly intelligent people secretly admire creative effort, realizing as they do that almost all the good in the world came from somebody's "foolish" ideas. When I can thus convince those whom

I coach, they become far less likely to let false dignity discourage their creativity.

3.

"A regular cock-a-hoop show-off" is what Musselman's grandmother called the man who created the coaster-brake. Paul de Kruif noted the "scornful cockiness" of Pasteur, and said of Leeuwenhoek who gave us the microscope: "His arrogance was limitless. In his day, Leeuwenhoek was regarded by all who knew him as the man with the swollen head."

The flamboyance of George Bernard Shaw may be due largely to a pose designed to attract the limelight. This suspicion comes from my first-hand knowledge of Alexander Woollcott and his ways. As his friend, I constantly had to defend his tendency to strut and hog the center of the stage. He several times embarrassed me when I was with him. Late one afternoon, we two called on William Paley, head of Columbia Broadcasting, to try to buy a time on which Woollcott could be aired. My job was to convince Mr. Paley that Woollcott would not go out of bounds as he had done during a previous sponsorship. The interview lasted so long that Paley, himself, showed us out through his ante-room. "I like that," cried Woollcott, pointing at a painting on the wall—and forthwith he took it under his arm. In the elevator I remonstrated, and Woollcott retaliated: "But he *loved* to have me take it!"

Deep-down, I knew Woollcott was not that way—that he was actuated in later life by an unnatural urge to play his part as a literary genius. The early backgrounds of both Shaw and Woollcott tended to excuse their cockiness. Both had been shy as boys and misunderstood by their playmates. Shaw was painfully bashful. "I suffered such agonies of shyness," wrote he, "that I sometimes walked up and down the Embankment for 20 minutes or more before venturing to knock at the door. . . . Few men have suffered more than I did in my youth from simple cowardice." To conquer his timidity, he learned to speak in public. His first few attempts deliberately made him seem to be a man of cocky confidence, even though his knees were shaking all the time.

Just because a few have stood out as exponents of self-worship in the creative field—is that any reason why any of us should let false modesty throttle our creative effort? As a matter of fact, the great majority of the notably creative have been modest to the point of over-humility. I have known more than a few men high up in creative research, and I have yet to meet one whom the world doesn't regard as a greater man than he regards himself. In almost every case, when asked the secret of their success, they have claimed that their imaginative talent is far below the genius level—and that whatever they have achieved has come mainly from just trying.

4.

Timidity is the arch gremlin. When due to our expecting too much of ourselves, diffidence may reflect conceit rather than modesty. One night, a group of us went into a huddle to think up a new radio show. All of us oldsters came through with ideas; but the youngsters just listened. I knew one of them to be gifted with far more creative talent than I, so I asked him: "Why didn't you do some pitching?" He explained to *his* satisfaction, but not to mine: "I was afraid you might not think my ideas were as good as you'd expect of me." He held back, not because he felt he was creatively sterile, but because he prided himself too much. What a shame! The chances are that at least one of his ideas would have been better than any of ours.

On the other hand, I have found that timidity usually stems from genuine doubts of one's ability to be creative. Such "doubts are traitors," quoth Shakespeare, "and make us lose the good we oft might win by fearing to attempt." Surely there can be no reasonable doubt that we do have imaginative talent, or that we can use it better if we will.

But even when we do think up, we are too often held

back by hesitation to give out. Years ago, a private secretary in a big company faced a dim future. His personality was meek and his duties were routine. And yet, over the years, I saw that man step ahead of scores of others and become one of the top three in his great corporation. Here's his own explanation of his success: "During the first 10 years I got nowhere because, even though I did think up ideas, I was afraid to suggest them to anybody. Then one day I made up my mind that the worst that could happen would be that somebody might laugh at me. After a few of my suggestions had been adopted, I became bold—so bold that I never hesitated to pass along any idea that I was able to think up."

He might not have lost those first 10 years if he had heard and believed Dr. Norman Peale when he said: "The trouble with the average person is that he does not sufficiently *trust himself* to create and deliver ideas." The meek ex-secretary also found, as he went along, that Carl Holmes was right when he remarked, "The more creative thinking we do, and the more ideas we *give out*, the more competent we become, and with this comes a most satisfying sense of accomplishment."

5.

Timidity tends also to halt us after we get started on a creative project. Even Edison had to fight off this gremlin. Charles Kettering's explanation of Edison's successes was that "he wasn't afraid of failure."

A man I had the honor to help coach, noticing his wife's difficulty in keeping labels on her home-canned fruits and vegetables, solved the problem by sandblasting a small area on the glass-jar. Thus, in this frosted space, the home-canner could write a description of the contents. My friend was so enthusiastic about his idea that he put up the money for a patent search, only to find that this same idea had been patented in 1882. I was afraid that might slow up his creative effort, but no. "Of course it was a disappointment," he said, "but I realize that any would-be thinker-upper is sure to run into dead ends, just as he's sure, now and then, to stumble on something good if he makes enough tries."

Many a creative scientist has had to whistle in the dark to keep himself going. Ronald Ross ran up against a stone wall in India while in hot pursuit of a way to overcome malaria; but, instead of being stopped, Ross kept on until he ran across a promising clue. He made the most of this by wiring back to London from Calcutta that the mystery of malaria was almost within his grasp and that, within a few weeks, he would solve it to the glory of old England. This turned out to be over-optimistic as to time, but not as to final achievement.

In the early days of the ethyl-gas research, the young scientists went to Boss Kettering with this protest: "We would like to do something in the world, and we don't want to be kept on this problem forever, because we don't see any hope of ever working it out." Kettering was about to leave for New York. "Let me have a couple of days to think this over," he replied, "and when I come back I'll see if I can't work out something for you." On the way back to Dayton, he picked up a newspaper which announced: "University Professor Discovers Universal Solvent." The next morning he showed this item to the boys and said, "Here's one we'd better try before we quit." So they went ahead again and that led, finally, to the successful use of tetraethyl lead. "The point of this story," said Kettering, "is that there will always be dark days, but if your conviction of the value of the problem is such that you go right ahead in spite of the difficulties, the chances are that you will achieve success in the end."

In getting going, keeping going, or giving out, we have every reason to sweep timidity aside and gird our efforts with courage. More than that, we will do best to carry that courage to the point of audacity, and here's why: In creative activity, the wilder we shoot, the more and bigger ideas we are likely to bag. Let's not forget that almost all good ideas are crazy at birth. Can you beat it?—they are going to put out a refrigerator which freezes ice with a gas-flame! What?—a ventriloquist on the radio! Yes, let's not only have the courage of our ideas, but let's risk them wild. There will always be plenty of people to tame them.

Chapter XIV

OTHERS CAN HELP MAKE OR MAR OUR CREATIVITY

"THERE SHOULD NEVER BE HEARD a discouraging word" when it comes to creative effort. Praise can help open our outflow and keep it open. Like trained seals, we need fish in the form of slaps-on-the-back to make us try again and harder. Although schoolmasters used to believe in canes and rulers as spurs, modern education "bases training on motivation by reward"—at least that's what Fryer and Henry concluded in their *Outline of General Psychology.*

Granted that Thomas Carlyle was right in saying, "a certain amount of opposition is a great help to a man," creativity is so delicate a flower that praise tends to make it bloom while discouragement often nips it in the bud. Any of us will put out more and better ideas if our efforts are appreciated. Unfriendliness can make us stop trying. Wisecracks can be poison—as brought out by Balzac's epigram, "Paris is a city where great ideas perish, done to death by witticism." *Every* idea should elicit receptivity, if not praise. Even if no good, it should at least call for encouragement to keep *trying.*

2.

A boss is at his best when both a suggestor of ideas and a creative coach. I had many a talk with E. M. Statler during the years when he was building up his staff from a one-hotel team to a national organization. Mr. Statler didn't pride himself so much on his own ideas as on his ability to coax ideas out of others. Here's what he told me on a train one night:

"When I was a bellboy at the McClure House in Wheeling, I got one of the best ideas I ever thought up. I had to run up and down stairs toting pitchers of water. I knew it could be cleaner, and I also knew that a lot of guests wanted ice-water but hesitated to call a bellboy. That's what led me to the idea of piping ice-water to each guest-room. Now that I am running my own hotels, I never fail to realize that some bellboy of mine could dish up just as good an idea as that. That's why I let everybody know that we *want* their ideas. And when anybody suggests anything, I make sure that he is praised for his effort—and ultimately rewarded if the idea is any good. In that way I coax them to keep trying."

E. M. Statler had come up from the bottom and was the owner. It is much harder to induce such an attitude in supervisory employees. Whenever a management can lead superintendents and foremen to act as creative coaches, a happier and harder-hitting organization is sure to result. "Ideas are generated best in an atmosphere of friendliness," said Ernest Benger of du Pont. "No stimulus to creative effort is as effective as a good pat on the back. We should do anything possible to encourage people to get more and better ideas."

The more encouragement we can put into suggestion systems, the better they will work. The B. F. Goodrich Company has gone so far in this that even a foolish notion still elicits encouragement, as in the case of this idea which landed in the suggestion-box: "I suggest that shude put Gloss windows in Dores in Mens and Women tolit for safty When two men mit nither one can see eich other and often makes cowlision." The head of the Suggestions Department tactfully pointed out that some privacy would be lost if glass doors were put on toilet compartments. His letter ended with,

"However, any time you have further ideas, we want to hear from you."

In another instance, a B. F. Goodrich worker who could hardly read or write seemed to have some kind of an idea. An engineer was assigned to interview him and after two hours of patient probing, got what the man had on his mind. The idea turned out to be so valuable that any engineer would have been proud to have thought it up.

What should an employee's attitude be toward ideas? I discussed this with a G.I. named R. L. Ryan who was going places in a firm owned by a friend of mine. "The best policy," said Mr. Ryan, "is always to keep suggesting. You may develop a reputation as a crackpot, but as soon as one or two of your ideas materialize your employer and co-workers begin to give you serious consideration. Then, when you suggest something which is impractical they will discuss it with you, instead of just brushing you off."

"The greatest lesson an employee must learn," continued Mr. Ryan, "is not to take rebuffs personally. Also, don't be too insistent. At times your employer may not seem to be receptive to your suggestions. Try again at a later time. Tell him you've been thinking it over and have some further evidence that your idea may be sound. Then again, sometimes it pays just to make a suggestion to the proper authority and let it lie dormant. It's surprising how often it will pop up in a new place. You may not get direct or complete credit, but your boss knows you're around and thinking. And that's a big step toward promotion."

3.

General Mills has made praise a company policy. Vice President Samuel Gale issues a citation for outstanding creative work. On a special form with "Good Deed of the Day" printed on top, he issues a bulletin to the executive staff in praise of whatever has come to his attention as worthy of an orchid. Most big companies fear that naming names in this way may stir up envy, but Mr. Gale's "Good Deed of the Day" specifically addresses itself to the individual to be congratulated; and the system works.

Unfortunately, a natural tendency among executives is to discourage rather than to encourage each other. The actuation is sometimes envy, or a desire to keep the other fellow from getting ahead. At the lower levels, the discouragement of worker by worker, too often arises from a growing tendency to keep down the working pace. "Let's not do anything more than we have to" is a sentiment that poisons many workers, and when such a one sees another going out of his way to make suggestions, he instinctively opposes his extra efforts.

But at all levels, the main cause is that old debbil, pride—pride in *judgment*. A sense of judicial superiority forces many a man to greet his fellow-worker's idea with a sneer.

4.

The discouragement that hurts the most is that which comes from those we love. Within a family, praise is at its greatest premium. Parents should stop, look, and listen before ever uttering the slightest discouragement of a child's creative efforts. Praise helps a child creatively when given face to face, but is even more powerful when spoken to others and overheard by the child.

Most of us start life with lots of imagination and yet many of us grow up to be men and women with "not an idea in their heads." Why is this so? One reason may be that as a nation we have not made enough of the *importance* of ideas, and have not admitted that creative power *can* be *developed*. Another reason is that oldsters so deliberately discourage youngsters. And why do we do this? Are we guilty of a touch of envy as in our old rule that children should be seen and not heard? No matter what prompts us, the fact is that as parents, nearly all of us are guilty either

of active discouragement, or, at least, of lack of active encouragement.

A friend who has prospered from his creative efforts told
me he got his start when, as a little boy, he showed his father
a gadget he had thought up so that he wouldn't have to stand
on a stool in order to turn off the gas light. All he had done
was to saw a notch in the top of a stick. With this, he could
reach up to the gas-fixture, slip the notch over the valve,
and turn off the gas without climbing. His father told him
his idea was "terrific"; and that night at the dinner table,
with guests present, he told the story over again with em-
phatic praise of his little boy's ingenuity. That encouragement made the lad realize that he *could* think up ideas and
that it was fun to try. This faith paved his way to success.

An associate of mine, highly creative himself and a firm
believer in the power of praise, has a daughter who at the
age of five revealed a rare talent known in musical terms as
"absolute pitch." Thus, when she heard any note, she could
tell just which it was—even though she could not see the
keyboard on which the note was struck. She easily learned
to play by ear, but, strangely enough, found it hard to read
notes. The parents divided each music-lesson into two parts.
First she had to go through with her note-reading instruction, and then, as a reward, she could "swing it" to her
heart's content. She got so she could create her own chords,
for which she was so heartily praised that she found a way
to simulate a locomotive whistle on the piano.

According to the late Justice O. W. Holmes, his father
made meals a training-ground for creative effort by offering
a prize for the wittiest remark his children could think up at
the table.

Dr. Roma Gans has stressed the need to build self-confidence in the young. Dr. Gans urged that the child be given
a chance to feel smarter than grown-ups—that any time a
child performed some stunt and demanded, "Can *you* do
that?" we should say, "No, I can't. What's more, I never
could." Dr. Gans further points out that there's a difference

between a child's willingness to try *three* things—getting two successes and one flop—and trying only *one* thing that can be perfectly done. In her opinion the perfectionist point of view makes for narrowness of living, and, of course, it can't help but cramp creative effort.

5.

Brothers and sisters tend to be somewhat sadistic toward each other, and to look for a laugh in anything the other has done or has tried to do. It may be too much to hope that a brother will *encourage* his brother in creative sallies, but how much less harm he would do if he resisted the temptation to *discourage*. This problem is a splinter in my flesh because of what happened in my youth.

As a kid I drew pictures and wrote jingles. On the playroom wall of our home there still hangs a framed continuity-strip, made up of six sketches, with a rhymed caption under each. A similar technique today leads all others in readership. I stumbled on it when about 11 years old, trying to create a Christmas greeting for my uncle and aunt.

About a year after I did that, my oldest brother came into my room one Sunday when I was at work on a drawing. "Gee, Alex," he said, "I saw a boy half your age yesterday who was blind in one eye and was paralyzed in both hands and he could draw better than that." I worshipped my big brother and therefore took him seriously. Years later I realized he had been joking. But the effect on me was withering. That one remark kept me from trying to draw or paint until 40 years later.

Uncles, aunts, and grandparents are less cruel in this respect. As a rule they instinctively tend to enhearten rather than to dishearten. An uncle I know found that his nephew, aged five, had gone to a fire with a pad and crayons and had drawn pictures of the flames, the windows, and the ladders. The uncle looked at the first sketch and said, "That's *good!*" The boy said, "Thank you!" The uncle looked at the second sketch and said, "That's *great!*" The boy said, "Thank you!" The uncle then shouted, "That's *wonderful!*", as he looked at the third sketch. The boy said, "Thank you!"

Strongly believing that there can be no such thing as too much praise in fanning the creative flames of the young, the uncle later wrote to the lad the first typewritten letter he had ever received, and in this he said: "Your pictures of the fire were so good that I showed them to the people in my office. They all felt the same as I did about how real you made the fire look. I am glad that you like to draw and hope you will keep on drawing. Perhaps some day you will be a great artist and we'll all be proud of you. For your birthday I am getting you some new crayons. Next Christmas I am going to ask Santa to send you a box of paints."

6.

Discouragement by outsiders is easier to take than that which comes from associates or relatives, but still we have to steel ourselves against even that. One way to gird our wills is to realize that most of the greatest ideas were at first greeted with sneers. Even Edison had to "take it" time and time again. When, at 32, he produced his first commercially practical electric lamp, the editor of the New York *Herald* greeted his claim as plain "bosh," and told his associates that the whole thing was "impossible and could never work." It was not long before he himself was working under one of Edison's new bulbs and had to eat his words.

When John Kay invented the flying shuttle, it was considered such a threat to labor that weavers mobbed him and destroyed his mold. When Charles Newbold worked out the idea of a cast-iron plow, the farmers rejected it on the grounds that iron polluted the soil and encouraged weeds. In 1844, Dr. Horace Wells was the first to use gas on patients while pulling teeth. The medical profession squelched this new idea as a humbug." When Samuel P. Langley built his first heavier-than-air machine—flown by steam—the newspapers dubbed it "Langley's folly" and scoffed at the whole idea of self-propelled planes.

Barney Baruch has provided our nation with ideas that have meant much to our welfare over a period of two world-wars. He is an exponent of the wisdom of encouragement and the folly of ridicule. His feeling goes back to an experience he suffered as a little boy trying to recite to a group of grown-ups. A smart-alec saw fit to make fun of the lad's inflections—so cruelly that young Baruch rushed out of the room in tearful humiliation.

Let's remember that we can throttle our own creative talent by self-discouragement. Let's also remember that we can throttle the creative talent in others in the same way. For all of us, a good rule is always to encourage ideas—to encourage speaking up as well as thinking up. Nothing else makes sense because the essence of creativity is to keep on trying and trying, harder and harder—and that's almost too much to expect of human nature if, on top of all other blocks to creative effort, we also have to surmount the curse of discouragement.

Chapter XV

EVEN *EXERCISE* CAN BE FUN—
ESPECIALLY IN CREATIVE THINKING

"JUMPING TO CONCLUSIONS" is the only exercise some minds get, and that's not even thinking; for to think is "to exercise the mind otherwise than by passive reception of another's ideas." So says the Oxford Dictionary, and thinking— especially *creative* thinking—*is exercise*. At first you get exhausted from just a little effort, but then, as you exercise more and more, you get so you can swing your mind from branch to branch without missing a single breath—and get to *like* it.

Bayard Pope told me how this principle was propounded by a white-bearded New Hampshirite named Jim Mills. Every night he and his cronies would sit in front of the general store, the silence broken only by the occasional splatter of tobacco juice. One day Pope asked him what they did and Mills replied, "We just think." Pope then asked, "But how can you possibly think that much?" Here was Mills' reply: "I'll tell you, son, thinking is like sin. Them as don't do it is ascairt of it. But them as do it *enough*, gets to like it."

"You must use it or you lose it" is a favorite expression of Bishop Norman Nash of Massachusetts. Mainly he uses it in connection with moral faculties; but it applies just as strongly to one's creative talent. For in thinking up, conscious effort *and exercise* are cardinal principles. Walt Disney ad-

111

vises us to look on our imagination-apparatus as mental muscles. "The more a muscle works," said Dr. Carrel, "the more it develops. Activity strengthens it, instead of wearing it out. Like muscles and organs, intelligence and moral sense become atrophied for want of exercise."

Albert Edward Wiggam has pointed out that in psychological experiments, subjects have been taught to improve their skills by just *imagining*. He related an experiment by psychologist R. A. Vandell and others. "They had persons sit in front of a target and imagine throwing darts at it. This 'mental practice' improved their aim as much as actual physical practice!"

Certain aptitudes like tonal memory are born in us and stay with us regardless of what we do or do not do to develop them. But personality, like creativity, can certainly be improved by practice as Dale Carnegie has proved. "And," says Johnson O'Connor as a result of his scientific testing, "one person may have a high degree of creative talent when young, and through lack of use or getting into the wrong kind of work, may let that talent atrophy." Add to that H. A. Overstreet's conclusion that by intelligent understanding, direction, and exercise, creative power "can actually be stimulated into growth."

2.

Reading packs the memory and thus enriches our power of association. As a creative exercise, it falls short in that it takes so little effort. It depends on *how* we read. Elliott Dunlap Smith recommends that we put enough energy into our reading actually to "*exercise* our power of creative thought."

Certain periodicals offer a helpfully creative climate. The *Saturday Evening Post, Life, Holiday* magazine, and most women's publications, are rich with material that stimulates imagination. The *American* magazine consciously sets forth the power of ideas. Most helpful, according to Walt Disney, is *The Reader's Digest.* "Your imagination may be creaky or

timid or dwarfed or frozen at the joints," said Disney. *"The
Reader's Digest* can serve as a gymnasium for its training."
Among specialized periodicals, *Popular Science* not only
provides a creative atmosphere, but also tends to give us
confidence that we *can* be more creative—since it shows us
such a myriad of new ideas thought up by so many unknown
people of average talent.

Biographies, through inspiration, can likewise help our
creative power. Certain books on thinking can make us better able to understand our minds, and through such understanding enable us to make more intelligent use of our creative gift. Most of our fiction-reading does almost as much to
deaden our sense of effort as to enliven our imagination. Of
all fiction, the mystery books seem to offer the most exercise
to our creative muscles—especially if we read them with an
attitude of participation rather than spectatorship. After the
mystery has been built up it is more creatively helpful—*and*
more fun—if we stop, and try to figure out "who done it"
all on our own.

3.

Games can be good exercise as well as fun. In chess, for
example, the players have to think forward—are forced to
pile up many alternatives before choosing the right one. And
chess also induces mental sweat.

Among parlor-games, "Twenty Questions" gives no creative exercise to those merely answering yes or no, although
the *questioner* does have to run his mind around energeti-
cally in search of alternatives. However, to the extent that
this game tends to keep the mind in a groove, it does more
for logic than for imagination.

A far better game is charades, as recently revised. My
married daughters tell me that Elsa Maxwell is responsible
for its modernized version, and they call it "The Game." This
provides creative exercise for all participants. It's a two-
team contest. Each team goes into a huddle and dreams up

a charade for each of the opposite team—five charades, if a five-man team. To keep the game within bounds, each charade is usually limited to eight words, and confined to well-known categories such as copybook maxims.

The five charades are written on separate slips of paper and tossed into a hat. An opponent draws a charade and—without showing it to his team-mates—acts it out for *them*. No props or sounds are allowed. Although the team-members are permitted to ask yes-and-no questions, all answers have to be *pantomimed*. The actor may act out the whole charade at once, or each separate word by syllables. It is all up to him. The object is to get the sentence across to his team in the shortest possible time, since the team with the lower aggregate time is the winner. The sides takes turns. First one player draws a charade from the other team's hat and acts it out for his team-mates. Then a member of the other team draws one from the opposition's hat, and so on.

Another game called "Inky Pinky" makes an exciting twosome and is excellent exercise for the imagination. Two of our most creative men, Al Ward and Carl Davis, play it together often. One day the three of us played it for five hours straight on the Empire State Express.

The best way to describe this game is by examples. For instance I say to you, "A stained finger," and you come back with "An inky pinky." If I say, "A frozen finger," you might qualify with "A frigid digit" or possibly "A numb thumb." The definition can be two words or more, each with the same number of syllables. For example, "a featherbrained young horse suffering from a cold" could be "a silly chilly filly." It is a hard game to catch onto at first; but once your mind gets going on it, you'll find it as insidious as eating peanuts. It may sound a bit puerile, but an Associated Press correspondent in London announced its introduction there, and ended with this paragraph: "Who plays the game? Not school-girls. It was the evening's entertainment one night this week for a group that included a psychiatrist, a radio writer, an artist and a newspaper-man."

Particularly in colleges there is need for games in which young people can use their idea-machinery. As an editor recently said: "Students spend too much of their time taking in and too little of their time giving out. For everything they sponge up from their books, they should squeeze out something on their own." There is hardly a college that doesn't have a German club, or a French club. Why not an "Idea" Club? The members could play creative games and hold contests in thinking up. They could brainstorm a problem such as "What is a better metaphor than 'the cart before the horse'?" They could take on as a project the patter printed in *The Reader's Digest* under "Spiced Tongue." Each could write similar pieces. All could then form a jury to pick out the five best. If one is accepted by the editors, the money received could be spent for eats and drinks at the Idea Club's next session.

4.

Quizzes and puzzles can likewise be creative exercises. Thomas Edison was a believer in these. According to his son Charles, Edison originated the first quizzes which became the forerunners of the crossword puzzle.

We can combine creative practice with relaxation by solving crossword puzzles, especially those as tough as in the New York *Times* each Sunday. What's the word for "Thus Shock Leaves Ophelia"? We think and think. "Demented" seems to fit. What's the six-letter word for "The Croxley Master Lasts Sixteen?" No idea. And so we go, with a letter here and a letter there; but the words won't come. How about 52 across? That may be the key. And 52 across says, "M. Lupin." That probably calls for M. Lupin's christian name. What in the world was it? We ponder and ponder. We pore through a reference book. Ah, there it is! Lupin's first name is Arsene. With that key, ten other words transform themselves from nonsense into sense.

In doing that puzzle, we have made our minds work

backward and forward. But mainly we have made them
work. And that, alone, is good for our creative souls.

Still better creative exercises are the Double-Crostics—
originated and carried on by Mrs. Elizabeth Kingsley—which
are printed weekly in the *Saturday Review of Literature* and
occasionally in the New York Sunday *Times*. Countless books
of these puzzles have been eaten up by the public. Their
publisher describes Double-Crostics as "an entertaining hy-
brid of the Crossword Puzzle, the Acrostic, and the Literary
Quiz. You use all three processes interchangeably, and when
you've got the solution, every millimeter of your gray matter is glowing the way a gymnast's muscles glow after a
work-out." Mrs. Kingsley's Double-Crostics puzzles have
made addicts of the most creative people in the country—
Kenneth Roberts, Christopher Morley, Elmer Rice and
Rupert Hughes, to mention only four.

5.

Actual *doing* is, of course, the best exercise. The way to
create is to create, just as the way to write is to write. John
R. Tunis, versatile free-lance writer, recently said this to a
college audience: "Any Hamilton student who is willing to
devote himself to writing eight hours a day, five days a week,
for a year and a half, will find himself turning out publish-
able material. It isn't whether you can *write* or not; it's
whether you can *take* it."

Some of us believe Winston Churchill to be not only the
greatest figure but also the greatest creative mind of our
time. The things he thought up to keep England out of Hitler's grasp are a lasting tribute to man's power of imagination. To a large extent it was his training in writing that made
him stand out creatively. While his fellow-officers loafed
through their Army days in India and other hot countries,
Churchill wrote and wrote and wrote.

Other men have simpler ways to exercise their mental
muscles. A college president told me about his "daily dozen."

Busy as he is, he makes himself think up one brand new simile each day. The night he told me this, I asked him what was the one he had thought up that day. Promptly he replied "As chaste as the kiss of billiard balls."

A young lawyer recently won a spectacular victory against one of the most experienced trial-lawyers in town. Much to everybody's surprise, the jury decided in favor of the weaker cause. When I asked a newspaperman about this, he said: "Based on knowledge of law, that young man could never have won that case. It was his ingenuity that turned the trick—his ability to think up new ways to prove to the jury that his client was right and his opponent's client was wrong!" That young lawyer is a neighbor of mine and I have observed him first-hand. His secret practice consists of *making up* stories for his children, night after night, year after year. His improvised tales may not be as good as the printed ones, but his children like them even better.

How about those odd moments when we have time on our hands? Why not use them for creative exercise? I am no great shakes as a mechanic, but one night when stuck on a railroad platform with an hour to kill, I gave myself a specific mechanical problem which had arisen at Oneida Community that morning. Up and down the platform I strolled, playing with this puzzle. Aboard the train I made sketches of some of the ideas I had thought up, and at breakfast the next morning I made another sketch of another idea. I gave this to my attorney at noon. It wasn't much of a patent but it brought $300. One moral of this incident is that it's good creative exercise just to think up creative exercises, and the weirder the better.

6.

The devil of discouragement is the enemy of creative exercise. Among other things, we are at first too apt to expect too much of ourselves. On this point we should heed the advice of Ray Giles: "What if your exercise doesn't yield a single worth-while idea at first? In exercising your mind, as in exercising your muscles, it's continuity, faithfulness, and persistence that get you there. Even the geniuses agree with that! Which is why so many of them keep right on exercising this way even after they've become famous."

Talk about a busman's holiday!—I spent a Christmas week at Lake Placid with Lowell Thomas. He skied every day, and every evening he aired his broadcast. To get that ready for the mike, he used up more creative energy than the physical energy in his skiing. On top of everything else, while there he created and conducted a contest for winter visitors at the Club—based on thinking up the biggest lies our imaginations could contrive. Lowell Thomas not only managed the event but participated with many an entry of his own.

Of course when you keep on creating, even trivially, you tend to form a habit. Getting started soon becomes less of a problem. The more you try, the more you instinctively do as Victor Wagner urged, when he said: "Ask questions, dig for facts, gather experience, watch the breaks. And at every stage of the game, peer beyond the end of your nose, learn that two and two can make 22 and zero as well as four—and above all get your Heaven-sent gift of imagination to work. Once that trick becomes a habit, as it always does, you will realize as the thousands who did it before, that imagination, like faith, can and often does moves mountains."

Chapter XVI

TO ATTACK A CREATIVE TASK
WE FIRST *GET SET*

NOW WE COME TO HOW to tackle a creative project. The first step is to *get set*—to establish the "working mood" which all agree is vital to purposeful creativity. To do this may be akin to pulling ourselves up by our bootstraps; but there are ways to do just that, and highly creative people consciously use these ways.

Even self-confidence can be self-induced to some extent. There is scientific proof that we can if we think we can when it comes to *physical* exertion. For instance, psychologists Muller and Schumann in Germany proved that our minds can even make a heavier weight seem lighter. They had people lift a light weight—then a weight three times as heavy—and then a medium weight. Although this last one was about 30 per cent *heavier* than the first, nearly all the people thus tested thought it to be much *lighter* than the first weight.

Thus we can build confidence in our weight-lifting ability by convincing our minds of something that is not true. But the reasons so far set forth in this book as to why you *can* be more creative are true reasons—and we hope these facts have helped you to induce in yourself more self-confidence than you otherwise might have felt in approaching a creative project.

119

2.

You've seen weight-lifters flex their muscles before lifting a 200-pound bar. Let's do likewise with our imaginative muscles, for many of us tend to become muscle-bound when approaching a creative task. I have watched ad-writer Alan Ward day by day for 20 years. Time upon time I have felt amazement at how many creative jobs he can start and carry through. You'd hardly believe that he has to wrestle with himself whenever he undertakes a project, but that's what he claims. How does he go about flexing his mental muscles? I asked him that, and here's his answer: "I have no sure way of uninhibiting myself for creative thinking. I wish I did. I would like to be able to press my thumb on my navel and think creatively by just doing that. By golly, I think I'll try it! But here's about the only way I've found to get into a working mood.

"I close my office door and try to limber up by filling a pipe and lighting it. I try to forget everything but the job before me. Then I pull my typewriter to me, wrap my legs around it, and start to write. I write down every line that comes into my head. Crazy, dull, or however it sounds. I find that if I don't, it may linger there and block others. One utterly useless line often pops into my head—'Fifteen men on a dead-man's chest!' When it pops, I set it down. If I am ever able to make good use of that line, it will not bother me any longer.

"I write as fast as I can," continued Ward. "And then, after a long while, some cogs that haven't worked start to whir, and something striking begins to tap itself out on the yellow sheet before me—like a telegraph message. That's the hard way and the only way I know on most days. Occasionally it comes easy when I happen to be 'hot.' Then, with no mechanics such as going for a drink of water, lighting a pipe, or picking the lint out of my typewriter's type, the right words pop into my head after about two tries."

Cub-writers say of copy-chief Ward, "*He* can't *help* but

be creative." They go ahead faster when they learn the truth
that even Ward *helps himself* to be creative.

3.

Albert Edward Wiggam has described the line between
"open-minders and tight-minders" as "sharp and clean-cut."
He rightfully declared the open-minded to be "the only
people who have ever contributed anything to human progress." If I had to say who *can't* be more creative, I would
nominate the morons and the tight-minded. But hardly any
intelligent mind is chronically closed. Nearly all of us are
more or less open-minded and can be completely so at times.
A good time to help make oneself that way is when starting
a creative task.

Even an open-minded man may have to ward off influences that could close his mind while in quest of an idea. It
would have been easy for Pasteur to have taken for granted
the cause of silkworm disease when he went to the south of
France to save it from ruin. The local silkworm-growers tried
to tell him just what the disease was and what caused it.
Had he heeded their theories, he might never have found the
answer that meant so much to France.

We sometimes have to keep our minds open by shutting
out environment, as does the ingenious head of a big manufacturing company. He built his success out of an ability to
cut costs by reducing the number of operations on a product.
He has decided never again to tackle such a problem while
in his plant. Instead he takes it home. "When I tried to do
that kind of thinking in the factory," he told me, "I heard
the machinery purring so beautifully, and saw the product
flowing out so smoothly, it tended to close my mind. As long
as there is anything in the shop that we could produce with
at least one less operation, I'm going to work on it at home
where my mind can see more clearly."

Dr. Suits of General Electric lays great stress on being
open-minded to one's hunches. "Aim to keep an open mind,"

he urged. "Be on the alert for hunches, and whenever you find one hovering on the threshold of your consciousness, welcome it with open arms. Doing these things won't transform you into a genius overnight. But they're guaranteed to help you locate the treasure chest of ideas which lies hidden at the back of your own brain."

4.

The German psychologists made much of what they called "Aufgabe." As I get it, this means interest sharpened to the point of all-out intent. This frame of mind is certainly important to a creative undertaking.

But how can we intensify our intent? Sometimes, some of us don't need to. I can't imagine any task more formidable than that of producing a double-crostic puzzle as done every week by Mrs. Elizabeth Kingsley. I asked her, "What do you do to make yourself start on one?" This was her reply: "I don't have to 'make myself start.' To me each start is like a game, with the same sort of fascination. I always *enjoy* tackling a new double-crostic." Thus, with habit, intent may become automatic in even the hardest creative work.

Intent is stronger when we have a goal, such as making money. We can make it even stronger by making our goal more graphic—like working for the wherewithal to buy a home. And we can intensify intent by making even a feeble start. "This snaps a trap," said Dr. William Easton. "It arouses interest which immediately attracts the imagination; and, from then on, one's mental energy is likely to devote itself to finishing the affair. A writer, for example, may intensify his interest by setting down various titles for a proposed composition; and a scientist may do the same by working out a diagram of apparatus to be used in an experiment; and so on. The creative thinker who wants to be master of his mental machinery must force himself into a working mood by some such process."

Such self-priming is not so needed by writers and artists

who engage only in work that interests them and just drop it when their interest fails. But there is no such easy escape for creative thinkers who have to work on assignments not of their own choosing. Industrial researchers, illustrators, advertising men, and others in commercial lines, are often given tasks which do not interest them, and they therefore have to force themselves into enough intent to start creating. Whether self-generated or not, an intense interest is needed for any creative task for, otherwise, we cannot fully command the services of our imaginations.

5.

All-out intent begets an all-around *awareness* which also helps to get us to first base creatively. This pays dividends even when not applied to specific programs. I have often wondered at the alertness of those in charge of the Abercrombie and Fitch windows in New York. There is almost always something in them that makes us stop and gaze. For instance, during war-time I noticed people packed three deep peering at one of the displays, so I wedged my way through. Guess what the magnet was?—a hunk of rag with a little card saying, "This piece of cloth came from the parachute of a bomb that devastated a large section of London."

In my newspaper days, such awareness was known as a "nose for news" and is still the distinguishing mark of star reporters. But even a chemist can set himself apart by developing the same power. Through awareness we can multiply our intake of materials for our minds to sort out and to apply to specific creative problems. In essence, a good idea is usually based on a combination of specific knowledge about the particular problem we're attacking, *plus* general facts we have accumulated in our cerebral warehouse. For this reason alone, we should consciously keep our eyes and ears wide open.

When awareness goes beyond receptivity, it becomes active curiosity. This may or may not kill cats; but it is certain that the greater our curiosity, the more lives we can live creatively. We should never apologize for or seek to discourage this trait which Dr. Alexis Carrel has called "a necessity of nature which impels us to discover."

Even "idle" curiosity is to be looked up to rather than sneered at. Veblen's ridicule of idle curiosity caused James Harvey Robinson to strike back at him with this: "Curiosity is idle only to those who fail to realize that it may be a very rare and indispensable thing. . . . Even occasionally and fitfully idle curiosity leads to creative thought."

But curiosity is not enough to insure enough awareness. Awareness at the best calls for conscious action. "Our creative urge," said Fryer and Henry, "has to be perpetually pricked and goaded and jogged into a wide-awake state of awareness. Get yourself seeing things about you, feeling things. By virtue of your very 'awareness' your mind will start effervescing."

So before we set our aim, let's flex ourselves, open our minds, intensify our intent, court awareness, encourage curiosity and then tug at that boot-strap marked "concentration." Thus we can get into a working mood where effort is more like a sport.

Chapter XVII

LET'S NOW PICK OUR TARGET
AND SET OUR AIM

ALTHOUGH, AT TIMES, AN IDEA is accidentally stumbled upon, it usually turns out that the stumbler had been hard on its trail. Only occasionally is it a case of aimless luck, as in the story of the plumber who carelessly dropped a piece of pipe into a batch of molten glass and, on pulling it out, found that he had stumbled onto a way to make glass-tubing. We cannot consciously increase the crop of fortunate accidents; but we can produce more ideas by conscious creative effort, and in this process, a good aim is needed as a starter and as a means of focus.

But first we must make our target clear. Often we must think up just what we are going to *try* to think up. At other times the problems are thrust upon us by force of circumstances. A crisis that beats us over our heads with its immediacy is likely to create its own target. Other problems are assigned to us by our bosses with targets clearly indicated.

In some cases, assignments even carry helpful hints, as when the National Inventors' Council during the war put out lists of "inventions wanted." Typical of such requests was the following: "A shockproof container which can be dropped from a plane without a parachute, and which is so cheap that it is not worth recovering. The National Inventors' Council suggests that the impact of the container can be cushioned with carbon dioxide gas, taken from a bottle on the plane."

2.

One reason why Americans get better and better goods for their money is that our manufacturers *reach out* for targets —are on the conscious look-out for problems the solution of which can spell opportunity. Recognition of shrinking as a shortcoming in men's shirts led to that multi-million-dollar idea of Sanforizing. Here's the story of how the target was picked and the aim set, as told by A. O. Buckingham, vice-president of Cluett, Peabody:

"When we decided to go into the shirt business in a big way, we felt that we should give the consumer as good a fit in shirts as we had given him in collars. The trouble was that collars had always been washed after being made, while if we tried to wash shirts that way, they would lose some of their fine finish—would look as though they were not new, but had been through the laundry. So we asked our research head, Sanford Cluett, to find a way to shrink cloth without putting it in water."

At the cotton mills Mr. Cluett saw that, in the finishing process, the cloth was always *pulled* through the various processes of bleaching and mercerization. In fact, the cloth was sewed together into strips as long as 14 miles, and then pulled through the mill. This naturally distorted the fabric. He discovered that if this distortion were taken out, most of the shrinkage would be eliminated. So he built a machine which automatically restored the cloth to equilibrium—in other words, pushed the stretch back.

The Sanforized process was designed for cotton goods only. Its success led to other aims. One result is a similar process called "Sanforset" which stabilizes rayon. A still newer process eliminates felting in wool. This case typifies how we can reach out for targets by grasping problems; and also how one target can create another.

3.

Creative triumphs have come from diving off the deep end in search of unseeable problems. Faraday went at it blind when, in 1831, he discovered how electricity could be produced. He had no target. He merely wondered what would happen if—between two poles of a horseshoe-magnet—he were to mount a copper disc and make it *spin*. To his amazement, electric current was what the spinning disc produced.

Dr. Charles M. A. Stine did not know what he was after when he started in the search for nylon. At Du Pont his associates have told me that his outstanding point is curiosity. There would probably be no nylon had he not asked this question: "I wonder what would happen if molecules were rearranged so that they would be in lines instead of clusters?" Dr. Stine thus created a target which he then handed to Dr. Wallace Hume Carothers. As leader of the scientific team which first synthesized Du Pont nylon, Dr. Carothers was highly honored by his company. When he died in 1937, at the age of 41, the Nylon Research Laboratory was dedicated in his honor as the "Carothers Research Laboratory."

Would Dr. Carothers' name now be immortalized had it not been for Dr. Stine's originality in setting the target for him? Who deserves the greater credit—the instigator or the worker-out-er? Surely, the aim itself is often more than half the battle.

Sometimes a man asks a question which leads to a precious answer, and yet his name is lost in oblivion. One example of this was reported by the Department of Agriculture. Baby pigs are often crushed by their mothers rolling over upon them. An unknown thinker-upper asked whether pig mortality in a farrowing house could not be remedied by simply tilting the floor. This led to a system which is now working well. Since mama pigs like to lie down with their backs uphill and piglets like to travel downhill, the tilted floor tends to keep the baby from under the recumbent old lady. The Department of Agriculture has reported that these tilted floors have cut down this cause of pig mortality by as much as 25 per cent. The price of our bacon would be higher had it not been for that unknown's going out of his way to create a target.

4.

Let's make the target clear. "Specify your problem consciously," urged Brand Blanshard of Yale. "Coin it at the beginning into a perfectly definite question."

As John Dewey has said, "a problem well stated is half solved." Clarification not only throws light on the target, but helps to put it in perspective. "It brings it into relation with other known facts so as to facilitate examination," as Matthew McClure put it.

By all means, let's *write out* the problem. To help force creative action, we might even write it to somebody else and commit ourselves to find *an* answer, if not *the* answer, by a certain date. And let's not stop with merely posing the problem. Certainly if it is true that "a problem well stated is half solved," it is just as true that the more we narrow it down, the nearer we get to its solution. So let's be sure to set the aim.

Dr. Walter Reed is one of our immortals mainly because he took pains to set the *aim* in the war against yellow fever. The *problem* was thrust upon him. On arrival in Cuba as head of the yellow-fever commission, he went over the latest death-list and asked about each case. He found that the latest to die had been near no other victim.

"You mean to say this man had no contact whatsoever with the disease?" asked Major Reed.

"None," was the reply. "He was in the guardhouse for six days with six other men and he was the only one to catch it."

"Well, if you are right about this," said the Major, "then something must have crawled or jumped or flown through the guardhouse window, bitten that prisoner, and then gone back where it had come from. I am convinced the time has come to set aside our microscopes and learn how yellow fever spreads from man to man. The poison is probably carried by an insect, and that may be a mosquito." After all the bleary-eyed efforts to track down the cause of yellow fever through the usual microscope techniques, Major Reed, in that one observation, had set the aim that led to its conquest. Through his finding the right focus—plus the heroism of the volunteers who served as human guinea-pigs—a vaccine against yellow fever was eventually produced. And 40 years later, our boys were able to chase the Japanese through infested jungles and swamps and yet be immune to the menace of that once dread disease.

5.

Let's not bite off more than we can chew. A creative objective should not only be narrowed down from the general to the specific, but may well be broken up into smaller targets. I ran across a Bronx taxi-driver who had been working in an office job all week, and asked him why he was driving me on a Sunday. "I'm buying a new Plymouth," he said, "and this is how I'm keeping up my payments." How much better than if he had taken on the aim of "making a million"!

Let's adopt Brand Blanshard's technique and convert our target into specific questions. Let's imagine ourselves to be the mouse-trap maker to whom Emerson is alleged to have brought fame. Out there in the woods we might determine to make a better mouse-trap, but we would be wise to narrow down this aim of ours before rolling up our sleeves. We could well ask ourselves a series of specific questions. "How can I make it better-looking?" . . . "Cheaper?" . . . "Easier to use?" . . . "Safer for the housewife?" . . . "Lighter in weight?" If we happened to have a research staff, we might well assign one of these aims to each man or group. That would put us further ahead than if we said to all of them: "Gentlemen, I want the world to beat a path to my door. Make me a better mouse-trap. Go to it!"

Walter Chrysler saved his small pay as a young railroad mechanic in order to buy a huge $5,000 Pierce-Arrow sedan. What for? Just to take it apart, put it together again, and see what he could see. He wanted to find a way to make a better motorcar and went at it, according to Ray Giles, by asking himself specific questions such as, "Why wouldn't brakes on all four wheels stop the car even better?" "Why not keep the lubricating oil in better condition by having it run through a filter all the while?" and "Wouldn't tires of bigger diameter give a smoother ride?"

"No wonder when that young fellow later brought out his first Chrysler automobile it was the sensation of that year's auto show," concluded Ray Giles.

6.

Just as one idea leads to another, one aim often leads to another. This has been true of even the greatest scientists. As Paul de Kruif has said, "Microbe hunters usually find other things than they set out to look for."

In June of 1922, I went through the General Motors research laboratory at Dayton. My guide was the lab's big boss, Charles Kettering. We peeked into a little room where three men were monkeying around a little stationary engine which was exhausting through the hole in a window. "What are they doing?" I asked.

"Oh, I told them they ought to be able to change gasoline so it would give the motorist five times as many miles per gallon." They never found what they were after, but they did hit on the idea of lead and that resulted in Ethyl gasoline. Their search had changed its aim and as a result, instead of increasing the mileage of gasoline, they had decreased its knocking.

The Corning Glass people aimed to make globes for railroad lanterns so strong that they would not crack even when bombarded by icy sleet. They hit that mark all right and railroads became safer as a result. But in doing that, they perfected a new kind of glass that could be used in millions of homes. Thus the aim to make better lanterns led to the aim to make glassware that could withstand the heat of ovens. The women of America have since bought over 300 million pieces of Pyrex ware in which to bake, serve and store.

Research directors recognize that aims often change. Dr. Howard Fritz of B. F. Goodrich told me how one of his scientists had started on a pursuit, which led to a by-product of his work, which then became his life's work. The by-product became the product known as Koroseal. This is not an unexpected turn of affairs in organized creativity, according to Dr. Fritz.

Not only a specific aim, but even a basic aim may change. Very few people know that Henry Ford planned not to go into the automobile business, but into the locomotive business. His first creative exploit as a young man on his father's farm was when he built a steam engine. His life's aim was to make railroad equipment. It was not until he was nearly 40 that he set his aim on passenger cars.

7.

It pays to assay our aims. The U. S. Patent Office is crowded with "good" ideas that are no good for anything. Countless people have spent countless hours and pounds of creative energy on projects of no useful purpose. Therefore, before we set our aim, we might well stop and analyze. For example, if we want to apply our creative energy to seeking advancement in business, let's be sure to select aims that will mean something. Put yourself in your employer's shoes and think of the most pressing problem he faces in your business. Carve off a corner of that problem, make that your target, and start shooting. As you pile up one idea after another, you may run into an even better aim.

As has been pointed out, judicial judgment is often an enemy of creativity and should be kept in its place. One of the times we should call in our judgment is right after we have tentatively picked a target. At this point, our judicial mind should tell us whether our target is worth shooting at.

Personally, I have too often set forth in search of will-o'-the-wisps. For example, I had in mind a certain new kind of dictionary. I talked with a few people who dealt in words and they were enthusiastic about my target. I set myself to the task and spent hundreds of hours working out the first 100 words. Then I talked to a dictionary publisher. It soon became obvious that it would take 10 men almost a lifetime to complete my work, the cost would be too great and the market would be too limited. Had I analyzed that aim in time, I could have invested those creative hours in something of greater promise.

Let's pick our target, set our aim, but let's beware of goat-feathers. And in narrowing our aim, let's not get the notion that all phases of creativity call for a sharp focus. For it is less important to *narrow* our aim than it is to *broaden* our search, after we get going.

Chapter XVIII

BREAK DOWN THE PROBLEM—
FILL IN THE FACTS

HAVING PICKED OUR TARGET and set our aim, we now need a plan of attack and a mobilization of facts. Our memories can bring up almost enough knowledge for most of our creative sorties; but, when waging any major campaign for ideas, we have to augment our memories with new facts.

To know what new facts are needed we have to break down our problem. This same analysis helps us plan a step-by-step attack—or a series of simultaneous attacks, as was done by the Manhattan District when General Groves split the atom-bomb problem into many problems and delegated each to a separate research-group.

Analysis of any kind can of itself bear creative fruit; for it tends to uncover clues which speed up our power of association and thus feed our imagination. And, in turn, imagination plays a guiding part in analysis. In fact, in *any* form of thinking, "imagination supplies the premises and asks the questions from which reason grinds out the conclusions as a calculating machine supplies answers." Dr. R. W. Gerard of the University of Chicago is the authority for that.

Just as effort is the core of creativity, so questions are the bone-and-sinew of analysis. "Why?" is almost always the main question, since cause-and-effect is usually the most important fact to find. So we have to delve into the *why-so* and the *what-if*, and in doing this let's not forget our pencils and pads. Let's heed the advice of Dr. Norman Vincent Peale—let's list on paper every fact and every factor in the problem. "This," said Dr. Peale, "clarifies our thinking, and brings various elements into orderly system. The problem thus becomes objective instead of subjective."

2.

"The *first* step is always to set up the problem," said Charles Kettering. "When we have done that, we say, 'Here's the way we think we ought to proceed,' and *then* we go to the library to see what others before us have thought about it. But if we go to the library first, few of us are strong enough to stay out of the rut that may be set up." Thus, just as judgment should be kept in its place, so fact-finding should be used at the right time and in the right way.

In setting up procedure, sequence is often important. Of course, if we have a large enough staff, we can tackle all phases at once. Such was the case with the Manhattan District—and likewise with the General Electric Company when called upon during the war to create a jet-plane almost overnight. G-E's research heads quickly broke down the problem of jet-propulsion and delegated one phase to each of about a dozen groups. But each group then had to create a plan for its procedure, and in this the factor of sequence became important. Much depended upon the right start.

Dr. William Easton stressed the need of what he called "framework"—a natural term for an engineer such as he. In speaking of the plan of attack for a creative project, he covered the "clearly defined objective" and as to the next steps commented thus:

"These steps will necessarily vary with circumstances; but in all cases, one of the first is to use the imagination to construct, out of data supplied by memory and observation, a framework of ideas that will serve as a foundation for further work. Thus the writer uses imagination to outline the composition he will write. The inventor uses it to determine the details of the device he is developing. The scientist uses it to draw inferences that will form the basis of a hypothesis. Without imagination, there would be no framework, and the thinker would never get started on his project."

3.

Carl Spier, a wholly creative associate of mine, is a great writer and a great believer in saturating oneself with facts. He recently said to me: "I seem to be unable to turn out anything worthwhile without the attendant agony of boning up interminably at first." This is especially true of scientists, according to Nobel Prize winner Ivan Pavlov who, just before he died at 87, wrote this: "Perfect as is the wing of a bird, it never could raise the bird up without resting on air. Facts are the air of a scientist. Without them you never can fly."

Henry J. Taylor once described Barney Baruch's creative thinking as following this pattern: "He gets the facts. He studies them patiently. And then he applies his imagination." But in talking with Mr. Taylor later, I found he agreed that Mr. Baruch's imagination must work in all three steps—that after he gets his basic facts, he has to think up what further information he needs, and in seeking those new facts, he likewise has to use his imagination.

Just as Kettering has held that we can get too many facts at the wrong stages of our creative projects, John Livingston Lowes has strongly pointed out that "facts may swamp imagination."

In one month I had to create two plans—one for an enlistment drive, another for a money-raising campaign. In preparation for the former plan I spent day after day digging into what others had done along similar lines. My exhaustive study of comparable programs lulled me into a willingness to adapt, and thus shut me off from thinking up anything really new. In preparing the other plan, I lined up the salient facts and then deliberately ignored what others had done.

Thus I found I could make my imagination work more radically. The resultant plan turned out to be far better than the other.

Such experiences indicate that, instead of doing an exhaustive job of digging before starting to create, we might well line up a few fundamental facts and then start thinking up all the ideas we possibly can. After listing 50 or 100 such ideas, we could go back to our fact-finding, gather all facts which might be helpful, and then turn on our imagination again. It is more than possible that an early idea, thought up by us while still shy on factual knowledge, might turn out to be the best idea in the end—and yet might have been drowned at the start in a premature and excessive flood of facts.

4.

There are two kinds of specific facts we should seek—those which are inherent in our problem and those which may have some bearing. Luckily, our analysis usually shows up just what new facts are needed. Luckily too, there are libraries to which we can turn to light up almost any specific phase. In our own business, for example, our Research Library, in addition to all the usual books, has on hand some 5000 special files on specific subjects. Day after day, our staff clips excerpts from all kinds of printed matter and tucks them into their proper folders. Well over a million such clippings are thus on tap.

Sometimes we realize we want new facts, but are at sea as to just what or where they might be. In this event, we can well prospect at random. For example, when we have a new package to think up, we might profitably meander through stores and just look over package after package. Or we might turn to some source that could serve as a check-list. For instance, in contemplating a package, or even the creation of a gadget, a good field for prospecting is a Sears, Roebuck catalog.

Good prospecting calls for an open mind and for wide exposure; and our prospecting should dig deeper than mere sensing. We should delve into the how and the why. Merely seeing a new type of fountain pen will add but little ore. But, by uncovering how the pen works and why people are buying it, we may strike a vein of thought which our mental mill can turn into gold. Our prospecting should also cover duds, for good ideas are often uncovered by digging into causes of failure.

Related facts are sometimes more helpful than facts directly in point and readily at hand. Before Dr. George R. Minot could establish a cure for anemia, he had to devise a way actually to watch the cells of bone-marrow as they busily created new red corpuscles. Only thus could he lay his hands on the essential facts attendant on his problem. It took plenty of analysis, plus creative sweat, plus new facts, for him to find that folic acid was what anemia needed. And then it took more new facts to arrive at liver as its best source for this purpose.

New facts as to *cause* are often all-important. When Dr. Robert Koch was challenged to find a cure for diphtheria he is said to have expostulated, "How can I cure diphtheria when I do not even know what causes it?" Personal problems are far simpler, but even these often call for new facts as to causes. For example, a boy is doing badly at school. It is up to his parents to think up a solution. Through talks with the teacher and the family physician, they could list a score of possible causes. One might concern the child's eyesight. In many such cases, eye-glasses have turned out to be the simple solution.

Medical analysis lays stress on contributory facts. A good doctor, in seeking a treatment to cure an ailment, often goes deeply into his patient's habits. Life insurance examinations may show a man to be a good risk, and yet his application may be turned down because of some facts in the history of his parents.

A conscious search for outside facts calls for imagination

galore but may lead to a winning idea. A young lawyer friend of mine won a spectacular case for a wealthy old man who was charged with incompetency by his relatives. My friend knew that his opponents could bring in just as much or more expert testimony. He asked himself, "What could we get that they couldn't have?" Just before the case went to trial he remembered that his client had a housekeeper. "I wonder what *she* would say about him?" he asked himself. Then he went to see her and asked her. "I am surprised you would ask me such a question," was her indignant reply. "You ought to know that if he weren't 100 per cent I wouldn't have stayed on as his housekeeper for all these 17 years." At the trial, her testimony turned the tide. The lawyer had turned up a new fact that turned out to be a winning idea for his client.

5.

The need for new facts may be so far-reaching that it calls for a new and complete education, as illustrated in the story of Alexander Graham Bell. "As a young, unknown man," said Dr. Bell, "I went to Washington to talk with Professor Henry, an authority on electricity, about an idea I had conceived for transmitting speech by wires. He told me he thought I had the germ of a great invention. I told him, however, that I had not the electrical knowledge necessary to bring it into existence. He replied, '*Get it!*'" Dr. Bell had studied sound all his life. More than any man, he knew the shapes of vibrations that pass through the air when we talk. But he had to—and did—absorb a new subject, electricity, in order to transform his notion into a telephone.

Paul Ehrlich had to go almost as deep into other fields to dig up what he needed to find his famous "606" cure for venereal diseases. His pursuit of new facts was less orderly than Dr. Bell's, but almost as exhaustive. He read book upon book in search of clues as to the kind of microbes he was fighting, and what might kill them without killing the patient.

In poring over the detailed reports of Alphonse Laveran, who himself had isolated the malaria microbe, Ehrlich finally got the information which ultimately led to his "606". The name is said to have come from the number of ideas he had thought up on his way to the final answer.

But again, it all depends. Charles Kettering has warned against leaning too much on text-books. Another leading researcher told me he guards himself against their over-use when on a creative pursuit, and added: "For one thing, the facts in a text-book may be out-of-date. It takes a year to write such a book, a year to get it out, and the chances are it's at least three years old when you hunt for helpful facts in its pages."

When Glenn Martin was at work on his first airplane model he studied the engineering of stationary bridges in order to get new facts on strains and stresses that might apply to flying. In search of similar new facts, Wilbur Wright built a crude glass-covered box at the end of which he installed a fan to create winds. From their effect on the miniature wings inside the toy tunnel, he could see just what happened. This was the world's first wind-tunnel. From it, the Wright Brothers got the needed new facts—true facts, even though they were at variance with the scientific tables in the text-books of that day. And that day was only about 50 years ago.

6.

As John Dewey pointed out, our creative thinking will improve as we relate the new fact with the old, and all facts with each other. That's why, in addition to finding new facts, we need to discover *relationships*. For instance, digging for *likenesses* can sometimes unearth a common factor which can serve as a *principle* in guiding our creative thinking. That's how Billy Rose got started on his career as a song-writer. Although he was the world's champion at shorthand, his heart was set on Tin Pan Alley. He realized how untutored

he was for a music-writing career, so he went into an orgy
of preparatory analysis which Maurice Zolotow reported as
follows:

"Billy Rose repaired to the New York Public Library and
each day, for many months, he studied the origins, history,
leading exemplars, and techniques of American threnody . . .
He scientifically divided the hit songs of 1890 to 1920 into
various categories . . . He then toted up the salient characteristics of each, and estimated which group made the most
money. The succession-of-sound songs—simple, repetitious,
easy to memorize—were the songs most likely to become
famous in the shortest span of time."

Thus Billy Rose hit on the principle that had proved
successful in songs like, *It's Mr. Dooley, Dooley-Dooley-
ooley-ooley-ooley-ooooo.* He decided not only that succession-of-sound was the best form for him, but also that the
most promising sound was "oo." Rose quickly won fame as a
tunesmith by applying this principle in his *Barney Google
with His Goo-Goo Googly Eyes.* Within the next 10 years or
so, he turned out nearly 400 popular songs including many
smash-hits.

Likenesses, yes, but differences, too, should be analyzed. In
fact there are about a dozen such headings under which relationships can be built. These categories are largely sub-divi-
sions of the three main laws of association. And logically so because the very process of relating facts and impressions is
an almost automatic function of our power of association.
Deliberate thinking-through on such relationships tends to
step up this power of ours.

As to the laws of association, let's first take contiguity—
and this includes sequence as well as cause-and-effect. Let's
ask these questions of any facts we have sought out: "This
is *next* to what?" . . . "What does this *go with*?" . . . "What
happens *before* or *after*?" . . . "This is *smaller* than what, or
larger than what?" . . . "What would *cause* this effect?"

Similarity, the second law of association, covers likeness,
sameness, composition and the common factor. Thus, under

similarity we could relate our data by asking: "What is this *like?*" . . . "What attribute has this in *common* with that?" . . . "Isn't this the *same* as that?" . . . "What about the *component parts?*"

The third law of association is contrast, which includes difference as well as oppositeness. Thus we can relate our facts through queries such as: "What is this *unlike?*" . . . "What is the point of *difference?*" . . . "What about the *opposite?*" . . . "How about *vice-versa?*"

And so it is that in a creative project, the final steps by way of preparation are these: (1) To break down our problem. (2) To build a framework. (3) To fill in the facts. (4) To relate our facts so as to give ourselves every chance of forming a *pattern.* For a pattern can become a magic map by which to reach the idea we pursue.

Chapter XIX

LET'S SEND FORTH OUR IMAGINATION IN SEARCH OF ALTERNATIVES

INSTINCTIVELY AND ALMOST UNCONSCIOUSLY, the imagination of the genius dashes down one trail after another in search of ideas. The rest of us need to give *conscious guidance* to our imagination and send it forth on the scores of trails where good ideas are known to be most plentiful.

How can we give directions to our imagination? One good way is to ask ourselves *questions*. The U. S. Army has successfully applied this method to both judicial and creative thinking. During the last war, the question-technique brought about far better thinking in the operations of all arsenals, motor-maintenance shops and many other war-production installations. "In only 50 installations which I happen to know about," said Bayard Pope, "that technique resulted in the saving of 6,000,000 man hours per year. As one example, it quadrupled the production of half-tracks."

"This is the way the technique works," continued Mr. Pope. "First you isolate the subject or problem you want to think about. Then you ask a series of questions about each step in that subject or problem." Here are the queries which Pope and other officers had to put to their minds: (1) *Why* is it necessary? (2) *Where* should it be done? (3) *When* should it be done? (4) *Who* should do it? (5) *What* should be done? (6) *How* should it be done?

Yes, as Charles Curtis, Jr. and Ferris Greenslet said in their *Practical Cogitator,* "There is a technique, a knack, for thinking, just as there is for doing other things. You are not wholly at the mercy of your thoughts, any more than they are of you. They are a machine you can learn to operate." But truly creative thinking calls for far more questions, and necessarily looser questions, than the Army manualized. Imagination has to be guided by stabs such as, "What *about* . . .?" and "What *if* . . .?" And always it must be prodded with, "What *else*?" and again, "What *else*?"

2.

It is a truism in golf that the lowest-scoring pros are not the best instructors. In most cases they acquired their swings as kids. In later years, their technique is so *instinctive* that they find it hard to tell a pupil what he should *consciously try* to do to better his score.

It's almost like that in creativity. The genius just doesn't know how he does it. A few even claim that there can be no techniques, and, rightly so, if technique means a rigid set of rules. Any attempt to lay down hard-and-fast methods would be naught but terminology masquerading as technology. But the genius is wrong if he holds that there can be no *principles,* or "guides to procedure" as defined by Webster.

The basic principle is *variation.* Almost all agree that the more changes we ring, the more likely we are to ring the cash-register. But variation is a helter-skelter principle which cannot be worked in any straight-line process. We have to weave our imaginations hither, thither and yon, uphill and downhill. Yes, and almost always into blind alleys; for, as psychologist Harry Hepner has said, "Creative thinkers make many false starts, and continually waver between unmanageable fantasies and systematic attack."

The active adjunct to the principle of variation is *plenty of alternatives.* To pile these up, there are scores of directions for our imaginations to take. About 10 of these are highways, each of which leads to about 10 by-ways.

How does the principle of plentiful variation fit in with *correlation* and *combination*—these being the two principles most frequently laid down by authorities on the creative mind? The answer is that variation includes both and more, too. Those who have espoused combination (or synthesis) have been largely right; because almost every new idea is a combination of old ideas. But if we limit our creative effort strictly to the field of combination, we cannot help but limit our resultant alternatives and thus restrict our creativity.

And what about the principle of correlation which Professor C. Spearman of the University of London described as the "educing of correlates"? *Relationships* of things to things and thoughts to thoughts are decidedly inherent in all good creative thinking. When we think of this instead of that; when we think of making that larger or smaller; when we think of changing attributes or relocating constituents—in all these mental thrusts we are "educing the correlates." And, of course, relationship is the basis of our power of association.

3.

As a rule, the more often, the *more freely* we swing our imagination, the *better*—with the one reservation that we should never overlook the obvious. For the best answer to a creative problem is sometimes as plain as a planet.

"No one rises so high as he who knows not whither he is going," said Oliver Cromwell; and this is largely true in creative soaring. There is even some truth in the oft-repeated wisecrack that "you don't have to be crazy to think up ideas, but it helps." Fred Sharp made an exhaustive study of thinking and came up with this conclusion:

"Ideas of the insane are the result of the functioning of associative mechanisms, with the associations of the most superficial sort—frequently nothing more than connections based on word-sounds. But maybe we could take a cue from the insane to improve our own creative thinking. If, when we search for ideas, we were to do our thinking out loud—holding back none of our 'crazy' associations—we might wander into just the thought we want."

Yes, it may pay to pay attention to the preposterous. Many a wild seed has reaped a harvest. Even scientists use more wildness than we realize. Of Pasteur, Paul de Kruif said, "This man was a passionate groper whose head was incessantly inventing right theories and wrong guesses—shooting them out like a display of village fireworks going off bewilderingly by accident."

The more freely we swing our imagination, the more likely we are to enlist the help of Lady Luck. Or call her Miss Inspiration if you will. If we shower her with enough ideas, no matter how wild they may be, she is likely to reward us with a new and beautiful hunch.

Let's start swinging and keep on swinging. "Let yourself go!" urged Ray Giles. "Plunge immediately into writing down every possible answer that comes to you. Force the drafts of your thinking. Forget quality; aim now to get a quantity of answers. When you're through, your sheet of paper may be so full of ridiculous nonsense that you'll be disgusted. Never mind. You're loosening up your fettered imagination—making your mind deliver."

4.

Quantity, quantity and more *quantity*! This is the surest recipe for ideas. "As in navigation, the more sights we take, the more likely we are to hit port" is the analogy used by John Caples, Annapolis graduate and a creative associate of mine. The principle of the machine-gun is another parallel.

The odds are that only a few of the many ideas we hit upon will be any good. Therefore the more alternatives we think up, the better our chance of success. Then, too, the more ideas we consciously gather, the more we prime our automatic power of association.

Of course, we should make a list of all our ideas. When we have piled up a good measure of alternatives, we can use this as a check-list to help us pile up *more*. Always we should keep asking our imagination: "What *else*?" and again, "What *else*?"

It may surprise you to know how many alternatives are thought up to arrive at the single product which the public finally sees. For example, here is what happens when Community Plate brings out a new pattern of silverware. In the first place, the artists turn out hundreds of sketches of all possible new designs. Finally, one of these sketches is chosen as a starter. Hundreds of more sketches are then made within a narrow range, with slight changes in this and that little detail. Actual models of spoons are then made by hand. Scores of these are then changed in this and that way until the final model is chosen.

And how about a name for a pattern—like "Morning Star"? Where did it come from? Was it somebody's first guess? Not at all. Over 500 names were considered and checked against names registered in the U. S. Patent Office. And the advertisement to introduce the new pattern to the public— did somebody just think up an idea or two and let it go at that? No! A dozen artists each sketched out a dozen or more layouts of how that advertisement should look. About 60 of these sketches were put into fairly finished form and then, by expert judgment and also by consumer testing, the final layout was chosen. But surely you would think the simple wording in that advertisement was done in a first or second try. No! There were 60 versions of the text created before the final wording was chosen.

In seeking a name for another consumer product, some 70 people in our shop thought up and wrote down a list of over 5000 possible names. By scientific testing, one was ultimately chosen as the most likely to click. But alas, it was then found that this name was owned by a little company in the mid-West. To acquire that one word, our client had to buy that business. Even on so trivial a project as finding a title for the book which you are now reading, 611 alternatives were listed and tested.

We think of Irving Berlin as turning out one masterpiece after another. But the fact is that in between hits he makes scores of mediocre stabs. He is a demon for quantity, according to Alexander Woollcott who said: "In his early days, he poured songs out so fast that his publishers thought it best to pretend that he was several persons. At least one song was thus launched under the name of Ren G. May. If you meditate on the letters of that implausible name you will see that they spell Germany, of which nation Berlin was the capital."

And when it comes to writing, the good author thinks up endless alternatives. For a headline for a short editorial, I have with my own eyes seen Bruce Barton write down over 100 possible captions. A century ago, a French novelist put the case for quantity in a nut-shell. "I require," said Stendhal, "three or four cubic feet of new ideas per day, as a steamboat requires coal."

"Yes, but what about quality?" you might well ask. For many intelligent people do fail to see the need of quantity. A man who is now a publisher once made this remark in my presence, "Don't bother about thinking up a lot of ideas. Just think up one or two good ideas."

But isn't it obvious that quantity breeds quality in creative effort? Not only are logic and mathematics on the side of the argument that the more ideas, the more likely it is that some of them may be good; but likewise it is true that the best ideas seldom come first. As Herbert Spencer said, "Early ideas are not usually true ideas."

My friend Welles Moot, among other things, is head of Sylvanite Mines. He tells me it takes four tons of ore to get one ounce of gold. Isn't creative mining like that—with the more ore, by way of alternatives, yielding the more gold by way of good ideas?

5.

Just as it's harder to work any part of our mind than to work any part of our body, so it is hardest of all consciously to keep the imagination at work piling up alternatives. For one thing, that devil judgment is likely to intrude with: "Whoa! That's enough alternatives. Let's look them over and see what's wrong with them." To which we have to cry "Hands off!" and blithely keep on piling.

We might even call on our imaginations to help seduce ourselves into piling up enough alternatives. To that end, I thought up a trick to play on myself. Having found that the first alternatives come easily, I wanted an incentive to make me strive for the next and the next and the next. So I wrote out a table of prices, all imaginary of course. By this my first idea would be worth one cent, my second two cents, my third four cents, my fourth eight cents, my fifth 16 cents —and so on, doubling the price for each additional alternative. Thus, when I have brainstorming to do and get 20 ideas written down on my list, I look at my table and see how much, on that basis, I would be paid for my 21st idea. Wow! It would be worth $10,485. For my 25th idea, my theoretical pay would be $167,772. This may sound childish, but it dramatizes to me the cold logic of the fact that the more alternatives I pile up, the more valuable my ideas are likely to be.

6.

The principle of plenty of variation is the essence of scientific experimentation. The Edisonian theory called for trying everything. No progress was made in alleviating allergies until the medical scientists started to scratch the skin with this dust and that pollen and countless other things to find the cause and thus find the treatment.

When experimentation calls for making models, the same principle applies. My friend Dr. C. W. Fuller was busy on his newest invention when I asked him, "How do you go at this kind of work?" "Oh," said he, "if I have any technique at all it simply consists of my making one new model after another until I happen to hit on the one that seems likely to work best."

Leeuwenhoek, famous for his invention of microscopes and his blood discoveries, not only believed in piling up alternatives, but in shooting wild. In one series of experiments he lost himself trying to find out what makes pepper taste as it does. One idea he hit upon along the way was that each speck of pepper has sharp points which prick the tongue and thus make the pepper taste sharp. Even this wild and fruitless experimentation turned out to be of help to one of his later achievements. And every modern scientist with whom I have talked is strong for plenty of alternatives or "tentative stabs," as one research-director calls them.

Charles Kettering told about a man who came to see his new Diesel engine. "I would like to talk to your thermodynamics expert about it," said the visitor. "I am sorry," Kettering replied, "we don't have anyone here who even understands the word 'thermodynamics,' much less be an expert on it. But if you want to know how we developed this engine, I'll be glad to show you."

He led the man to the dynamometer room and showed him a single-cylinder setup. Kettering's explanation included this remark: "We tried one thing after another for about six years until the engine itself finally told us exactly what it wanted."

Six years of trying one thing after another, endless piling up of alternatives—that, said Kettering, "is the only way we know." Can there be any doubt that the more ideas we pile up, the more likely we are to arrive at the right idea?

Chapter XX

"TO WHAT OTHER USES
COULD THIS BE PUT?"

"TO WHAT OTHER USES could this be put?" is a good question to ask of our imaginations in regard to a thing, a thought or a talent. For by adding uses we can often add values. Then too, by piling up alternatives by way of other uses, a *better* use is likely to come to light.

"In what other products could my material be used?" This is an obvious question to ask ourselves when we have a certain material and want to widen its market. Dr. George Washington Carver thought up over 300 useful articles in which peanuts could be used. For the home alone, he worked up "105 different ways to prepare peanuts for the table."

Every manufacturer is constantly on the hunt for other things to make out of his own basic material. This has been particularly true of rubber. Out of thousands of ideas considered, here are a few that have been turned down by one big company: rubber bed-blankets, rubber bathtubs, rubber bathtub covers, rubber curbstones, rubber clothespins, rubber bird-houses, rubber door-knobs, rubber coffins, and rubber gravestones.

The success of most synthetic materials is based on thinking up new ways in which other people can use the product. Du Pont's neoprene has been built up into great volume through thousands of new applications, some of which could come only from shooting wild. For example, a toymaker makes a chocolate-flavored bone out of neoprene for dogs to chew upon. A doll-maker has covered some of his creations with a magic skin of neoprene and in a color so natural that a child thinks of it as a real baby. The list is endless— a lamb with a coat like wool; a duck; a dog named Poochy; baby chicks; a whale that spouts water; a whale-like submarine; a ship with three smokestacks.

Likewise with cellophane and nylon. The latter, for example, has already displaced catgut on most tennis rackets. Fishing-lines of nylon have become more and more popular. Every woman knows about nylon clothesline. Huge hawsers and mammoth grommets are made of nylon too.

Along about 1935 I happened to be in on the start of Fiberglas. Our big creative problem was, *"To what uses could glass-thread be put?"* We dreamed up hundreds of applications; but hundreds more have since been thought up. And through these other-use ideas, that tiny thread of spun glass has been developed into a great industry. One use none of us foresaw was for fishing-rods, which the Shakespeare Company perfected by imbedding glass threads in a plastic binder. Nor did any of us pile up enough alternatives to hit upon by far the largest ultimate use of Fiberglas, which came when Hitler forced us to build a two-ocean Navy, and Fiberglas was adopted as a new and better insulation for our warships.

2.

"In what other ways could this be used?" Sometimes this trail leads to re-designing a product so as to give it extra functions. My friend Ed Barcalo had long made conventional pillows. He thought up a new one called the "6-Way," a triangular cushion for reading in bed, for sitting up in bed, and for four other purposes. Gadgeteers have gone so far in incorporating extra uses that some became the butt of Ed Wynne, Rube Goldberg, and other laughmakers.

But, without change of product, it pays to think up new and added uses. Listerine was built up as a mouthwash. Someone in Lambert Pharmacal must have asked, "Where else on the human body could this be used?" Out of the alternatives that were piled up came the idea of its application to the hair for the alleviation of dandruff. The same with Absorbine. The product sold well as a liniment for sore muscles. The makers swung their creative searchlights around in search of new uses and hit upon "Athlete's Foot."

Sometimes the new use is even more extreme. During one period, Procter and Gamble started a fad of using Ivory Soap for sculpturing. Lemons are now sold for a mild laxative as well as for lemonade and garnishing fish.

Scotch Tape has grown from a little specialty into a great industry. It is made by the Minnesota Mining Company, whose executives created a list of 325 unduplicated uses. Tom, Dick and Harry thought up a lot more. I happened to be the beneficiary of one of these ideas. The side of my face became partially paralyzed as the result of an icy draft. A nerve specialist in Canada told me that only time could cure my ailment, but that I could help myself meanwhile with Scotch Tape. He showed me how, before retiring, to push my face into proper shape and then strap it there.

Some great advances in science have come from finding a new use for an old thing. In London, along about 1620, a woman was having a hard time delivering a baby. A doctor named Chamberlain appeared with something under his coat. He covered it with a sheet and quickly brought forth the baby. For nearly a century, the doctor's "iron hands" were kept a secret within the Chamberlain family—and yet similar tongs were on almost every hearthside. According to an obstetric friend of mine, "forceps have done more to shorten labor-pains and to preserve life than any other surgical gadget ever thought up."

At one time I was given the task of trying to discover a new and better rat-poison. I failed. Thanks to scientific research in recent years, Du Pont has developed a product unusually fatal to brown rats. Its use is the same old use—to kill rats. The *way* the rats use it is the new idea. This latest rat-killer, "Antu," is known as a tracking poison. For some strange reason, rats like to lick their feet. When this tracking poison is sprinkled where the rats walk, they lick their feet and that's their end.

3.

New uses sometimes lead to progressive changes in product. The Corning Glass Works, as already mentioned, developed a stronger globe for railroad lanterns. In seeking new uses for this new glass, a Corning researcher named J. T. Littleton next hit on battery jars. One day in 1913 he cut the bottom off one of these jars, took it home to his wife and asked her to bake a cake. It was thus that glass began to be used for baking. This led to the question of still other uses. "How would it do for top-of-stove cooking?" was one of the questions asked. Dr. Eugene Sullivan, chief chemist at the time, decided that the ovenware glass was not strong enough to stand the heat of direct flame. Four years of experimentation followed. This included thousands of actual kitchen tests in which 18,000 pounds of potatoes were boiled and fried in experimental saucepans and skillets. Out of this came Flameware, with a brand new use for glass.

When Du Pont found out how to use coal, water and air to make water-gas, the next creative problem was what to make with water-gas. Thousands of uses were thought up, with the result that in just one department of the company, 100 new products were added within 10 years. Of course, each of these products differed slightly. But all were based on new uses of the new technique which made the fixation of nitrogen possible.

Most of us think of Koroseal as one kind of product that is always the same. The fact is, however, that in multiplying the uses for Koroseal there has been a vast progression in kinds of Koroseal. Dr. Waldo Semon, who had most to do with creating Koroseal for the B. F. Goodrich Company, estimates that since 1926 nearly 10,000 rubberlike materials have been created in order to adapt the original product to new uses. The raw materials of the process are still limestone, coke and salt. The basic characteristics of the product are still the shedding of water and insulation against electricity. But variation of product has had to go along hand-in-hand with multiplication of use.

Similar progression has marked the multiplication of uses for electric lamps. For many years, bulbs were solely for illumination. Then came the change in wave-length that led to duplicating the ultra-violet rays of the sun. Also came another change which gave us infra-red heat-rays. But the creative researchers at Nela Park, headquarters of General Electric lamps, kept on the hunt for still other uses. One of them asked: "I wonder if we could find a wave-length that would kill germs without harming people?" This led to the new Germicidal Lamp, which is successfullly killing air-borne bacteria. When the product was modified for this purpose there came the question, "*Where* could these lamps best be used?" Out of the alternatives thus piled up, came new uses for this same lamp in hospitals, schools, military barracks, doctors' waiting-rooms, meat-coolers, hotel-kitchens and homes. Yes, even in hen-houses. On the Casler Poultry Farm in Ohio, within six weeks, 240 baby chicks grew 14 per cent heavier than 240 others in a control-pen without benefit of G-E Germicidal lamps. Three times as many chicks died in the lampless house.

4.

"*To what use can waste be put?*" Along this trail, the piling up of alternatives is particularly important. America's packing industry has been built on ingenuity in finding new uses for by-products—almost all by-products except the "pig's whistle."

Likewise in the steel industry. Slag used to be a costly

waste. Now it is salvaged for ballast in railroad beds, for making cement, and for processing into building-blocks. The slag from the Tennessee plant near Birmingham is so rich in phosphorus content that it is now packaged and sold throughout the south as a soil-conditioner.

"What use could be made of those gases?" was the question some steel man must have asked himself long ago as he stared at the ugly fumes arising from his stacks. What a development that started! Today, through the use of by-product coke-ovens, those gases are saved and are the source of literally thousands of products in the chemical and drug field. While most people think in terms of 50,000 end-products from such salvaging, a friend of mine in the steel business believes that as many as 500,000 more uses may be developed in the future.

What to do with rejects is another creative challenge. Often it is easy to sell them as seconds. Ingenuity can sometimes provide a more profitable answer. And what to do with scrap likewise calls for imagination. L. A. Conley of B. F. Goodrich saw pieces of surgical tubing being thrown into the waste-barrel. "Why not cut them into rubber bands of the size and width used by the millions to hold small items together?" he asked. Conley got $150 for his new-use suggestion. The profit his company made from that idea was velvet —velvet scraped from stuff which otherwise was worthless.

And then, too, there are cases where a new use may turn a dud into a triumph. George Westinghouse thought up about 400 inventions, of which the only dud was a rotary engine. But he refused to throw it away. Instead, he added a new invention and started another business—simply by turning his useless engine into a new and better water-meter.

5.

The other-use trail need not be limited to things. When it comes to intangibles like principles, we might also ask our imagination, "To what use could this thought be put?"

Pure science becomes practical science by thinking up ways to use an academic discovery. Lord Lister thought Louis Pasteur was more or less guilty of boondoggling in trying to find a way to make wine stay sweet. But this work of Pasteur's led Lister to wonder whether a more important use could be found for Pasteur's findings. Specifically, he asked himself: "If germs ruin flavor, could germs be the cause of so many unexplained fatalities in surgery?" This other use of Pasteur's new theory led to proof that germs did invade wounds and this truth became the key to the antiseptic surgery which immortalized Lister's name.

Roentgen was indulging in pure science when he hit upon the X-ray. He had no way of knowing what the ray was and that's why he called it "X". He had no *use* in view. It is said that he himself was surprised when he found how widely his discovery could be used—not only as a therapy in itself, but as eyes to enable the surgeon to look deep into the body before applying the knife.

In modern science, the alert researcher is ever on the lookout for ways to apply old principles and new principles to new uses. Management no longer looks at pure research as a waste of money; because too many "worthless" theories have been turned into profitable improvements by asking and answering the question, "To what use could this be put?"

6.

Piling up alternatives by way of new uses can do much to make the most of talents. Along this trail, imagination can help a lot in vocational guidance. Parents can well send their creative minds in this direction. For instance, a little girl in the house behind ours loves to make things with her hands. Every Thanksgiving the windows in her room are alive with turkeys she has cut out and crayonned. At Halloween the windows are plastered with pumpkins, and at Christmas they are gay with stars and bells. Her mother showed me a list she had worked out of the vocations in which her daughter could best use this talent, and toward which she might steer her.

In some cases, new uses for a talent come about more or less by accident. Daniel M. Eisenberg set out to find two rich great-uncles with whom his family had lost touch. Although he searched for months he never located them. But what he did find was that he had a talent for turning up missing relatives of others. He asked himself, "How to use this talent?" That led him to the idea of operating a "missing persons" business. More than 65,000 wives have since paid him to find their husbands.

Having gone broke as a rancher, John Gast was feeling lower than a weed. He knew he had an artistic touch and drove himself to think up a way to use it. Among his musings came this thought: "Even a weed can be quite pretty when you look at it the right way. Dressed up it might even become a thing of beauty." As an experiment, he silvered some eucalyptus and smoke-tree branches, and a Los Angeles department store snapped them up for window decorations. That started a lucrative career for Mr. Gast. It is said that he now makes $50,000 a year out of weeds which others find a nuisance. Although many of his materials come from California, his staff goes to Kansas for lotus-pads, to Florida for sea-oats, and to other distant points for many special items.

Mrs. Joseph Watson was a fair photographer. She saw a newspaper picture of three rats sprawled on a cat. She decided that the photo was faked. "Why can't I make just as interesting animal pictures that are *not* faked?" she asked herself. From that idea, Mrs. Watson built a hobby which has yielded her around $5,000. Her first picture was of a Shetland pony modeling a straw hat. She has successfully combined as many as 13 animals in one shot.

Ray Giles tells an interesting tale of four young artists who found their landscapes not quite good enough to sell. They decided to think up all the different ways in which they could use their skills. One became a well-paid painter of pictures on drums used in bands. Another specializes in clay models for museums. The third does well by painting faces on "character" dolls. The fourth now names his own price for portraits of dogs, cats and horses owned by people who love pets more than money.

"What *new* use?" . . . "What *other* use?" All of us have enough creative power to pile up alternatives galore by sending our imagination along this highway and into its many by-ways.

Chapter *XXI*

WHAT CAN WE BORROW AND
ADAPT TO OUR NEED?

NOW LET'S MAKE OUR IMAGINATION pursue the *parallels* in search of ideas which we can *adapt*. Let's ask ourselves: "What is there *like* this, from which I might get an idea?" . . . "Is there something *similar* I could partially copy?"

Ah—but how about plagiarism and infringement? True, it is legally and morally wrong to steal outright from the other fellow, especially if by so doing we do him harm. But just to take a lead from what someone else has thought up—this is a legitimate practice. And its sanction is good public policy; for without such adaptation, there would be far fewer ideas of benefit to the people. It is a common and inescapable practice, as Wendell Phillips pointed out: "In every matter that relates to invention, to use, or beauty or form, we are borrowers."

The patent office is full of overlapping inventions. Larry Parker, Washington patent attorney, once told me: "One of the toughest jobs of government officials is to draw a line between that which infringes and that which is similar and yet new."

Plagiarism means passing off as original something which someone else has created. The word comes from Latin meaning kidnapping. As in infringement, the line between

159

plagiarism and legitimate adaptation is sometimes shadowy.

A queer case of *reverse* plagiarism was related to me by my associate, Robley Feland, who was once a ghost-writer for Elbert Hubbard, internationally known publicist of a generation ago. Hubbard, according to Feland, coined a new word, "kabojolism." It meant the opposite of plagiarism. Here is Feland's explanation:

"Hubbard was a lavish user of the famous 'mouse-trap' quotation. He even had it carved on the great door of his Roycroft shop. Usually he worded it thus: 'If a man can write a better book, preach a better sermon, or build a better mousetrap than his neighbor, though he build his house in the woods, the world will make a beaten path to his door.' Always he credited it to Ralph Waldo Emerson. The quotation became so popular that humorists offered such para-phrases as 'If a man will build a grass lawn around a curving walk, his neighbors will make a beaten pathway to his door.'

"From Emerson fans there came a ground-swell of quer-ies: 'In which of Emerson's essays did this appear?' 'At what time was it written?' 'What was the context?' Finally, in 1911, Hubbard publicly confessed that he had committed 'kabojolism.' It had seemed immodest, wrote he, to admit that he himself had created this line, since it obviously re-ferred to the national success of his own village printery and craftshop. So he had deliberately ascribed it to another writer of recognized greatness who had died 13 years before Hub-bard had founded the Roycrofters."

Incidentally, doubt was thrown on Hubbard's explana-tion when, a year or so later, the same mouse-trap quotation came to light in a privately printed brochure called "Bor-rowings," which claimed to be made up of excerpts from lec-tures which Emerson had delivered but had never published.

2.

There are many cases where ideas are almost bodily trans-planted. The "Book-of-the-Month" became the "Fruit-of-the-

Month" and the "Candy-of-the-Month." Then came the "Hobby-of-the-Month" in which the first selection offered was an assortment of sharks' teeth for jewelry-making hobbyists.

More often the adaptation is but partial. Baseball, for instance, was adapted from the English sport of "rounders." Football came from rugby. Basketball is about the only game originated in America. Dr. James Naismith deliberately set out to devise a brand-new sport that could be played in a gym. The basket, however, was not a product of his imagination, but was an accident. The janitor, when asked to get some boxes, couldn't find any; so he came back with peach-baskets instead. Hence the name and the goals for the game.

It is well-nigh impossible for writers not to adapt. A novelist is forced to use a well-used basic plot. James N. Young counted 101 of these. Goethe claimed there were only 36. Willa Cather said,"There are only two or three human stories, and they go on repeating themselves as fiercely as if they had never happened before." Don Marquis held that there is only one basic plot. "The world hath just one tale to tell," wrote he, "and it is very old—a little tale, a simple tale, a tale that's easy told: 'There was a youth in Babylon who greatly loved a maid!'"

As to humor, George Lewis of the Gag Writers Institute claimed that in every "new" joke he could detect the skeleton of one of six basic gags. That's all there are, according to him—every new joke is merely a new version of an old one.

"Whose style can I emulate?" is not a bad question for a creative writer to ask himself. Robert L. May contemplated the perennial success of *The Night Before Christmas* and in the same style and meter wrote *Rudolph the Red-Nosed Reindeer*. In 1939, Montgomery Ward put out 2,365,000 copies of this. Seven years later, a reprint of 3,776,000 copies was hardly enough.

And here we come to adaptations of an adaptation, which is not unusual in the world of ideas. The epic of *Rudolph*, patterned after *The Night Before Christmas*, led manufacturers to make use of the red-nosed reindeer. RCA put out a *Rudolph* record. Other manufacturers produced *Rudolph* slippers, bracelets, sweatshirts and games, even a new flashlight with Rudolph's nose supplying the beam.

Composing music is largely based on borrowing. Sometimes it is a bodily transplantation of an old melody into new words. At other times the adaptation is so different that the public—yes, even the composer—may fail to recognize its parallel.

Of the many hits which have been re-births of classics, one example is *Till the End of Time.* This was taken bodily from Chopin's *Polonaise. Andantino in D Flat* was the source of *Moonlight and Roses. The Star-Spangled Banner*—which was "created" to defy England—was substantially the same as a tune then popular in the pubs of London.

Sigmund Spaeth has detected many musical borrowings in songs supposed to be original. The truly new tunes are exceptional, and among these exceptions Dr. Spaeth has cited *I Didn't Know What Time It Was,* by Rodgers and Hart, and *Smoke Gets in Yours Eyes,* by Jerome Kern.

And yet, said Spaeth, "Both of these titles illustrate the trick of giving a new twist to an old idea. Essentially they are expressing the most popular of all vocal thoughts, which is 'I Love You.' But they succeed in suggesting this basic thought in an entirely new way, Lorenz Hart expressing the confusion of young love, while Otto Harbach supplies Mr. Kern with a fanciful legend that conveys a similar thought in an entirely different way."

3.

"What can I make this *look* like?" . . . "What can I copy into this?" These are legitimate and helpful questions when it comes to fashions. Plucking ideas from parallels is a conscious part of creativity among stylists.

Swim-suits are a striking example. A recent style was unblushingly based on diapers. Another was the strapless swim-suit. The man who thought this up told me just where he borrowed his idea. "We badly needed a new number for the next season," he said. "So I kept looking over magazines for a lead. I ran across a picture of a strapless evening gown. Immediately I drew a sketch of a strapless swim-suit. We put it into production right away and it turned out to be a wow."

Winston Churchill's overcoat inspired a box-shaped six-button creation. General Eisenhower's battle-jacket was femininized into a dressy coat tied at the waist and garnished with military cuffs, lapels and a shoulder-medal.

New York's Metropolitan Museum of Art offers a special service to creators of fashions. From its treasury of ancient art, New York designers take many ideas. The shape of an angel's wings in a fifteenth-century painting was the basis of Marcel Vertes' creations. Designer Lina Harttman found inspiration in the warriors pictured on a Greek vase of around 800 B.C. And in Hollywood, one of Adrian's great hits was a design taken from the helmet and eye of a warrior of around 500 B.C.

And so it goes with hats and everything else that women wear. And it goes with furniture too. In many a fine living-room you will find a table which simulates the cobbler's bench of long ago. A new electric lamp-post to light up an entrance or a driveway is a black replica of the gas-lamps against which our grandfathers leaned. The new Rotiss-O-Mat is an electrified version of the spit on which King Henry VIII cooked his meat. The new Robot Cigarette Holder, to insure against setting fire to your bed, is a frank copy of the long-hosed water-pipe which the Arabians smoked when Aladdin was in short pants.

Sometimes an adaptation is a frank copy, but in far cheaper form. Mrs. Edith Holmes of Conley, Georgia, heard of an expensive doll supposedly owned by a child in a Czar's family long before the Russian Revolution. The doll was a princess in royal raiment until you turned it upside down. Then it became a peasant in rags. Mrs. Holmes told me, "We jut took that idea for our Topsy-Eva doll and cut the costs down to where we could sell it far and wide at $1.00."

A stirring deed in style-adaptation was performed by a young friend of mine, Richard Moot, in order to save the lives of Navy fliers. He was Landing Signal Officer on one of the big airplane-carriers. His responsibility was to control and direct the boys in landing on the ship after their combat flights. In the black of the night, the fliers could not see the signals controlling their landings on the deck of the ship moving at 30 knots; if enough light were used, it would disclose the ship's location to enemy submarines.

Richard Moot remembered "Black Magic" at the New York World's Fair and recommended an adaptation of that idea. Senior officers were skeptical but, nevertheless, permitted him to contact the General Electric Company. The final result was that landing signal officers on aircraft-carriers thereafter wore uniforms and carried signal paddles of a material which became luminous and visible to the pilots when invisible black light was used. And yet such luminous uniforms and signals were visible only for the short distance required by the plane pilots coming in on radio signals and were of no use as a guide to enemy submarines.

4.

Not only new styles but epoch-making new products are arrived at via the adaptation highway. Rudolf Diesel wanted to burn fuel directly in the cylinders of his engine, but did not know how to ignite the fuel. In piling up parallels he thought of a cigar-lighter. He analyzed one which had these essential features: 1.) Both air and fuel were in its cylinder. 2.) A piston suddenly compressed the air in the cylinder. 3.) This caused the fuel to ignite. From this parallel he thought his way through to the invention of the first Diesel engine in 1892.

In preparing for this chapter, I thought there might be a good case in the way the airplane pioneers had adapted the flight of birds. So, through a friend, I made inquiry of Orville Wright; but, alas, he replied as follows: "I cannot think of any part bird-flight had in the development of human flight excepting as an inspiration. Although we intently watched birds fly in a hope of learning something from them, I cannot think of anything that was first learned in that way. After we had thought out certain principles, we then watched the bird to see whether it used the same principles. In a few cases we did detect the same thing in the bird's flight."

Descending from the sublime to the ridiculous, I made a fool of myself in trying to adapt a woman's garment as an aid to golf. When about 35 I started to play, and my pro told me that I had to keep my left arm straight. This I could not do. So I had a miniature corset built to lace around my elbow. In my first try-out, I teed up my ball, took a full swing, and fell flat on my face. I should have known that a swing's centrifugal force cannot spend itself unless the left arm can collapse at the finish.

The idea of stretchers for stockings probably came from coat-hangers. A further adaptation was sweater-stretchers. In St. Louis the Lee-Rowan Company was looking for something to make. "As long as frames to hold sweaters in shape are so popular, why not a frame to hold pants in shape?" Such parallel thinking was the basis of their trouser-creasers. Over a million pairs of these have already been sold.

Years ago I knew Dr. William More Decker. He had left a lucrative medical practice to build his Hygeia Nursing Bottle business. Until then, all nipples had been narrow. He based his new ideas on copying the rounded surface of the mother's breast. This wider nipple called for a wider bottle, far easier to clean. This sanitary feature plus the more natural nipple proved to be a winning combination.

5.

"What other *process* could be adapted to this job?" . . . "Could we make this better and cheaper with an assembly-line?" Questions like these have led to ideas that have raised America's standard of living.

Straight-line assembly has been adapted to almost every industry, even for baking bread. Some 30 years ago I heard a violent argument between William Deininger, head of the General Baking Company, and Louis J. Kolb, his largest stockholder. Colonel Kolb held out for keeping on with the age-old stationary ovens. Mr. Deininger wanted to put the unbaked loaves on a belt and have them travel through a long oven and come out at the other end baked to a turn. Mr. Deininger won out. In practically every bakery in the country, you will now find this adaptation of the assembly-line in the form of traveling ovens.

Likewise, the finding of the right machine often calls for exploring the parallels. When Wildroot Cream Oil was created, the problem was to emulsify it so as not to separate. No machine in the pharmauceutical industry could do just that. One morning Harry Lehman said to his production manager: "I want you to visit a dairy and see what machinery is used for homogenizing milk. Maybe something like that is what we need for Cream Oil." Sure enough, the adaptation of a machine from another industry turned out to be the answer.

In the same way, tools meant for one purpose can be successfully adapted for something else. An extreme example of this took place in the Dallas plant of the North American Aviation Company. The war was raging and the armed forces were crying for planes. But each plane had to be right, down to the last nut. Girls had to string the steel nuts on wire, spray them with graphite, and pass them through an induction coil in order to reveal faults in the metal. It took tedious hours to string those nuts that way. One of the workers, pondering what to use for a better tool, thought of a corkscrew. He took a long wire, and curved it into corkscrew turns. This device, when swiftly rotated in a box of nuts, could pick up over a hundred per minute. The production of planes was thus sped up by adapting something similar to provide a better tool.

6.

"Out of whose book can I take a leaf?" This is a question which can send our imagination down the adaptation-trail to the end of brightening our personal lives. "*What* leaf?" is important, as I found out to my dismay. One of our young men —I accidentally discovered—sought to emulate me. He noticed that I got along, and that I smoked cigars. He decided to smoke cigars, too. That leaf got him nowhere.

But in personal problems, it does often pay to peer into parallels. One case, by way of example, is that of a father I know whose daughter thought she was in love with a gigolo. Her dad was at his wits' end as to how to break up the romance. In casting his mind around in search of a solution, he remembered that when he was a youngster his cousin Eloise had involved her parents in a similar problem, and her mother had wisely sent her to Europe for a course in music. While in Paris the girl came to her senses and called off her engagement. So my friend took a leaf out of his aunt's book. With the war on, a trip to Europe was out of the question, so he persuaded his daughter to go to the University of Arizona. "I thought that would be even better than a trip to Europe," he told me, "because out in the Southwest she will meet a lot of real red-blooded fellows and see by contrast what a mistake she would have made." His idea worked.

A barber I go to is a staunch American who came from Italy when in his teens. Among his many children is a son with a high I.Q. The boy went to war as a private and came out as a top-sergeant. Then he went to medical college. One day I asked old Joe how his son was. "He breaks my heart," was his reply. "He won't talk with me any more. Before he went to war, he and I used to talk sports all the time. We used to discuss batting averages, football scores, Joe Louis, and even the wrestlers. But now he won't talk. He studies hard to be a doctor. He wants to be a doctor in the Army. He doesn't care about sports any more and he keeps his thoughts to himself."

That bothered me, so I tried to figure how I could help Joe with his son. In thinking of parallels, I thought of their mutual interest in sports, and by way of natural sequence, that led me to ask, "Why not develop a mutual interest in the Army?" Joe thought this was a good idea, so he started to learn a new subject. He diligently read up on military affairs. Then he started to ask his son questions, to which the boy sparked. Now when the boy comes back from medical college, instead of giving his father the cold shoulder, the two of them discuss military affairs with almost as much gusto as when they used to discuss sports.

What is experience but a wealth of parallels upon which our imagination can draw? Nor does it have to be first-hand experience. Few psychiatrists have had as many personal problems put up to them as has our minister, Dr. Butzer. Vicariously he has lived hundreds of lives—lives in distress. He can counsel because he can take leaves out of many books, and the right leaves. He knows what works and what fails in trying to rehabilitate a life. He knows what ideas to transplant from one case to another.

To step up our creative power we need to pile up alternatives. Whether for better writing, better music, better product, better process—or for a brighter life—let's pile up plenty of alternatives by way of parallels. Let's borrow ideas right and left and adapt them to our needs.

Chapter XXII

LET'S LOOK FOR A NEW TWIST—
LET'S *MODIFY*

HAVING PILED UP ALTERNATIVES through adaptation, as well as through other uses, now let's deal with *modification*. Let's ask ourselves: "What if this were somewhat *changed*?" ... "How can this be *altered* for the better?" ... "How about a new *twist*?"

Ever so slight a change can often add much to a thing or to a thought. The jokesters make much of the new-twist method of modification. The ones who write the gags for the big network shows are paid around $100,000 a year and yet, hardly once in a dog's age, do they think up anything really new—mainly they think up a new twist to an old tale. For example, remember the old favorite: "Who was that lady I saw you out with last night?" The gagsters have modified that into at least six jokes, according to Joe Laurie; and of these, here's the latest:

SHE: "Who was that lady I saw you out wit' last night?"
HE: "That was no lady, and I didn't outwit her!"

Fred Allen is an outstanding switch-doctor. According to Laurie, Fred thought up several new twists to the old gag about the man who had been operated on so often that his surgeon sewed a button on his stomach to make him easier to open up. When zippers became common, Fred dug up this old gag and switched it to: "The fellow had so many opera-

169

tions, the doctor was going to put a zipper on his stomach." Then when a subway was being built in New York, and contractors kept opening and filling the streets, Fred thought up still another switch: "The Mayor is going to put a zipper down Eighth Avenue."

"The same gag," said Laurie, "later turned up in his radio script as: 'Luther Burbank crossed a banana seed with part of a key-chain and grew a banana with a zipper in it.'

"So you see, there's nothing to it. Just give an old joke a few new words, a new setting, and you won't be able to tell *which* is *switch*," concluded Joe Laurie.

A good mother uses the new-twist wizardry. She makes her old hat new with a brighter flower or a bit of veil. She turns her drab dress into a costume with a colorful belt or some inexpensive jewelry. And where did that new davenport come from? It's the one that was so dingy, but which she made resplendent by re-covering.

No matter what our creative problem, let's ask ourselves, "How could we do this differently?" Even when we have to make a speech, we might well challenge every feature of our talk with that question. For example, should we start out with a bang, or should we begin hesitantly—as some of the best speakers deliberately do?

"What change can we make in the *process*?" This is a good question to ask when it comes to technology or even to cooking. A very slight change by way of toasting has added much to bread, as well as to other things such as cereals and cigarettes. Many process-improvements have come from mere changes in temperature. For the fermentation of wine, Pasteur found just the right heat to kill microbes without spoiling the flavor. When this slight change in process was later applied to milk, it became a momentous idea. How many lives have been saved by pasteurization, nobody will ever know.

Sponge rubber was unsuitable for cushioning. Then someone thought of cooking latex like bread; so now we have rubber seats and mattresses that are thermally comfortable.

2.

"How about changing the *shape?*" . . . "In what *way?*" . . . "In what *other* ways?" Along such lines, we can profitably pile up alternatives when pondering a product.

Roller-bearings go back to about 1500 and Leonardo da Vinci. For four centuries they were straight-sided cylinders, of less use than ball-bearings. The revolutionary improvement came in 1898 when Henry Timken first patented his *tapered* roller-bearing. This entailed but a slight modification of shape in the cylinder type. But the new design took care of both radial and thrust loads, and thus surpassed all other forms of bearings.

A manufacturer of drinking glasses asked himself, "How would it be to make them square?" At first, his square glasses looked likely to sell well. But people quickly found it too hard to wrap their lips around a straight surface. So now you find *square* glasses with *round* tops.

Soap manufacturers have run the gamut of changes in shape. Soap first came in square-cut oblongs. Ivory won the market with the same shape, but beveled at the edges. Fairy came along with an oval soap and did well. Lever brought out Olva soap in round form, and at the same time introduced Lux in oblong form. The public preferred the more conventional shape, and Olva failed, while Lux toilet soap succeeded. Soap has also been shaped in the form of flowers, faces, golf-balls, and even baseballs. The latter, with a round-the-neck cord through it, sells well with men who like bigness and love shower-baths.

It might even be well to ask of a product, "Would this be better symmetrical or unsymmetrical?" For example, when squeezed for space, a washbowl has to be so small that its top surface on each side is too narrow to hold toilet articles. A manufacturer of plumbing might ask himself, "Why not make the bowl off-center?" In this way, there could be a broad enough surface on one side, with a narrower surface on the other.

In brainstorming the question of shape we might also ask, "What if this were *curved*?" An appliance-maker did that to good effect and designed a bacon-grill with a curved center. The cover keeps the bacon from curling, while the curve serves to drain off the grease into the base of the grill.

Curving, or coiling, did much to give us the high-efficiency electric lamp. Dr. Langmuir of General Electric had to find a way to use a thin filament which would work as well as a thick one. By shaping it in coils—and with a new gas instead of vacuum—he created a bulb nearly 15 times as efficient as the first carbon lamps.

3.

"In what *form* could this be?" This is another byway which our imagination should explore. Two cleansers in cake form held the lion's share of the market when I was a boy. The better-known was Sapolio. The other was Bon Ami. To-day, Bon Ami is going stronger than ever, and Sapolio is relatively unknown. What happened? According to Eversley Childs, chairman of the Bon Ami board, here's the story:

"Bon Ami was making gains on Sapolio, but we were not satisfied. Then, one day, someone said, 'Why don't we put Bon Ami out in powder form too? Maybe a lot of people would like it better that way.' Well, it seemed to me that it might be well to have two horses instead of one in the race. So we tried it. A lot of people still like the cake form, but many others prefer the powder. More than two-thirds of our business is now in Bon Ami Powder."

Sugar was first granulated, then powdered, then put into square lumps. Someone in the American Sugar Company then asked a shape question, "Wouldn't these dice-like lumps look more attractive if made into oblongs like dominoes?" Except when slowed down by the war, Domino has gone stronger and stronger ever since.

In my boyhood, a liquid dentifrice held the lead. Called Sozodont, its name was painted on barns throughout the country and was even written into songs. Then came powder, and Dr. Lyons' took the lead. And then came dentifrices in paste form. And, strangely enough, the American public is about equally divided as to which form it likes better. Dr. Lyons' now offers both powder and paste, lest one of these forms may lose out.

Shaving soap has gone through the same evolution. At first it sold best in a round tablet. Then came Colgate's stick. About the same time, powder form was tried. But in this case, paste proved to be by all odds the form that most men preferred.

"What other *package*?" is a question that should go with "What other form?" Lustre Creme beat out Drene in the shampoo field. Drene's makers then came out with a paste form like Lustre Creme, called it Prell, but put it up in tubes instead of jars.

Let's also ask, "Could the package be *combined* with the form to provide a new twist?" Eskimo Pie was a triumphant idea along this line. It is one bit of our Americana which Russia has adopted inside her iron-curtain. Dr. Willard Dow believes that many more edibles will be in edible packages. Said he: "We have learned to make synthetic sausage-coverings and ice cream cones. Why stop there?"

4.

"What other changes can we make to provide more *sense-appeals*?" Let's explore what to do to attract the eye and the ear, as well as the taste, the sense of touch and the sense of smell. But first let's ask ourselves questions about eye-appeal and start with color.

One of my fiascoes was an attempt to give a new look to golf-balls. Edward B. Germain, manufacturer of Dunlops, is a playmate of mine on the links. One Saturday afternoon I said to him: "Everybody makes white golf-balls. Why don't you use a color that's different, more pleasurable to the eye, and easier to see among the leaves—a bright color that will pop up and cry, 'Here's your ball!'" He gave me no encouragement.

That was in the fall. During the golfless winter I painted a dozen balls, each in a different color. The yellow one seemed to be it. The spring came and I met Ed for our first game of the season. "Here's where I prove to you that you should make yellow balls," was my boast as I teed up. Wham! My drive went straight down the fairway. But alas, it took us 10 minutes to find my yellow jewel. Why? Because the course was covered with dandelions.

But there have been successes in going to a new color, even yellow. Have you ever faced the problem of how to light up the outside of your house without attracting all the bugs in the neighborhood? A scientist solved that for you by changing the color of an ordinary mazda lamp from white to yellow. Thus he found a way to make lights say to bugs, "Scram!" instead of "Come hither!"

In decorating, white is often the loser even when backed by tradition. Shouldn't operating-rooms be in white as they always have been? No, this is no longer so. A surgeon showed me his new operating-room with walls tinted in a soft green. "This color," he told me, "reduces glare and, as a result, the nurses and I can work here more comfortably and more efficiently."

More and more the manufacturers of machines are asking, "What color would be better?" Nearly all machines used to be black, but the new ones are in bright colors which soak up far less light. Many a plant has increased production, reduced its rejects, and heightened morale by such a change. The trend toward newer and better colors has led Du Pont to establish a color-conditioning service which scientifically creates plans to make seeing easier, to cut down glare—to make hot rooms seem cooler, and cool rooms warmer.

Du Pont has taken its medicine by using color for safety. Electric blasting-caps are now fired by wires colorfully coated with nylon plastic. The bright colors—red, yellow and blue—show plainly against the rocky walls of a mine tunnel.

For coal mines, which are black, the nylon plastic is gleaming white. For salt mines, which are white, the nylon is black.

And how about red-white-and-blue tape-measures instead of those hard-to-find buff ones? Don't bother. It's just been done. Yes, many articles are being made more useful through greater impact on the eye. Luminous paints come under this head. But the makers of Scotch Tape have gone much further. They have produced a new material which, when used on road-signs, reflects your headlights so lustrously that the signs seem to pounce upon you.

5.

To achieve more eye-appeal, let's also ask, "How about *motion?*" Have you seen the new Christmas-tree lights which not only shine colorfully, but also actively *bubble?* "Anybody could have thought up that idea." Sure, but how we wish we had been the one.

Motion will make a window display stop far more people. Douglas Leigh has won fame and fortune by putting movement into spectacular signs. You can actually see the bubbles rising in his ginger-ale display. Steam arises from his gigantic cup of coffee. Smoke-rings as big as a street-circle come puffing out of the mouth of his cigarette-smoker; but it isn't smoke, it's steam.

Leigh recently talked to a women's club. After the applause had died down, the chairlady asked him what he would most like to do from here on in. Said Leigh: "I'd like to take a good-sized dirigible, light it on one side with 'House of Morgan' and on the other with 'Standard Oil' and fly the darn thing over Red Square on May Day."

6.

"How about more *ear*-appeal?" . . . "What can we do with sound?" Elmer Wheeler has won fame and fortune by sending his imagination down this trail. "Sizzling" steaks were his idea. He has delivered 4000 addresses on "Sell the Sizzle."

Last Christmas I bought a woolly lamb for my grand-daughter. How she loved it! It bleated. Dolls which say "Mama" bring an extra price beyond the cost of the sound.

In selling, many attempts have been made to add sound. One of these is the latest caper inspired by the National Institute of Diaper Services. A number of diaper laundries have installed on their trucks a new type of musical horn that plays the tune *Rock-a-Bye-Baby*.

Sponsors have gone to great lengths to use sound in their selling messages over the air. They believe it sparks attention and makes for memorability. The Lucky Strike auctioneer, the penguin yodeling "Kooool" cigarettes, the choo-choo train puffing "Bromo Seltzer," the Rinso-white whistle, the Lifebuoy foghorn—these are a few of the many ways in which sound has been used to strengthen words.

7.

What about smell, touch and taste? We might well ask, "What could we do by way of odor?" . . . "How can we appeal to the sense of smell?" Too little has been thought up along this line. Take bread for example. If you ever walked through a bakery you would know what a delicious aroma fills your nostrils. No eloquence could make you hungrier for that bread. Some day, someone will devise a bread-wrapper with that same fragrance. The housewife then will still pinch the loaf to see whether it is fresh, but the odor of the wrapper will also attract her.

Even the question of touch-appeal might be worth exploring. And taste-appeal is obviously important. In all the surveys made on foods, flavor is by all odds the main reason why people buy this instead of that. The French are noted for the imagination they have put into their food. The creative ability of American women is more and more demonstrated by their origination of so many new recipes which make commonplace foodstuffs taste like party fare.

Chapter XXIII

WHAT IF WE ADD, OR MULTIPLY— OR *MAGNIFY?*

LET'S SEE WHAT IDEAS we can bag by sending our imaginations down the *magnification* trail. Among the many questions along this line, let's ask ourselves: "What about making it *bigger?*" . . . "What strength can we *add?*" . . . "How about extra *value?* . . . "Could this be *multiplied?*"

There are, of course, no clear-cut boundaries between the different hunting-fields. For instance, through *addition* we may arrive at an idea, only to find that its value depends upon thinking up a *new use.* Such was the case when Pittsburgh Plate sought a bigger volume in mirror-glass. The first idea was to sell *larger* mirrors. Fine, but where? A relatively new use was thought up and tried out—large mirrors to cover *doors*—and this turned out to be the answer.

In piling up alternatives through addition, we should go beyond size. "How about *more time?*" This might well be one of our queries. Many a process has been improved through longer aging, and in human affairs, more time can often be a helpful factor. We do better when we count three before we talk back. Cooling-off periods have proved to be wise measures in labor-disputes. The answer to little Willie's tummy troubles may be more time for eating. More time for sleeping may be the answer to little Lillian's failure to grow as she should.

177

Greater frequency may also be worth exploring. "What if this were done *more often*?" Some wise doctor, name unknown, must have asked that question when up against the problem of treating stomach-ulcers—with the result that eating less each time, but far more often, became an approved practice.

"How can we *add strength*?" is still another key. More specifically we might ask, "How could this be *reinforced*?" Interwoven Hosiery shot ahead by reinforcing heels and toes of hosiery. Oneida Community added a new sales appeal by reinforcing the points of wear on teaspoons. By heat-treating the rims of table glasses, Libby made a success of no-nick tumblers.

"What can we *add* to make this *stronger*?" This query has often led to lamination. We must admit, however, that the adaptation of lamination to shatter-proof glass was largely an accident. The accepted story is that a chemist tipped over a bottle of collodion, tried to pick up the pieces of glass, and found that they stuck together. This led to shatter-proof glass, which is simply a sandwich of plastic material between layers of glass.

2.

Size is the simplest key to ideas through magnification. When brainstorming a product we should ask: "What if this were *bigger*?" . . . "What if it were *higher*?" . . . "Should it be *wider*?" . . . "Suppose it were *longer*?"

With the fair sex getting taller, more and more men are embarrassed by their lesser height. The makers of Adler Shoes sensed this and designed men's models with *higher* heels; and out of this idea came a profitable appeal. "Nunc quam illam ALTIOR esse potes" is the Latin wording sometimes used by Adler, but more often it is: "Now You Can Be Taller Than 'SHE' Is."

Some unknown designer in the automotive world must have asked the question, "Why can't we make our seats *wider?*" This changed five-passenger bodies into six-passenger jobs, with the front seat wide enough for three. Recently a new model came out of California with only one seat, but with that seat wide enough for four.

Tires used to be much smaller. Their narrowness made ruts a menace, and their cushion-effect was but meager. About 25 years ago, a tire-maker asked, "Why not make 'em *fatter?*" This led to the balloon tire. Sensational at first, it won its way so fast that by 1928 the balloon tire became the conventional type. "Why not make it *still fatter?*" led to the recent super-balloon, which Chrysler featured on the newest models, and for which buyers of replacement tires are now gladly paying a premium.

Years ago, Pall Mall Cigarettes were finding the going hard, despite the fact that the name was favorably and widely known. Someone in the American Tobacco Company asked himself, "Why not make them *longer?*" This started king-size Pall Malls on the road to success.

A fountain-pen has recently been enlarged into a "brush" for addressing packages and writing signs. Its felt nib can pen lines one-half inch in width. It even fills like a fountain pen and the ink dries instantly.

"How about a *bigger package?*" may often be asked with profit. Chain-stores have made great gains along this road. Lever recently introduced a large-size Lux toilet soap for use in the bath. The latest beauty soap in larger size is Camay.

Rubber factories use quantities of rubber-cement. Customarily it came in one-gallon cans, used once and discarded. A workman suggested that it be put in 50-gallon drums with removable heads, and that each workman be given a refillable can. Since the former cans could never be scraped clean, this saved waste. It also saved tin. The suggestor was awarded $500 for his big-package idea.

"How about a *jumbo?*" This is a key to much of Russia's propaganda. Outdoor portraits of Soviet leaders are usually as big as a house. The Statue of Liberty was Lafayette's forerunner of this jumbo technique. England almost got a colossus of Churchill. A Yankee engineer offered to raise $100,000 here to start a fund for the erection of a 300-foot-high statue of Churchill on the White Cliffs of Dover—with a cigar in his hand and an electric beacon at its lighted end. The former prime minister scotched the idea.

3.

When on the more-so trail it might be well to think in terms of "How can I *add value?*" Although many of us object to double-features in movies, exhibitors know that an added attraction fills more seats. Adding more of the same kind has likewise crept into sports. Nick Altrock's clowning has upped the gate-receipts of many a baseball park.

Larry McPhail went further afield in adding attractions to baseball games in the Yankee Stadium. "McPhail's Circus" included professional tennis matches as curtain-raisers. He even made his stars blindfold themselves and push teammates around the diamond in wheelbarrows.

The usual way to add value is to give more of the same for less. But adding something *else* may sometimes pull even better. I remember how, when I was a kid, I made my mother go far out of her way to patronize a clothing dealer who put free whistles in the pockets of little boys' suits. Added value in the form of premiums is a big part of American business. In a normal year the amount of money invested by sellers in premiums exceeds $500,000,000.

Another question to ask is: "What *ingredient* could I add?" Many a woman instinctively asks this of herself while cooking. Many a hostess has made herself a reputation for salads by adding a touch of garlic or burgundy.

When it comes to products, the plus of a new ingredient is often worthwhile. The addition of lanolin to Wildroot Cream Oil helped this hair tonic to rise from nowhere to the top of its field in less than ten years. Charles Luckman, head of Lever Bros., seems to think highly of adding new ingredients. While pushing Pepsodent to its heights, he built fast by adding irium. On taking the presidency of Lever Bros., one of his first moves by way of product-change was to add solium to Rinso.

What to add by way of pleasant environment is a key-question in employee relations. In many cases, more light and more paint have done much to make workers like their work better. In other cases, cosier restrooms, some with free coffee, have helped. Music through the plant, to offset the ugly clatter of machines, seems to be a sure-fire morale-builder.

4.

Along the more-so trail we might also ask, "What if I should *duplicate* this?" . . . "What about *more* of the *same?*" Let's make our imaginations look into multiplication.

"How about doubling it?" My friend John Oishei originally thought of only one windshield wiper to a car. He doubled the use—two wipers became standard equipment on each windshield. He is now on his way to having a third wiper installed on rear windows.

My western associate, John Cornelius, was confronted with the problem of introducing a new grocery product in a tough field. He sought a different and harder-hitting mer-chandising hook. Wisely, his first approach was to mull over the obvious. He toyed with the tried-and-true idea of a money-back guarantee, and then tried to think how to make something excitingly new out of so threadbare a device. By multiplication he came to the idea of *"Double* Your Money Back." This worked so well that at least 16 advertisers have since copied the device. One of its latest users is Arthur Mur-ray, who recently promised double your money back if you can't foxtrot after one hour in his dancing school.

Multiplication has been the source of many new products, the latest of which is a boon to those of us who paint. We would-be Rembrandts no longer have to scrape the pigments off our palettes. John Anthony supplies us now with a palette made up of 50 sheets of impervious paper. We just peel off the smeared surface and presto! we have a fresh-clean palette.

And, of course, multiplication is the basis of America's wizardry in production. Gang-drills are only one of the many manufacturing setups based on the multiple principle. Here are two little instances of how this works. In a B. F. Goodrich plant, a four-hanger rack was used to dip small metal pieces in acid, preparatory to plating. "Why not *six* hangers instead of four?" suggested a workman. Production was thus increased 50 per cent. Similarly, an employee asked, "Why can't we use a *double* die instead of a single die to cut out this piece?" That *doubled* production.

In addition to asking, "How can I kill two birds with one stone?" a good question to ask is, "What if this were duplicated on a large scale?" Along this line I hit upon one of my best ideas. During the depth of the depression I was a volunteer worker on the Mayor's Committee for the alleviation of unemployment. My mind was set on the problem of creating jobs. One morning I noticed old Angelo, the man on our block who took care of lawns and furnaces for about a dozen of us residents. At our committee meeting that noon I asked, "What if neighbors on *every* block in the city were to hire a man to do chores at a small stipend per home per week?" Out of that came the Man-A-Block plan which gave work to thousands of jobless men.

The Soap Box Derby is a more noteworthy example of how the "snow-balling process" can turn one little idea into a nation-wide event. Myron Scott got the inspiration for this while watching youngsters race home-made cars in his home-town of Dayton. At first the Derby attracted only local interest. But, godfathered by Chevrolet, it moved to Akron in 1935 and took over a new concrete track of its own. Over 170,000 boys have taken part in Soap Box Derbies.

New techniques of testing now facilitate the multiplication of plans. Long before Pearl Harbor, Admiral Francis

Whiting called me to Washington and said: "We may be at war before we know it. We're already on our way to a two-ocean Navy. We need twice as many volunteers right now, no matter what it may cost to enlist them. What do you suggest?" We quickly created a campaign for testing in a few towns. Almost over night, the rate of enlistment jumped in those localities. The figures were so promising that Admiral Whiting and I reported the results to Secretary Knox and Admiral Nimitz with the recommendation that the plan be multiplied through the nation. Colonel Knox quickly agreed, and so did Admiral Nimitz.

By way of an aside, after we left the Secretary's office, Admiral Nimitz turned on me and exclaimed: *"Such audacity! And on such slim evidence!"* In peacetime the costly expansion of that plan did look bold. But, during the war, I often thought how little courage that decision took compared to the daily feats of audacity performed by Admiral Nimitz in his superb leadership of our naval war against Japan.

5.

Almost every figure of speech gives us a lead for new ideas, and *hyperbole*, the rhetorical term for *exaggeration*, is no exception. So let's ask ourselves, "What if this were blown up to the *n*th degree?". . . . "What if this were preposterously *over-stated*?"

The carrying of more-so to the point of exaggeration is a cardinal trick of cartoonists. Carl Rose, my favorite pen-comedian, has often used this multiplication *ad absurdum*. One example was his picture which told a story of hoarding. The scene was that of a hostess serving tea to two guests in a living room crowded with commodities. Row after row of flour-barrels were piled to the ceiling. Canisters of lard covered the mantel. The grand piano was groaning under a huge pile of hams. And beneath the picture was this explanation: "We're terribly cramped since John got to worrying about inflation and began to convert his assets into *things*."

Stan Hunt, who has drawn so many comics for *The Saturday Evening Post,* admits that exaggeration is his best stock in trade. In a course in abnormal psychology, Hunt said, "I once learned that the characteristics of the insane were merely exaggerations of normal characteristics. Cartoon characters develop in much the same way."

Disney's art has been partly based on exaggerated multiplication. In his movie-short of an orchestra playing William Tell he showed one violinist playing five violins at once, and then five violinists playing one violin.

Most of us want to be like everybody else and not stand out in personality. But those who have sought the limelight have often used sartorial exaggeration. Fiorello LaGuardia did this so successfully with his headwear that he won a nickname of "The Big Hat." Diamond Jim Brady did it by wearing an oversize sparkler on his shirt-front. Woollcott did it by wearing a huge billowy cape.

In personal problems the idea we want may sometimes be found in the realm of exaggeration. When coping with a serious fault in a child, we might ask, "How could I carry this to such an extreme that it would really make a dent?" In this way a mother I know dramatized to her daughter how selfish she really was. The little girl had received from her aunt a one-pound box of candy as an Easter present. That night her father asked her for a chocolate. The daughter snapped back, "They are not for the family. They are all mine!" The next day, the mother brought home two *two-*pound boxes of chocolates, one for herself and one for her husband. The little girl got the point and it made a dent on her.

Exaggeration can be a powerful club in driving home a point and is sometimes so used by Charlie Brower, our super-chief of creative activities. One of our writers of radio commercials had fallen too much in love with the notion that sales-messages had to be disliked by listeners in order to make a dent on their purses. Charlie thought up this parable:

"A man went to town to do the week-end shopping for

his wife. He entered a grocery store where the clerks had been taught the psychology of selling through dislike. The first clerk stamped on his foot as he mentioned a popular brand of soap. Another clerk pulled the customer's hat down over his eyes because there was a special on canned soup that day. A third kicked him right in the shins about a new and different kind of shortening."

Exaggeration is but one of the many byways which lead off from the magnification highway. By sending our imaginations down these trails we can add more alternatives; and the more numerous the alternatives, the better the ideas. In turn, the conscious effort we put into such quests tends to step up our creative power.

Chapter XXIV

LET'S SUBTRACT AND DIVIDE—
LET'S *MINIFY*

MY FRIEND JAMES MURRAY manufactures speed *reducers* which *increase* power when hooked up to motors. Just so, we can *magnify* our creative power by thinking of ways to *minify*. That's why, after having beaten the bushes of *more*-so, we should shift our hunt to *less*-so. In seeking ideas along this trail, we ask ourselves questions such as: "What if this were *smaller*?" . . . "What could I *omit*?" . . . "How about *dividing*?"

In pondering a product, here's a specific question to explore: "How could we make this more *compact*?" Thinner pocket-watches and tiny wrist-watches came from such thinking.

In the early days of radio, A. Atwater Kent made and sold over 1,000,000 sets in one year. He did almost everything himself, including his designing. At the height of his success, he said to me as one of his advertising counselors: "Next year I am going to make my leading model one-*half* the size." I doubted the wisdom of this. To get backing for my judgment I interviewed merchandisers in big stores, and they agreed with me that such a move was dangerous. But Mr. Kent went ahead. His smaller model, called "The Compact," was an even greater success than its predecessor.

"What if they were smaller?" can even be asked of holes.

186

New York papers played up Walter Irving when he created ready-made landing fields for our air-forces in Africa. I got in touch with him and asked him for his story. "We used to make big iron gates for banks, public buildings and country estates," he told me. "Then we made sidewalk gratings for subways. We found that women's heels were getting caught in these, and that baby carriages were being upset. So I thought up our newer and better kind of grating, with openings too small to catch the high heels."

Under more-so, we asked, "How about a *jumbo*?" Here we should ask, "How about *miniatures*?" You've seen how the makers of chocolates successfully followed that trail. Parker Pen made a hit with a miniature version of "51" called "demi-size" for women to carry upright in their handbags. Sperti now offers an ultra-violet lamp as small as a lunchbox.

Let's also ask: "How about *condensing*?" A striking example of a good idea along this trail is the new full-size umbrella that can be folded up to fit a woman's purse. Another is the new vest-pocket book made up of filmy sheets of soap, with pellets which expand into washcloths when dropped in water.

2.

Just as on the more-so trail we looked into questions of height and length, we should also ask ourselves, "What if this were *lower*?" My cigar-dealer, Bill Mathias, was a widower with nine children. On arriving home after work, he was put out by the way the kids had failed to hang up their coats and hats. He solved this by lowering the hooks according to the height of each child.

In designing new cars, a constant challenge to engineers is how to cut down the height. To make a car even a quarter-inch lower, a manufacturer will go to the expense of almost redesigning a new model.

Another good question is, "How about *less length*?" The

ultimate in this has to do with sound-waves and light-waves. One of Nela Park's creative achievements has been the shortening of wave-lengths to make lamps perform functions which formerly only the sun could perform.

The sun's radiant energy comes in three broad groups: (1) Long-wave energy, such as heat. (2) Visible energy which produces light and color. (3) Short-wave energy such as invisible ultraviolet. In dealing with wave-shortening, the scientific unit of measurement is an Angstrom—1/250,000,-000th of an inch!

G-E. engineers produced the sun-lamp by shortening wave-lengths and using a special glass. Still shorter rays of the sun can kill germs. About 95 per cent of this germicidal energy is in wave-lengths so infinitesimally short that they measure only 2537 Angstroms. With the help of special glass, the new G-E. Germicidal Lamps reproduce the waves which so effectively kill germs. But these shortening triumphs stemmed from the original idea of isolating the different bands of the sun's wave-lengths. This suggests that we might also ask ourselves, "How about *separating* this from that?"

3.

"What if the *weight* were *less*?" is likewise a good question. Early in his career, Henry Ford asked that about freight-cars. Unfortunately, it was not until 30 years later that even a slight start was made along this line. A crying need of the nation is lighter, faster freight-cars, and lower freight-costs. Tariffs have become so high that ingenuity is now aroused to lighten the weight of packaging.

Part of Kettering's genius has been to ask, "Why does this have to be so heavy?" It was an accepted belief that Diesels had to weigh too much ever to be used on automobiles. Kettering ignored the text-books and asked, "Why not make them *lighter*?" With the help of his researchers at Dayton, he found the main answer was a new injector so infinitely precise that it would blow into the engine just the right amount of vaporized fuel, at high pressure and at just the right intervals. Diesel engines, in relation to their power, can now weigh 10 times *less* than before Kettering asked his unorthodox question.

There's big business in fire-hose and competition is keen. B. F. Goodrich had its share but wanted more. A creative engineer asked, "Why can't we make our hose lighter?" It takes more time to drag heavier hose up a ladder, and a minute thus lost may mean a lost life. B. F. Goodrich created a new rubber compound that is lighter yet stronger, and also lasts longer. The new fire hose is 18 per cent lighter than ever before and can be put into action in far less time. With this, a new Koroseal gasket was developed—one which can be tightened by hand and coupled in half the time.

Such time-saving is important, and suggests another question along the less-so trail, "Could this be done *faster?*" That's what led Birdseye to his triumph. The freezing of food was not new. Birdseye's discovery was a way to freeze so much faster that the freezing would penetrate the *inside* of the tiniest cell. He then brainstormed the question of how to adapt this technique to the *drying* of food, and after years of effort found a way to reduce the time of dehydration by over 16 hours.

America's efficiency in producing low-priced goods at high hourly labor-cost has partly come from questions like, "How could this be *speeded up?*" . . . "What waste motions could be *cut out?*" Without creative thinking and time-studies along this line, prices would be higher and purchasers would be fewer. Similar attacks on the time-element have likewise improved retailing. The success of cafeterias has been due to saving time as well as money. The growth of Super Markets is based on time-saving as well as other elements.

Even in home-problems, the time-question may be worth exploring. The child who does badly at school may be spending too much time on listening to radio or on some other time-consumer. It's a wise parent who, in her attack on such a problem, includes a query as to how to shorten such periods.

4.

The less-so highway now leads us into the *omission* by-way. Here we ask ourselves, "What can we *eliminate?*" . . . "Suppose we leave this *out?*" . . . "Why not *fewer parts?*" This latter trail led to safer goggles during the war when a manufacturer worked his mind something like this: "Goggles have two lenses. Why *two?* Why not *one* lens, straight across both eyes?" The result was the Monogoggle, made of "Plastecele."

Instead of eliminating parts, even whole units can sometimes be omitted. Home-laundry always looked to me like more work than it should be. Helping my wife do our washing during the war, I found our Easy Spindrier offered no hope for improvement. The part of the process that tempted my creative attack was the tedious task of hanging up the clothes. My "brilliant" discovery was that by overlapping the corners of adjoining pieces, I could use *one* clothespin to fasten *two* corners. When I proudly demonstrated to my wife how this meant a 33⅓ per cent saving in clothes-pinning time, she remarked with a smile of forbearance, "Why, *every* woman knows *that* little trick!" If I had tried hard enough to think up how *altogether* to do away with clothespins, I might have hit on the idea of the new clothesline called *Zip Grip*. It's a dustproof steel cable which runs over a pulley and through a device which spreads the strands apart. You slip the clothes between the strands and as you move the line, the strands come together and grip the duds. When the process is reversed, the line releases one corner at a time as each piece nears the spreader.

Martin Pearson, author of Western stories, was honored by the War Production Headquarters for thinking up what to cut out. As a war-worker in the Yellow Truck plant at

Pontiac, he made two suggestions which saved 76,000 feet of lumber in 60 days. One was an improved method of boxing Army trucks for shipment. The other idea was to stencil information directly on trucks and thus do away with separate boards. This saved 242 work-hours each month.

Elimination of the objectionable is an obvious creative challenge. Dr. Alex Schwarcman did this when he decided that castor oil didn't have to taste that way, and developed a tasteless type. C. N. Keeney noticed that string beans were hard to prepare, and unpleasant to eat if not stripped of their coarse strings. He had also noticed that some beans which came into his canning plant were stringless. He decided to seek these freaks. So in the growing season, he donned overalls and went through field after field on his hands and knees, examining every plant. He found a good many stringless beans, which he saved and replanted; and then he repeated the process until he had what he was after —a string bean without a string.

Ideas are often needed to eliminate barnacles from ships of progress. One instance is the jet plane. Sound travels about 12½ miles a minute. The new jet-propelled planes fly right along behind the sound they make. When a plane travels nearly as fast as sound, air is unable to get out of the way—is compressed and piled up around the leading edges of the wing. Behind this "shock" wave, the air is so rough that a ship may be torn to pieces. Wright Field is at work on an entirely new type of wing construction to help overcome this hazard. To reduce skin friction to a minimum, the outside is finished and polished like a mirror—free from rivets, overlapping joints and other projections. The wing surfaces are made from several layers of glass-cloth cemented together.

In seeking ideas through elimination, a good question is, "How can this be *streamlined*?" Our thinking in this direction should be, not only in terms of increased efficiency as in jet planes, but also in terms of greater eye-appeal and less cost, as in the automobile industry.

Part of the genius of American industry is simplification; and nearly always this means thinking up what to cut out. Streamlining of design is good, but streamlining the steps in production is even more important.

"Leave-it-out" ideas need not be limited to making things. The factor of omission is often important in human relations. It is well to ask ourselves, "What could be left *unsaid?*" Such silence is often golden in diplomacy, and certainly plays a big part in the everyday tact that helps to brighten our lives.

5.

In addition to thinking along lines of deletion, let's look for alternatives by way of *division*. Let's ask ourselves, "What if this were *divided?*" . . . "Suppose we *split this up?*"

My daughter's infant would not go to sleep unless covered with a certain crib blanket. This had to be washed; but how could it be washed when in use almost all the time? Little Barbie knew instinctively whenever a substitute was tried, and she rebelled. My daughter hit upon the idea of cutting the blanket in two and washing one half at a time. Her idea worked like a charm.

Let's also think of separating into *assortments*. This idea seems to work well in the chicken business. In New York, many shops specialize in splitting up fowl and selling legs to those who want legs, and breasts to those who want breasts. This same merchandising idea is now taking hold in Super Markets all over the country.

Years ago, I happened to be in on the start of the pre-slicing of bread. That simple idea made over a basic industry. Sometimes, instead of thinking of complete cleavage, as in pre-sliced bread, we may well ask, "How about *partial division?*" Thomas Olsen of General Baking found himself faced with a poser when, during the war, the pre-slicing of bread was outlawed. He knew that busy housewives, many of them at work in war-plants, more than ever needed bread they could slice more uniformly and in less time.

"On the night we got the non-slicing order," related Mr. Olsen, "I took a pencil and made lists and sketches of every crazy idea I could drive myself to think up; and thus I forced myself to the idea of slice-marking." This became an overnight success. It merely called for indenting the bottom of each loaf with cross-lines—shallow grooves which served as guides for the housewife's knife. Thus she could more easily and more evenly slice her bread for war-time sandwiches.

"Divide and conquer!" was Hitler's master strategy. "How can we go at it *piecemeal*?" is a good question to ask even in everyday problems of human relations.

6.

Another less-so trail worthy of exploration is that of *understatement*. We might well ask ourselves, "What if this were said far *short* of the expected?" Understatement often gives strength to writing. Shakespeare used it when he made Caesar say, "Et tu, Brute!" Instead of "I came, I saw, I conquered," the Count of Turenne, after destroying the Spanish army, sent this message to His Majesty Louis XIV, "The enemy came, was beaten. I am tired. Good night!"

In dramatic criticism, stings through understatement are common. Brooks Atkinson once wrote this, "When Mr. Wilbur calls his play *Halfway to Hell*, he underestimates the distance." And when Robert Benchley was covering plays on Broadway, he often used understatement to combine a jab with a smile. For instance, he described a certain drama as "one of those plays in which all of the actors *unfortunately enunciated very clearly*."

In caricature, the less-so technique often takes the form of understatement. The artist leaves out all possible details and creates the picture with the fewest possible strokes. Likewise, understatement is often used in the idea itself and in the wording, in order to point up the humor. Carl

Rose caricatured an advertising executive glaring at a young copywriter holding a layout which was headed, "*It really isn't bad.*" His big boss is shown as saying, "Understatement has its place, Burton, but I'm afraid it's not in advertising."

And yet that statement is less and less true. Humor is proving an ever stronger appeal in advertising and understatement goes with such humor. Some ads in this tenor were reprinted by *The Reader's Digest.* One said, "Leave us no longer pretend these mops are worth more than 10¢." In another, house-dresses were eulogized as "fine for scaring away door-to-door salesmen." Kitchen stools were lauded thus: "They'll tip over if you stand on them. Buy some insurance and then buy one of these $3.50 stools for $1.50."

The best brains in advertising are thinking more and more in terms of understatement to achieve forcefulness. But this trend is still so new that the advertising world was startled when McCall's ran a full-page in metropolitan newspapers under this headline, "McCall's Magazine has been sort of dumb for four or five years."

A so-called joke of my high-school days asked the question, "Why is a mouse when it twirls?" The answer was, "The higher the fewer." In an inane way, the "more" was thus joined with the "less." And it is true that the less-so trail and the more-so trail often cross each other. Arrow Shirts followed both and arrived at the idea of *fewer* pins and *larger* pins—each pin with a head so big that it obligingly sings out, "Here I am, Sir!"

Chapter XXV

LET'S SEEK "THAT" INSTEAD
OF "THIS"—LET'S *SUBSTITUTE*

WE'RE STILL PILING up alternatives—still listing more and more what-else ideas. An obvious key to more what-elses is *substitution*—changing *this* for *that*. So let's ask ourselves questions like: "What can I *substitute*?" . . . "What else *instead*?"

The search for substitutes is a trial-and-error method all of us can use in our everyday creativity. The same technique is vital to scientific experimentation.

What a series of successive substitutions Paul Ehrlich went through in his search for the right dye to color the veins of his laboratory mice! In this one phase of his long hunt for something that would kill trypanosomes, he used one dye after another—over 500 different colors all-told.

The change of this for that is not limited to things. Places, persons and even emotions can be substituted. Even ideas can be transferred. The classic example of this is the "eureka" story about Archimedes. He had to find out whether a crown was all gold. How to figure the cubic area of the crown was too much for him. So, as often helps in creative thinking, he took a hot bath.

"My body makes the water rise. It displaces exactly the same cubic area. I will immerse the crown in water, measure how much it displaces, and thus find its cubic area. Multiplying that by the known weight of gold, I can then prove whether the crown is a counterfeit. *Eureka!*" I wasn't there at the time but I imagine that's how his mind worked when interchanging an idea by substituting water displacement for metal measurement.

2.

Many worthwhile new ideas have come from seeking a *substitute component*. So let's inquire, "What other *part* instead of this?" Driving-gears illustrate this obvious avenue for creative achievements. Transmission was improved on trucks by substituting metal worms for conventional cogs. Why not use a fluid instead of metal gears on motorcars? That sounds far-fetched, and yet that's just what they did to make our newest automobiles easier to drive.

Substitution has even gone so far as to replace something with nothing, and then to replace nothing with something. This dramatic feat of changing components helped to give us our improved electric lamp. Dr. Irving Langmuir started his search for better bulbs by first finding out why the original Edison lamps tended to blacken on the inside. Theoretically there was nothing there except the filament—not even air. Langmuir worked out a better vacuum, but still the lamps tended to blacken. Then he tried one gas after another, and finally hit on argon as the one best gas. The substitution of that gas for vacuum—plus Langmuir's discovery of just the right coiling in the filament—resulted in a gas-filled lamp "twice as efficient as the ordinary vacuum tungsten lamp," according to John Winthrop Hammond.

"How about making parts *interchangeable?*" Cadillac made its first spurt by making the parts of one car quickly changeable into another. But there are many instances of interchangeability within the same article. Tom Olsen wanted to find a way to pre-slice fruit-cake. The only complaint the public ever uttered about Bond Fruit Cake was that it crumbled when you tried to cut it. Olsen looked into every slicing device his industry offered; but none would work. When he finally hit on a machine meant for a different purpose, its maker discouraged its use on the ground that rich fruit-cake would gum up the knife.

Olsen then considered parallels. "I thought about my own safety razor," he said. "I suggested that the knives be made interchangeable so that when one got gummed we could take it out and replace it with another." The result is that millions of families can now buy fruit-cake as rich as home-made, without grumbling about crumbling.

Multi-use is another phase of interchangeability. The new electric Beautiator is made up of five attachments, instantly interchangeable. A revolving disc files the nails, a "wand" rolls the cuticle, a "whisk" brushes away the dead skin, a buffer provides a polish-base and a massager stimulates circulation in hands and fingers. Thus "in 15 minutes," say the makers, "you have a professional manicure without leaving the house."

3.

Let's also ask ourselves, "What *other ingredient?*" For many centuries, soap was soap. Then one improved soap after another was arrived at through substitution of ingredients. The newest idea is "soapless" soaps. They're grand for woolens, they don't leave rings around the bathtub, they wash dishes sparkling clean so you don't even need to wipe them, and they work in the hardest water—even in cold salt water. These have come from the substitution of a new chemical compound known as fatty alcohol sulfates.

Who would ever think of putting glue into a cleaning compound? You might expect a great research-laboratory to think of that. But, no. It was thought up by two Milwaukee men who were out of work and at their wits' end. They and their wives produced Spic and Span. The women packaged it, the husbands peddled it. Housewives tried it and bought more. Procter and Gamble noted its meteoric success in the mid-west and paid the amateur chemists a fortune for their product.

In talking to a glue manufacturer, I found this to be the first time that glue was ever used as a cleaning ingredient. The animal-glue industry had long been alarmed by the inroads of vegetable-glues and synthetic glues. Their researchers had racked their brains as to what big new uses could be found for animal-glue. Was the idea of its use for cleaning purposes too far-fetched to expect of them? Didn't they fail to shoot wild enough and to pile up *enough* newuse alternatives in their creative thinking?

The price of chicken and eggs would be even higher if poultrymen could not get vitamin-D in the form of Du Pont's Delsterol. The material from which this food-element had usually been extracted was liver-oil from tuna and halibut. But Du Pont substituted mussels—an abundant, cheap and hitherto unused source. It was lucky for us that this change was thought of, because just at the time the supply of tuna and halibut was shut off by the war, America needed poultry and eggs more than ever. Likewise Du Pont did us a good turn by substituting as a source for camphor, old treestumps in our South—just in time to supply our camphor needs when war shut us off from our traditional source, Formosa.

The invention of the zipper was a highly creative feat. For several years I made frequent trips to Meadville, Pa., as advertising consultant to the Hookless Fastener Company. No one ever thought of substituting some other material in place of metal for Talon Zippers. But recently, zipper-fasteners made of Du Pont nylon plastic have appeared on women's clothing. They are so light that they can be used on the sheerest marquisettes and chiffons, and yet are durable enough for heavy garments.

When Du Pont created nylon no one in the company would have predicted that it would one day be used to make zippers. The ingenuity of people in another business, however, saw in nylon a superior substitute.

4.

"What other *process?*" is another idea-finding question. Should it be roasted? Or should it be toasted? Or should it be steamed? Should it be processed in vacuum or under pressure? Should it be cast, or should it be stamped? These are but few of countless ways in which we can challenge a process to the end of a better idea.

Yes, there are many ways to skin a cat and too often the obvious is overlooked. As an illustration of this, I liked Harry Henderson's story of the trailer-truck that got stuck between the pavement and the overhead girders of an underpass in Oklahoma. The traffic was stalled far back on both sides. State Highway experts worked in vain. Someone suggested burning off part of the girders with an acetylene torch but the railroad officials forbade. Finally a little boy suggested a substitute method—that of letting air out of the tires. The trailer got loose. Hundreds of horns blared their cheers. Obvious, wasn't it? "Out of the mouth of babes . . ."

"What other *power* might work better? Although the foot-driven sewing machine called for but little exertion, the substitution of electric-power for leg-power was a worth-while achievement. Our homes are full of similar examples.

On new automobiles you will find air-powered devices for raising and lowering windows. This radical improvement stems back to a little idea hunted and caught by a friend of mine, John Oishei, about 30 years ago. He was then the manager of the old Teck Theater in Buffalo, and so highly creative that the Shuberts liked to open their new plays there. He could not only sense the faults in a show but could suggest what to do to make it click.

Spurred by an accident while driving his 1912 model through the rain, he thought up a hand-operated windshield-wiper which became standard equipment on all motorcars. Despite this success, he kept asking himself, "Why does this have to be worked by *hand?*" Search for a simpler and surer source of power led to a discovery which he likened to "finding a gas-well in the front yard." By tapping the intake-manifold he pulled air through a tiny hose, and this air operated a motor on the windshield top. Thus a radically new "air-belt" made the blade and arm move back and forth across the glass.

John Oishei then adapted his engine-vacuum-power to varied automotive uses. Automobile horns were one of the early applications. Fans for defrosting the interior of windshields were next. This same source of power was then used to squirt water on the windshield and thus wash and wipe the glass while driving in dry weather.

Recently, Mr. Oishei's company set aside over $8,000,000 for plant expansion. The newest success is the air-device which provides instant touch-button control for raising and lowering car windows. Thus, the last remaining hand-cranks on cars are about to take the air. In these several ways, air-power, freely available from the intake manifold of the engine, has been substituted for hand-cranking to the end that we drivers can now keep our hands on the wheel and our eyes on the road. Many lives have been and will be saved because John Oishei thought up that substitute power.

5.

"Who else?" In piling up alternatives through substitution, we might ask ourselves questions along that line. Carl Rose even substituted an animal for a person in his cartoon of a Southern family celebrating the birthday of a horse. The scene is an elegant dining room. The butler is bringing in a cake with three lighted candles. The horse, with a ribbon on his tail, is eating at the table. Apparently there is a Yankee guest because the host is saying to him, "I suppose you No'theners think us just *too* sentimental for words."

"Who else could do this better?" is a good question to ask. I had to write a circular to raise money for a war-memorial. The more I thought of it, the more I realized that this called

for more spiritual power than I could command. I made a list of those who might write a better letter and chose a man whose son had been in the air corps and whose heart was in the cause for which the letter would seek funds. "My" letter was twice as good as if I had not thought of "who else?"

It is also well to ask, "*Where* else?" Family problems sometimes arise as to what vocations would be best for sons or daughters. Here, as in many other cases, a check-list can be helpful. The classified section of a telephone book will automatically provide hundreds of alternatives.

In advertising, "where else" is an important question. "Should our message be put on the air, or on the billboard, or in the newspaper?" "If in the newspaper, where?" In piling up alternatives, we may even think of front pages. Although most dailies will not sell such space, some 300 of them will accept front-page reader-notices. And surveys have proved that these tiny advertisements are exceptionally well read.

A change of place may change the emotional setting. For nearly 30 days the nation had been crippled by the 1948 coal strike. John L. Lewis of the miners and Ezra Van Horn of the mine-owners were irreconcilable. House Speaker Joe Martin arranged a new and unconventional place for them to meet—his own office. In 13 minutes, the two gladiators agreed on the point that led to the end of what could have paralyzed the nation.

The most vital need for where-else thinking is in military strategy. No campaign could be soundly planned without probing every possible place at which to attack or to expect attack from the enemy.

6.

Substitution of one interest for another is often a key to personal betterment. A mother I know had a little son who loved to play with matches. She turned her mind to "what instead?" and hit on drinking-straws as substitutes for flame-makers. The idea worked.

The success of Alcoholics Anonymous is at least partially based on the substitution of altruism for alcohol. One of our best men kept falling by the wayside until at last he joined A. A. "As you know," he told me later, "I tried all kinds of substitutes for booze, like eating candy, drinking pop, and all that. But you don't have to worry about me any more. I have a new zeal which has a stronger hold on me than alcohol ever had. I am spending all my spare time pulling other fellows out of the gutter and I'll be a dry from now until I die." And he proved it. He successfully substituted an evangelism for an otherwise unconquerable thirst.

A basic principle of psychiatry is the substitution of something higher for something lower, a technique called *sublimation*. A bestial desire can sometimes be sublimated into a lust for good music. Even an inferiority complex, says Dr. Harry Emerson Fosdick, can be sublimated into "insight, understanding, sympathy, kindliness, efficient ability." Dr. Albert Butzer, once an assistant to Fosdick, places great stress on sublimation. Especially in the loss of a loved one, he urges his parishioners against unduly choking down emotions which naturally go with grief. Instead he recommends the *substitution*, in due time, of another interest, or even another person to help fill the gap.

In most cases of juvenile delinquency, the best answer would be to change the child's parents. The practical though partial answer is to change part of the environment—to substitute innocent pleasures for dangerous influences. Much of the creative thinking which brought about the "teen-age" movement has come from Willard Pleuthner whom I was privileged to coach for many years. He thought up many of the ideas which the Nehi Corporation and Royal Crown Cola bottlers have used to spread "teen-age" clubs throughout the nation. He helped to produce the first complete plan book entitled, "How to Organize a Teen-Age Club," a free manual now in its fifteenth printing. In this way, creative minds have helped to offset juvenile delinquency with "what-instead" ideas.

The substitution-trail is an endless road to an infinite number of ideas. No matter what our problem, let's make our imagination go on the hunt in the many fields into which that road leads. But don't forget your pencil. And you'd better have a pencil-sharpener ready, too—you will find so many, *many* alternatives to write down.

Chapter XXVI

LET'S CHANGE THE PATTERN—
LET'S *RE-ARRANGE*

THE SIMPLEST QUESTION OF RE-ARRANGEMENT is whether whiskers should be tucked inside or outside the bedclothes; but even this opens up more than these two alternatives. Another one might be to shave off the beard.

Re-arrangement usually offers an unbelievable quantity of alternatives. For instance, a baseball manager can shuffle his team's batting-order 362,880 times—362,880 ways of re-arranging the same nine players! Yes, there are countless alternatives—countless leads to ideas—to be had through questions like: "How *else* can this be *arranged?*" . . . "What if the *order were changed?*"

The urge to re-arrange is an inborn trait. Children pile up the same blocks in endlessly different patterns. Mothers continually shift the living-room furniture and this, plus a new lamp-shade or doily, creates an entirely new room each time.

And dads are the same way. This was ironically brought out in Jimmy Hatlo's cartoon of a big-shot in his office, saying to his staff: "Roll up your sleeves! We're going to re-arrange this office so there's some system around here." The next scene shows confusion, with the boys and girls carrying desks and books hither and thither. The third scene, four hours later, shows everything right back where it was at the start;

and the big-shot is bellowing: *"There!* That's more *like* it!"

Modern girls even re-arrange their looks. Using the same elements with which they were born, they do things to their lips, eyebrows and hair to create one new face after another. Not only the exterior, but the contents of the head are now subject to re-arrangement. A psychiatrist finds out what is in his patient's mind and then re-arranges the thoughts and feelings into a healthier pattern.

2.

"What about *sequence?*" . . . "What should come after what?" Authors and playwrights always have to think hard on such questions. Chronological order is the simplest and often the best; but a plot can sometimes be enlivened through flash-backs—by jumping the hands of the clock backward and forward.

Re-arrangement of sequence is a frequent problem in radio, especially as to just where to place commercials. The sponsor, of course, wants a maximum audience for his advertising messages, but not at the cost of making people tune out. For 20 years, we had to rely solely on personal opinion in this dilemma. Then a friend of mine, Arthur Nielsen, worked up a system of scientific guidance. Through recording devices attached to home radios, he now reveals just how many people listen to a program *at each minute,* and how many tune out at each minute. With this factual help, sponsors can now re-arrange sequence and place their commercials so as to insure maximum listening and minimum tuning-out.

We can solve many a home-problem by asking ourselves questions such as, "Should this come before that?" For instance, one of my daughters was frail in her early years and the doctor insisted she eat more vegetables. Notwithstanding all our scolding and coaxing, she would invariably eat her meat first and let her vegetables go uneaten. This impasse was solved by the question: "Why not give her the vegetables *first*?" From then on, while the rest of us ate both our meat and vegetables, she had vegetables only. And she ate them in order to get her meat. Strangely enough, when she became a mother, her little daughter presented the same problem; and this was recently solved through the very same strategy of re-arrangement.

An old business was revived by a similar idea of putting something else first. Welch Grape Juice was not going too well as a beverage. The management wanted to sell it as a weight-reducer. Since each ounce contains 20 calories, grape-juice is not too slenderizing of itself. But Welch sold the idea of drinking a glassful *before* each meal. The result was that Mrs. Wouldbe Thinner became less hungry for other food, and to that extent reduced.

Re-arrangement has likewise proved profitable for cafeterias. They have found that desserts sell better when shown near the *start* of the line instead of at the *end*, where they used to be and where seemingly they would belong.

3.

"What other *layout* might be better?" . . . "Where should this part be *placed* in relation to that?" Such questions will help us pile up alternatives via re-arrangement of constituent elements.

"Should the cart be put before the horse?" used to be an academic query. "Should the motor be in the front or in the rear?" is a live and practical question. William Stout was one of Ford's most creative engineers. About 15 years ago I rode with him in his then new model called the Scarab, which had its motor in the rear. Every now and then this same idea is re-agitated, but so far, the disadvantages seem to outweigh the advantages—except on buses. Buses with engines in the back became common. But re-arrangement never stops and now the newest buses have their motors in the middle.

Likewise, in the early days of airplanes, a heated controversy developed over the question whether the pusher type was better, with the propeller in the rear—or whether the tractor type was better, with the propeller out ahead. The latter type won out. In the new jet planes, however, the power comes from behind; whereas helicopters have their propellers on top. All of which adds strength to the fact that there is always some *other* alternative, especially in the field of re-arrangement.

"What other *floor plan* would work better?" This question is at the core of all architecture. For new buildings, the architect takes old and new ideas, alters proportions, and considers thousands of alternatives. It's the same in remodeling; except that here there are more fixed elements to limit the alternatives. In merchandising, "tried-and-true" floor-plans are being challenged by questions of re-arrangement. Even the best stores formerly ran their counters lengthwise and parallel. It was observed that customers would travel between two counters and "go down the slot," with too little chance of being tempted by other merchandise. The new idea is to run counters *across* the store, with narrow ends on main aisles. The patron is thus exposed to a greater variety of goods. In chain stores, the corner position on square counters is now used for features. A popular item thus placed brings traffic to the counter and, in turn, this re-arrangement results in more items being sold over the rest of the counter.

4.

"What about *cause* and *effect*?" . . . "What if they were *transposed*?" Even such questions of re-arrangement can be sources of ideas. One reason for this is that we do not always know what is cause and what is effect; we still are not sure which came first, the chicken or the egg.

There is the same confusion about sequence even in matters that should be scientific. Take medicine, for example.

A person is toxic and runs a fever. Diagnosis traces the cause to an inflammation of the urinal system. In one case I know of, that "cause" was ultimately found to be the effect. The real cause was sluggish elimination, which put too big a load on the kidneys and resulted in inflammation of the bladder. By speeding elimination, the bladder was cleared up and the toxicity and the fever were stopped.

That true history illustrates why it is well to think in terms of transposing cause and effect—of asking of an apparent effect, "Is this perhaps the cause?"—of asking of an alleged cause, "Is this perhaps the effect?" Carried into personal relations, such a creative challenge is often worthwhile. Many a person has given way to the alibi, "People don't like me—that is why I am morose and sensitive." Again, this may be a confusion of cause and effect. If such a grouch should try hard enough to be cheerful and objective instead of glum and subjective, the effect would probably be that people *would like him.*

By challenging sequence we can break vicious circles. For example, I come home from work all tired out. The effect of my fatigue is that I quarrel with my family. The effect of this becomes a cause—it upsets me so that when I go to bed I cannot sleep well enough. This effect then becomes a cause. I am tired when I go to work the next morning. This, in turn, causes me to go home even more tired and more crotchety than ever.

Obviously, I can change all that by simply changing the first effect. Even though tired, I could make myself act pleasantly when I get home. I could then sleep better; I would go to work the next day more refreshed. Therefore, I would be less tired at the end of the day; therefore I would be less quarrelsome.

Since cause and effect are not always immutable, it is always well for us creatively to think up changes we might ring even in this relationship.

In addition to such transposition, let's also make ourselves think in terms of *other* possible *causes.*

5.

"What method of *pay* would provide the most *incentive?*" The nation is in need of better ideas as to how to re-arrange *compensation* in order to inspire utmost production. The proven fact is that by working harder, nearly all of us would be healthier as well as happier. The shortening of our hours in recent years is far less of a threat to American prosperity than the fact that so much less effort is put into those fewer hours. Since without utmost production we cannot hope to keep on bettering America's standard of living, the question of how to stimulate productive effort is a challenge worthy of the nation's best creative thinking.

A neighbor of mine demonstrated to me the magic of ideas in this regard. He loved to practice short golf-shots when he got home in the evening, or at odd hours during week-ends. He would take 30 balls and hit them over the fence into a vacant lot next door. His five-year-old son liked to watch him and one day spoke up with: "Dad, how much will you give me for getting those balls for you?" The father was about to offer 10¢ but, instead, said: "I'll give you one penny for each three you find."

The boy went at this enterprise avidly, but time after time would bring back only 27 or 28 balls; he seldom stuck at it long enough to find the last two or three. The father feared this might induce a slipshod habit in the lad, so he re-arranged the compensation. He told his son: "I will pay you 15¢ instead of 10¢ for finding all my balls. You'll get nothing for the first 28 balls that you pick up. You'll get 5¢ for the twenty-ninth and you'll get 10¢ for the thirtieth. The result was that all the 30 balls were retrieved each time and the little fellow enjoyed the hunt far more. More than that, he began to grasp arithmetic well ahead of his years.

That father-and-son scheme is not meant as a formula, but merely to illustrate how re-arrangement of compensation can accomplish more top production, with more satisfaction to the toiler. New incentive plans of industry follow this same principle. Some of them are working well from the standpoint of the employer, the worker, and the national economy. But re-arrangement of compensation is still, and always will be, a creative challenge as long as the siren of human nature keeps seducing mankind with her insidious whisper, "Let's take it easy."

6.

"What about *timing?*" . . . "How about a change of pace?" . . . "What if the *tempo* were different?" Such re-arrangement is part of the genius of the stars among pitchers, speakers, preachers, and actors. Change of pace plays a big part in the mastery of radio comedians like Jack Benny, Fred Allen, Bob Hope, and Edgar Bergen. Music-arrangers find that re-arrangement of tempo can add as much novelty as modification of the notes themselves.

How about *schedules?* Business might well brainstorm the question, "What working-hours would be best?" Especially when it comes to office-work, there are opportunities to re-arrange work-schedules for the better. Those whose jobs are primarily creative should devote their mornings to problems which call for imagination and use their afternoons for more routine matters which call for judicial judgment.

When Fred Frazier was head of General Baking, he found himself unavoidably swamped with details during regular hours. So he made it a practice to arrive late and stay for two or three hours after the office closed and then do his really creative work. William H. Means, a lawyer, had a summer-cottage near mine about 40 minutes from his office. During the hot weather, he always drove to work at 5:30 A.M. so as to spend the afternoon at the lake shore. In the same way, many stores have re-arranged shopping hours to the better convenience of the public and with less pressure on transportation facilities.

In family problems, it is often well to ask, "Should this be done earlier or later?" . . . "What would be the best time

for that?" One mother found her daughter slacked her homework because she listened to the radio too long after supper.
That problem was solved by arranging that the child start
studying right after the evening meal and then listen to the
radio after she had finished her homework.

Even the time and place of irritations can be profitably
re-arranged. One of our ablest woman writers left us to marry
a lawyer. Although resolved that she would allow no mundane details of housekeeping to mar their comradeship, she
soon found herself greeting him on his home-arrival with
anti-romantic subjects, such as a new pane for a broken
window, a new washer for the kitchen faucet, and even a
needed repair of the toilet. She went on the hunt for an idea
to put a stop to all that. One evening she greeted her husband with nothing but pleasant topics and, although he wondered at this change, he said nothing about it. The explanation came to him as he was leaving for work the next morning.

"Darling," said his smart wife, "no one can run a home
without lots of irritating odds and ends which need attention,
and which I can't take care of myself since I am keeping up
my writing. I know that you are willing to help me on these,
but you hate as much as I do to make these chores the bane
of your homecoming. So here is an envelope. In it I have
typed the little things that need to be attended to today. If
you will just turn this list over to your secretary, I am sure
she will be glad to take care of most of the items without even
bothering you." Years later, I got to know this husband in-
timately. It was he who told me the story, and how well this
little idea had worked throughout their married life.

Thousands of alternatives are lurking in the fields of re-
arrangement. By sending our imaginations thither on the
hunt, we can bag many an idea. This is only one of many
ways in which we can step up our creative power.

Chapter XXVII

THERE'S LOTS OF GOOD HUNTING IN *VICE VERSA*

IT WAS A HOT SUMMER EVENING when Mike came home from work tired and hungry, and greeted his good wife with a genial smack. "Don't try to jolly *me*," she bristled at him. "Here I've got to *slave* from morn till night over my red-hot cook-stove, while *you*—you just *loaf* all day in that nice *cool* sewer!"

There we have antithesis, another example of how a figure of speech can serve as a creative guide. Through such reverse twists, we carry re-arrangement to radical extremes, usually to the point of *vice versa*. To that end, we ask ourselves such questions as, "What about the *opposite*?" and "What if this were *reversed*?"

In the early 30s, we sought a man for a zany radio program to advertise doughnuts. I found him in a stock-broker's office. His name was then Chase Taylor. Now known as Colonel Stoopnagle, he built his fame on wacky reversals like this: "A West Ghastly, Vt., butcher who shall be nameless—George H. Nameless, to be specific—has invented a machine for ungrinding hamburger back into steak. The steaks thus made are boneless, of course, and Nameless is now at work on some bone-glue, with which he hopes to restore the steaks to their original shape, bones and all."

That topsy-turvy form of creativity is what Hollywood calls *switcheroo*. Many a movie plot has been thought up, or sparked up, by having the man bite the dog instead of *vice versa*. Rub two movie-writers together in a story-conference, and you ignite thinking like this:

"I've got it," one will cry. "Instead of having *him* fall in love with his stenographer, we'll have him be the steno, and make his boss a *girl* who gets crazy about *him*. When *he* sits on *her* lap to take dictation, it will kill 'em. It's *terrific!*"

At lunch with Groucho Marx some years ago, I asked him about switcheroo. "It's 'The Thinker' as done by Rube Goldberg," was his explanation. Groucho certainly has a knack for the topsy-turvy. Remember when the Marx Brothers took a night at the opera, turned it upside down and inside out? What a masterpiece of incongruity that was!

Such creative thinking is based on a search for the opposite of the conventional, and Leo Nejelski has stressed the need of this even in business executives. "Many men," he said, "have found that they get original ideas when they systematically challenge the obvious." Such thinking often leads to "stoppers" in advertisements—like the man wearing a baby-bonnet, the bathing beauty fishing through the ice, the *rabbit* pulling a *magician* out of a hat.

Thomas S. Olsen uses a slightly different version of reverse thinking. "When hunting for an idea," he told me, "I always go from the positive to the negative, and vice versa." By trying first to think of the obvious, and then of opposites of the obvious, he uses an alternating current to step up his creative power.

Since contrast is a cardinal principle of association, the more we try to think in reverse, the more we enlist the help of this automatic power of ours. Thus consciously and subconsciously we can pile up plenty of alternatives by way of vice versas.

2.

Another reverse twist is literally to turn things upside down. So let's ask ourselves, "What if this were *up-ended?*"

When, on a Southern Pacific diner, I ordered a bottle of beer, the empty glass came filled with cracked ice. That wasn't anything new. What *was* new was that the ice-filled glass was turned *upside down* in a cereal bowl. The steward was Carl Johnson, and I gave him a slap on the back for that neat idea. Upside-down cake is another example of this type of thinking.

Cartoonists like to up-end now and then. Robert Day pictured a Christmas gathering in a tiny flat. The incoming guests are staring at a Christmas tree suspended upside down from the ceiling, while the hostess is explaining: "In a one-and-a-half room apartment, every inch is precious."

We might also ask this, "Why not *turn it around?*" A furrier friend of mine, Tom Leous, challenged his label in that way and now sews it into his coats upside down. This makes for distinction; but, more than that, when the fur coat is draped over the back of a chair, the Leous name is right side up and easy to read.

"Why not try it on the *other end?*" The nub of Howe's invention of the sewing machine was that instead of putting the eye of the needle at the end opposite the point, he put the eye at the point.

"How about *building it upside down?*" Through such reverse thinking, Henry Kaiser spectacularly sped up the construction of ships during the last war. His idea was to build whole sections such as deck-houses *upside down,* so that the welders could work downhand instead of overhead. Cranes turned the completed units rightside up and then dropped them into their proper places on the ships.

Gene Commery of General Electric Lamp Works was in search of new ways to illuminate; so he asked himself, "Why not have the light go *upward* instead of *downward?*" The result is a brand new idea for lighting dinner-tables. No lamp is in sight. The light is on the floor. The beam rises through a hole in the table up to a mirror on the ceiling. The mirror reflects a soft light which covers exactly the area of the table itself. Regardless of how high the ceiling may be, the mirror is always just half the size of the table, a fact which may appeal to Robert Ripley.

3.

"How about *reversing* the *roles*?" Let's also ask that question. Carl Rose does this often, as instanced in his cartoon of a father reading a newspaper *inside* a play-pen while four brats are rough-housing *outside* the pen.

Hollywood would be crippled without its man-bite-dog switcheroo. Movies could do with more high-hatted gentlemen throwing snowballs at urchins instead of vice versa.

"How about *transposing* the *use*?" is a corollary question. Walt Disney often uses this, as when he showed Donald Duck walking in his sleep with a shoe on his *head*. Olsen and Johnson rely on props in which the laugh-getting twist is usually a reversal of use. For example, Chick Johnson picks up a telephone; but he doesn't talk into it. Instead, the receiver squirts him with one beverage after another—coffee, milk, pop and even bourbon.

Serious use can also be made of reversal of roles. Dr. Henry Sloane Coffin heard General Marshall address a crowd of Chinese in Shanghai. "He revealed to the audience," said Dr. Coffin, "that whenever he ran into a problem too opaque for him to see through, he would ask himself, 'How would Christ have tackled that?' "

"Into *whose shoes* should I put myself?" can be a good business question. In talking of ideas, E. M. Statler once told me: "I try never to look upon myself as a hotel proprietor, but always to put myself in the shoes of my guests. By thinking in terms of *their* wants, I have arrived at some of my best ideas." In competitive thinking, we might also do well to put the shoe on the other foot by asking ourselves: "What can my competitor do to go me one better?" . . . "What *plus* could he add which might put my product behind the eight-ball?"

Reversal of roles can even be carried into teaching. Dr.

James B. Conant of Harvard suggested: "Bring back to life the great figures of the past. . . . Ask them to view the present scene and answer whether or not in their opinion there has been an advance. No one can doubt how Galileo, Newton, Harvey, or the pioneers in anthropology and archaeology would respond. It is far otherwise with Michelangelo, Rembrandt, Dante, Milton or Keats."

A wife did well by successively reversing her husband's roles. One of our creative women married a naval officer. Here's the story she told me:

"After many months at sea my husband came home for shore-duty. Our child was two years old. I decided that a quick adjustment into our then nursery-home would be too much for him, even though he had survived some ugly shocks from the Japs. So I suggested that during his first month at home the baby and I would conform to him—that I would go out with him almost every night—that we'd give cocktail parties at home and let the radio blast, no matter how disturbing to the baby.

"But I arranged that during the second month he would have to conform to us—that he could not then be the ship's captain *giving* orders—but would have to *take* orders from Mama, the nursemaid and the baby. Then for the third month and thereafter, we arranged a 'give-and-take' relationship." All of which suggests the wisdom of asking: "How about a turnabout?"

4.

We might also ask ourselves: "How about *saying* it in *reverse?*" This is one of the humorist's bag of tricks. When used seriously, it comes under the head of *irony*—the figure which drives home a point by stating one thing and meaning the opposite. Unlike sarcasm or satire, irony can be kindly. We can often use it to add power to what we say.

Irony can take the form of *action* as well as words. Such dramatization can carry far more than verbal force. I remember reading somewhere about a husband who was a model of conduct, a strict monogamist, and yet henpecked by his wife. Nothing he could say would stop her from carping at him from the minute he returned from work until the lights went out. So he tried to think up something to shock her into sense. That night he came home late for dinner. He knew his wife would be at the table when he arrived, because she always insisted on starting supper at exactly the same minute each night. The garage was under the dining room. He drove his Ford hell-bent through the driveway and crashed the side of the garage doorway with a terrific bang. When he reached the top of the cellar-stairs, his wife was just about to jump on him; but then she noticed his crooked necktie, his tousled hair, and the drunken leer, as well as lip-stick marks on his face. She changed her tune by sweetly saying, "You had better eat right away, dear." At the table he pulled a whiskey bottle out of his back-pocket, and, against her gentle protest, took swig after swig until it was empty; then he went to bed. Luckily she never learned that the bottle was filled with cola, and never knew how gladly he paid for his new fender.

On a nobler scale, the Albright Art Gallery encouraged good taste with a chamber of horrors. It was called *"This Is Bad Design,* being an exhibition to end exhibitions." The event attracted crowds for three afternoons and three evenings. The horrible examples consisted of household pieces so outlandish that only their unique appeal had saved them from the scrap-heap. Completely irreconcilable with modern standards of good taste, most of the designs were monstrously mongrel. A critic described the collection as "the most incredible gingerbread that a preceding generation ever cooked up." Object lessons based on opposites hit home.

5.

"How about doing the *unexpected*?" . . . "What *surprise* can I pull?" Questions like these are also worth asking when sending one's imagination down the vice-versa trail. Here again we simply challenge the obvious. We think up the opposite to the usual. We reverse the traditional.

In military strategy surprise is everything. Had it not been for putting Hitler off the track by mobilizing fake armadas, and by choosing the unexpected place to land in Normandy, the last war would have cost many more American lives.

"How can I turn the tables?" Along this line, imagination can come into play in the practice of law. George Wharton Pepper tells in his autobiography about one of his first trials. Amateurishly and over-elaborately, he presented his case. His opponent, John G. Johnson, arose, peered at Pepper with pity, turned to the judge, picked up his papers, grunted, and left the court without saying a word. Johnson had done the unexpected, had turned the tables and had won the case.

Years ago a Hollywood press-agent was asked to pinch-hit for a friend as commentator on a news-reel. One shot showed a baseball player coming to a sudden stop. "Put screeching brakes under it," he called to the sound man. When the reel was exhibited, movie patrons rolled in the aisles at that unexpected touch. From this idea, ex-press agent Pete Smith went on to develop his series of comedy-shorts, and to establish a new school of sport comment. Some of his one-reelers made more money than successful full-length features.

Unexpected kindliness can do wonders in business. Harry Lehman of Wildroot continually surprises people with slaps on the back. During the pre-war buyers' market, he treated all his suppliers as if they were doing *him* a favor in selling him their bottles and other materials. When war turned the tables, and those vendors had fewer goods to sell and more customers to buy, they *favored* Harry.

Edward Hamilton drives a taxi in Chicago and treats his passengers like royal guests. He provides free newspapers, cigars, cigarettes, matches, safety pins and cleansing tissue. "With all this service," said a surprised patron, "you should

serve coffee." After each five trips he brooms the interior
and opens a bottle of air-purifier.

"It pays me well to jolt the public with these extras," explained Hamilton. "And it makes my days more pleasant in
the bargain."

John Wanamaker likewise believed in doing the unexpected. In his biography Joseph Appel wrote: "Wanamaker
deliberately planned to do the unexpected thing, or to do a
thing in a different way. So much was this true that some of
his associates used to figure on the very opposite of what he
was expected to do, and this opposite would be the best
guess."

The personality of Lord Beaverbrook looms above London. He, too, built his prominence by doing the unexpected.
Perhaps the most dramatic example of this was when he
hired David Low, who frequently caricatured Lord Beaverbrook in vitriolic art for a rival paper. Beaverbrook took him
on at $50,000 a year and with the clear understanding that
Low would ridicule Beaverbrook in Beaverbrook's own
pages.

6.

Still another phase of vice versa has most to do with human relations and is summed up in the Golden Rule. Christ
carried this principle even further when he told us to "turn
the other cheek." To do this may seem weak, but, because
of its unexpectedness, it often carries force. So let's add to
our questions, "What if I turned the *other cheek*?"

In handling a child or a grown-up, it is well to pile up
alternatives and the right idea may sometimes be found
along the vice-versa trail. For example, molasses is often
better than vinegar, and praise is especially powerful when
unexpected. Laudation behind one's back reaches one's ears
with far more force than if expressed face to face.

Dr. Herman Mantell, high-school principal in New York,
demonstrated how unexpected tact can bring unexpected

action. When the wrist-watch of one of his students was stolen, he addressed the school assembly: "I believe in boys. Nearly every boy is good at heart. Someone took that watch when he wasn't himself. Tomorrow morning I will not come to my office until 10 o'clock. Nobody will be in the office. Nobody will be watching. I will leave the top right-hand drawer of my desk wide-open. I am sure I will find the watch there when I arrive." He did. In fact, he found seven watches in his top drawer.

My train to Chicago arrived too late for me to catch my train to Los Angeles. In the station, wondering where I could spend the night, I saw our late conductor. He tried to duck me, expecting that I would take it out on him. Instead, I handed him a cigar and a few kind words. The surprised look on his face gave me a glow, and what a hit my unexpected gesture made with him!

There are so many little ways in which we can work via vice versa in our relations with each other. For example, a woman about to leave on a long trip invited friends for tea and gave each of *them* a "going-away" present. A daughter I know always gives presents to her mother and father on *her* birthday.

It surprises me how many people believe that to get ahead in business they must grab and shove and call attention to themselves. In my own experience, the opposite has worked far better at every turn. The fact is that we serve ambition best when we bear in mind the old saying: "The average run of men fret and worry themselves into nameless graves, while here and there a great unselfish soul forgets itself into immortality."

To get ahead, to brighten our lives, to step up our creative power—let's cover the vice-versa trail and its many branches. Let's heed the score of questions we have listed as guides to our imaginations—guides which can lead us to countless alternatives and probably to the very idea we seek.

Chapter XXVIII

YOUR CREATIVE KEY MAY BE
A *COMBINATION*

"IMAGINATION," SAID SAMUEL COLERIDGE, "gives unity to variety—sees all things in one." Modern authorities have likewise stressed synthesis. *Combination* is probably the most useful of the several creative principles; so let's spur our imaginations with questions like these: "What if this and that were put together?" . . . "What *other* commodity might well be merged with this?"

Even combination of *ideas* is often fruitful, as in the conception of the program sponsored by the Association of National Advertisers and the Advertising Agency Association of America—a program which seeks to create a better understanding of our economic system. My associate, John Cornelius, played an active part in the birth of this project. Here's his story: "Years ago, our Hiene Haupt worked out a way to educate the profit-sharing employees of the Hormel Company on the economic soundness of spending so much money on Spam advertising. His plan of persuasion attracted such nation-wide attention that he was invited to repeat his presentation before business-groups in Philadelphia, Chicago, and many other cities.

"While I was head of our advertising agency association, we tackled the problem of how to teach Americans the many good things about the American way. Hiene Haupt's job for

Hormel served as our springboard. We organized a group of creative aces to go on from there and suggest dramatic ways to point up the pro-America theme. Continuing along that line of thought, Attorney General Tom Clark hatched the idea of the Freedom Train."

Thus these men combined Haupt's idea with others, added touches, and gave birth to brand-new ideas. And then, inspired by public acceptance of the *Freedom* Train, the *Friendship* Train was adapted from that. So let's not fail to prod our creative minds with questions such as, "How can this *idea* be *combined* with another to make a still better idea?"

"How can our *appeal* be *hooked* to another appeal?" is a question we often ask ourselves in advertising. We call this *fusion of ideas,* which merely means the linking-up of our appeal with something which of itself has an appeal. On this score, our hats are off to a competitive agency which handles "Four Roses" whiskey. The very name and all the ads have been built on effective fusion of ideas. In hot weather, the appeal of *ice* is also combined. Real roses in real blocks of ice are displayed in liquor stores, cocktail-lounges, night-clubs, bars and restaurants. Even flower-shops feature this "live" display. All-told, according to J. Baxter Gardner, Frankfort's vice-president in charge of advertising, "40,000 roses have appeared in 1,000 tons of ice."

Such fusion of ideas makes the most of the consumer's power of association. Even ideas often combine themselves automatically through this same power of ours. "An idea grows by annexing its neighbors," observed Ernest Dimnet.

2.

"What *materials* could I *combine*?" is another idea-starter which can lead to endless alternatives. According to Albert W. Atwood, the last war "was largely a war of alloy metals." For instance, after Pearl Harbor we needed lots of cannons in a hurry. The old method was to cast and bore each barrel;

but this took so long and needed so much hand-labor that our cannon-quota looked impossible of fulfillment. Luckily, a certain new alloyed tubing had been developed. It was so strong that the tube itself could be quickly turned into barrels, even for the big guns on the battleships.

Alloys have played a big part in our industrial progress, especially in the automotive field. On over a score of places in Chrysler-made cars there are bearings which combine many metals *and oil*. We think of tires as rubber, but they too are a mixture. The best crude rubber would fall far short unless combined with chemicals such as the accelerators and de-agers originated by B. F. Goodrich. And, of course, the beads in tires are metal while the carcass is mostly fiber. At first this was cotton, later converted into cord. Then rayon was substituted for cotton in certain tires; and in some others nylon has now been substituted for rayon.

New fabrics come from combination. "Blended fibers" is a term we will hear of more and more, now that increased production has made nylon available to clothing manufacturers for combination with other fibers. Apparel has long been made of mixtures of wool and cotton, or wool and rayon. Nylon opens up still newer and more interesting possibilities for combination. For example, you may like a very soft woolen fabric such as a fluffy angora sweater; but, since this is so delicate, it may wear out too fast. Now, by combining nylon with the other fiber, such a sweater can be made durable; it can still be soft but at the same time will last much longer. Manufacturers of men's socks can likewise now blend nylon threads into toes and heels.

3.

We should also ask ourselves, "What other *article* could advantageously be *merged* with this?" . . . "What goes with this which might better be *combined into a single unit*?" An example of the latter is the modern shirt for men. We don't have to be too old to remember what a chore it was to put on a separate collar and separate cuffs. Now that those three units are combined into the shirt we take it for granted. If we stop and think, we'll gratefully admit it was quite an idea.

Until recently we also took for granted that tubes and tires had to be separate. Then the creative engineers of the B. F. Goodrich Company found how to *combine* the two, and the tubeless tire resulted. At the same time, they combined into the new tire the self-sealing safety-feature of the punctureless tubes which had been made under the name of Sealomatic.

Soap and water go together. Why can't we design a shower-bath head to combine both? That was the trail down which my friend Emanuel Gundlach led his mind. As a result you may soon have a shower that will drench you with either a soapy foam or clear water at the twist of your wrist. This same idea is adaptable to a dish-washing hose that can be hooked to the kitchen faucet—just as a new water-heater called "Thermojet" now combines an electric element with a tap.

Another such combination is now seen in train yards for washing car-windows. It's a big brush with a built-in water-hose which thus combines two operations in one. The newest adaptation of that idea is a self-feeding paint-brush. In this, the liquid is fed to the bristles much as it is fed to a nozzle in a paint-sprayer.

Combinations come in clusters. More than one mind must have asked, "With what can I combine a bedside radio?" With a receiving set inside a new Latex pillow, you can now have music for your ears alone. A Sonora is now combined with a lamp which you can clamp on the head of your bed so that you can listen to radio and read as you rest.

Such combinations bring together *purposes* as well as products, and therefore suggest as an idea-starter this question: "What can I *combine* to *multiply* the *use?*" Many of us might still be switching back and forth from distance glasses to reading-glasses had it not been for Benjamin Franklin. He got tired of changing from one set of specs to another, so he cut his lenses in two and stuck them together, with the reading halves below. Thus he became the first man to be confused and heartened by bifocals. Two centuries later some Dayton men combined a third lense, a trifocal through which we may gradually adjust our vision from arm's length to reading.

A big new idea was worked out by Edwin H. Land for consolidating a developing-room with a camera. Through this invention, a camera of normal size is equipped with two rollers, one carrying the film and the other the sensitized paper. The picture is taken, developed and printed with this combined camera, all within a minute or less.

About the weirdest example I ever saw of double-purpose gadgets was in a British war-museum which exhibited a shovel used by Army engineers along about 1800—a digging shovel with the edge of one side serrated to serve as a saw. Multiple-purpose combinations can become ludicrous, as Rube Goldberg has often proved in his complicated cartoons. Robert O. Thoesen of New York, dreamed up a combination to end combinations. Called the "Cocktail Caddy," this is a sort of harness for guests to wear. It combines places for salted nuts, olives, an ashtray, a glass, a plate of canapés, and an address-book. Its main merit is that it enables us to smoke and drink and gesture with both hands, as long as we don't turn handsprings.

4.

"What could be done with *combination* in *packaging*?" is a question that can lead our imaginations to still more alternatives. A brush-top on a bottle of spot-remover was a natural; and so was the idea of packaging cheese in tumblers.

An over-night success in the food business was the combination of pie-ingredients by General Mills under the name of Pyequick, with dried apples of better flavor than we can usually buy fresh. Another manufacturer has introduced a mixture of all ingredients, except the crust, for making pumpkin pie. A neighbor of mine, William Cease, built a business of freezing pies after he baked them. William L. Maxon carried combination in food to its ultimate when he introduced entire meals, pre-cooked, frozen, and delivered to the home. His first application of this idea was to supply the Navy with "Sky Plates" for fliers to eat while in flight.

Combination has been the key to novel packaging for human adornment. Boutonnières are now sold in moisture-holding vases, for men to wear in their lapels or women to wear in their hair. Perhaps the most novel idea by way of applying combination was that of a young New Yorker named Armand Winfield. He started a new trend in self-adornment by packaging bits of beauty. Into transparent plastic he "floats" flowers, bits of fabric, all kinds of metals, plants, butterflies, and even bees. He now employs artists to make miniature figurines as well as paintings. When packaged in his new plastic these make attractive jewelry.

Let's also ask: "What could we do by way of putting things together in ensembles?" One simple example is what Cluett Peabody did in offering Arrow shirts, neckties, and handkerchiefs, in combinations of matching colors.

Who would ever think of combining dry goods with a book? A handkerchief-maker did this with his version of *The Night Before Christmas*. Tucked into each large colorful illustration, you find an appropriate hanky. A double-page shows Santa's eight reindeer prancing across the sky and this spread is bedecked with two hankies—one of yellow with a picture of St. Nick in his roomy red suit, the other of blue and adorned with pink reindeer. An adaptation of the hanky-book is a new soap-book, with the story lithographed on the inside cover, and the characters portrayed by illustrations molded on cakes of soap.

"How about an *assortment* of *assortments*?" This was the basis of a new business in Detroit which exemplifies how a simple idea can lead to a highly profitable service. With most employees being paid by check, the cashing of these became a headache costly to banks. B. F. Studebaker brainstormed this problem. As a result, many banks are now collating paper-money into assortments of $10, $20, $25, $50, $60, and so on. This assortment is slipped into a paper-band with the total printed large. These packages are then pigeonholed in special racks on tellers' counters. Thus during busy hours, instead of counting money, the tellers can simply hand out the right bundle plus the change. According to Mr. Studebaker, "even inexperienced tellers can now cash an average of 110 checks per hour, their first time at the window." Banks are more than happy to pay royalties to the Fast-Cash system for this service.

5.

Science creates largely by combination. Chemistry is mainly based on compounding. We find it hard to realize that nylon is made from air, coal and water, and that koroseal is made from limestone, salt, coke and water. Admittedly, to put it thus is to over-simplify; but the fact is that the basic elements are as stated.

As has been said, many scholars have stressed *combination* as *the* key to creativity, and have slighted the importance of the several other principles which can serve as guides to our creative thinking. One reason for this is that in science, especially in chemistry, compounding *has* been *the* stepping-stone to so many new ideas. On this point, Robinson wrote in his *Mind in the Making*: "Up to date the chemist has been able to produce artfully over 200,000 compounds, for some of which mankind formerly depended on the alchemy of animals and plants." That was over 25 years ago. Who could estimate how many more compounds have been created since then?

Incidentally, in that great book—written 20 years before Pearl Harbor—Robinson made this prophecy: "The day may not be far distant when, should the chemist learn to control the incredible interatomic energy, the steam engine will seem as complete an anachronism as the treadmill."

Biologists combine blood-streams through breeding. Horticulturists create new plants by grafting. Most of us think of John Burroughs solely as a botanist, although he claiméd to be primarily a poet. The imagination that made him so great as a poet was what made him great as a botanist who brought into being over 100,000 new varieties of plants.

There is a certain Scotchman, practically unknown, who carried on a course of combination by grafting for which I am most grateful. It so happens that I am a lover of apples, especially McIntoshes. In 1796, when John McIntosh, from Scotland, was clearing land on his farm near the Canadian side of the St. Lawrence, he found a clump of about 20 apple trees. They thrived for a few years; then all but one died. This continued to bear an abundance of fruit. About 40 years later, his son began grafting from the original tree. And year after year since 1836, this has been repeated. The resultant apples became so famous for their flavor that by popular subscription, a monument was erected in 1912 at Dundela, Ontario, to commemorate the creation of the McIntosh.

6.

In thinking up ideas to help us in our personal living, we can well make use of combination. Ray Giles suggested one way to do this for better entertainment. "Perhaps you're to be hostess at a party. Recall the most enjoyable parties you have been to. Now take their details. Ask yourself, 'How might I combine the best features of my most enjoyable parties into a new kind of affair?'"

But there are many other and more important ways to prime our minds for ideas through combination. Here, for example, are some questions we might well ask ourselves: "How can I combine self-improvement with baby-tending?" . . . "How can I combine more civic activity with my housework?" . . . "How can I lead my children to combine more good works with their good times?"

Well, there, in these last nine chapters, we have guide upon guide to help us make the most of our imaginations. It all boils down to piling up alternatives in one way or another to the end that we have *plenty*—so many that among them there is a mathematical likelihood of our finding the ideas we seek. Even the *effort* invested in sending our imaginations down these trails will of itself step up our creative power.

Chapter XXIX

IDEAS WILL FLY IN OUR
WINDOWS—*IF* WE'VE *OPENED* THEM

HURRAY! WE CAN NOW RELAX. At this point we stop piling up alternatives and let our minds go blank in order that stray ideas—"butterflies," John Masefield called them—may be tempted to fly in through our mental windows. All creative thinkers pay homage to this phenomenon which produces bright ideas so often that it is called *illumination*. Because of the *suddenness* of its flashes, it is also known as "the period of luminous surprise."

Although illumination is effortless, we sometimes need to use a bit of will-power to set the right climate for our butterflies and to shoo away their enemies. For instance, when I sit down for a haircut, I usually say to my friend the barber: "If you don't mind, Joe, I'd like to do a little thinking." But I don't really *try* to *think*, but rather to let myself *dream*. Usually, by the time the hot towel is pulled off my face, something by way of a sought-for idea will have mysteriously flown into my mind.

Such short snatches of illumination are like naps compared to a long sleep. After a sustained creative drive, we should coast far longer—long enough to brood, for brooding helps to woo an idea. Although Newton called this same process, "thinking of it all the time," he, too, believed in periods of star-gazing between his spells of conscious straining.

2.

Many scientists have stressed illumination. Said Darwin in his autobiography, "I can remember the very spot in the road, whilst in my carriage, when to my joy the solution occurred to me." Hamilton, describing his discovery of equations, reported that his basic solution came to him as he "was walking with Lady Hamilton to Dublin, and came up to Brougham Bridge." But Darwin and Hamilton had put in years of deliberate thinking to reach those points of illumination.

In literature, the same phenomenon has been marveled at by Goethe, Coleridge and countless others, and often referred to figuratively. Stevenson spoke of his "Brownies" as helpers who worked for him while he slept. Barrie gave much credit to "McConnachie"—whom he described as "the unruly half of me, the writing half." Milton dubbed as "droughts" his periods of illumination. He actually courted these spells by just brooding over a theme and deliberately writing nothing. Sometimes in the night he would awaken his daughters and dictate his poetry to them.

Modern authors have similarly attested. "A story must simmer in its own juice for months or even years before it is ready to serve," wrote Edna Ferber. A newer novelist, Constance Robertson, told me this: "I have found that it pays to hold a plot in suspension, and not to worry it or force it. At the right point, I go into a long lull. *Then*, I tackle my typewriter and write whatever comes. My story then seems to reel itself off in a most extraordinary way."

Illumination has been explained as "intellectual rhythm"; but that seems more poetic than expository. It has also been described as the "*subconscious* at work." But isn't this too general, and isn't the subconscious hypothetical?

A clearer psychological explanation was put forth by Elliott Dunlap Smith in an address: "If the knowledge of the inventor and the clues which will bring the invention into being have been brought nearly into position to provide the inventive insight, his inner tension will be strong. . . . As he nears his goal he will become increasingly excited. . . . It is no wonder that the sudden release of such inner tension is often described as a 'flash.' "

Unconscious effort in the form of *inner tension* appears to be a most likely theory. But there may be other ways to explain illumination, and one of these has to do with motivation. Creative thinking thrives on enthusiasm, and this tends to lag when we force our minds beyond a certain point. By letting up a while, we tend to regenerate our emotional urge.

Another explanation is that our power of association often works best when running freely on its own. During time-out, this untiring helper is more likely to scurry around in the hidden corners of our minds and pick up the mysterious ingredients which combine into *ideas*.

Even a *physiological* explanation may lie in the fact that our gray-matter, as well as the rest of us, is subject to fatigue. The neuron is technically indicated as the basic unit of our nervous system, and the exertion of thinking calls upon these neurons to work upon each other. They, too, can do with rest-periods.

However, when all is said and done, illumination will probably remain a mystery like life itself.

3.

As to how to woo illumination, one good rule is to *take enough time;* and a good way to do that is *to start sooner.* Monday is supposed to be my minister's day off, but he finds he can turn out a better sermon if he makes a good start on Monday instead of later. By spreading his creative work over a longer span, he gives illumination more chance to help. Henry Ward Beecher is said to have conceived every one of his sermons at least two weeks in advance of delivery.

We can sometimes induce illumination by deliberately *stopping* our conscious thinking. In my travels I ran across a story about a boxer named Beau Jack. It struck me that this might suit *The Reader's Digest,* so I got the facts and consciously tried to work up my narrative. When I failed to find the right angle, instead of forcing myself further, I dashed off the tale in a letter to my son and thus deliberately brushed it off my mind. Two days later, the needed idea came to me and I quickly wrote my manuscript almost exactly as published.

Sleep, above all else, helps court illumination, for it tends to unleash our power of association as well as to unweary our mind. While William Deininger was turning the General Baking Company from failure to success, I had free access to his office, even though I was less than half his age.

"My boy, do you know that I nap here now and then?" he asked me one day. I sheepishly confessed that I knew. "Well, my lad," he went on, "I want you to realize that those naps of mine are not wastes of time. I keep pondering a problem and don't get the answer. Then, if I feel like it, I doze off and when I wake up the solution is right there looking at me."

While naps may help, a good night's sleep will do more. But if we rush at it too hard on first arising, we may lose some good ideas. It is better to breakfast leisurely, or even to loaf a bit, and thus prevent premature pressure from nipping the buds of our nocturnal illumination.

Burdette Wright had to turn out more and more warplanes every day during the time when Hitler had our backs against the wall. I knew Mr. Wright and wondered how, with his mind so tortured by pressure, he could do the creative thinking his job demanded. So I asked one of his right-hand men, Charles Augspurger, who told me this: "He would eat with us at noon, but very lightly, and then would lock himself in his office for an hour. During that time he would lie on a sofa and—as he later told me—would just dream with his eyes open. Almost every afternoon, after one of these siestas, Mr. Wright would bring into our conference at least one good idea he had thought of in his 'do-nothing' period."

To cultivate illumination Lowell Thomas recommends a prescription from Yoga which calls for "a deliberate, sustained period of silence—just an hour of silence, sitting still, neither reading nor looking upon anything in particular."

4.

Illumination can also be coaxed by shifting our minds to another subject. Psychologist Ernest Dichter has warned against staying too long with one task: "If you have difficulty in sticking to a certain goal, give in to your natural desire to change to something else. This is particularly important when you do creative work." Edison habitually switched from one project to another and worked on several simultaneously.

"Among the best ways to relax," said Dr. Suits of General Electric, "are hobbies, provided they are not taken too seriously. Mine are skiing and playing the clarinet. I have friends in the laboratory who botanize, collect Indian relics, study the stars. One business executive I know has discovered that his mind is more likely to be full of fresh ideas at the morning conference if he spends the evening fiddling with his ship models instead of poring over the company reports."

For a year before Pearl Harbor, I worked from time to time with Admiral Nimitz. Even then, his problems were almost too much for any man's mind; what a mental strain he must have been under when later directing the strategy of our fleets against the Japs! One of my former associates, Nate Crabtree, was on his staff. "The Admiral would work feverishly and for long hours," Nate told me recently. "But he would take time out, morning, noon and night. Before breakfast he would take a hike, each morning he would practice for 15 minutes on our pistol range, once a week he would swim for at least a mile, and almost every day he would either play tennis or pitch horseshoes."

Most creative advisors counsel us *against* diversion through reading while on a creative quest. "Who knows if

Shakespeare might not have *thought less,* if he had *read more?*" asked Schopenhauer. At another time he wrote: "To put away one's own original thoughts in order to take up a book is to sin against the Holy Ghost." Graham Wallas likewise regarded passive reading as "the most dangerous substitute for bodily and mental relaxation during the stage of incubation."

Since there is something mystic about illumination, we might well relax in ways that can kindle the *spiritual* in us. When in 1697, William Congreve penned "Music hath charms to soothe a savage breast . . ." he might have added that music also helps to woo the muse of illumination. Concerts are recommended. A record-changing phonograph is a good accessory. Pile up a dozen platters of good music *without words,* sit in your favorite chair and just listen. If, before this, you have put in enough steady effort on your creative problem, you may soon see "butterflies" circling around your living room.

An even more spiritual lull can be had in church. A friend who won success in real estate recently confessed to me that he can get more ideas there than anywhere else. Robert G. Le Tourneau, who climbed to the heights through his inventions of earth-moving apparatus, received an urgent order from the Army for a device to pick up shattered war-planes. He and his assistants went to work feverishly, but ran up against a stone wall. "I am going to prayer-meeting tonight," he told them. "Perhaps the solution will come while I am there." Thus, as far as he could, he erased the problem from his conscious mind. Before the closing prayer, the picture of the wanted design suddenly flashed before him. He went home and made a working sketch of it that very night.

5.

When ideas come through illumination, what should we do? Should we reach out and grasp them, or should we sit back and do nothing? At least one authority on creative thinking recommends inaction, even to the point of restraining oneself from making a notation; but the weight of testimony seems to be on the side of those who favor action, even to the point of quickly pinning down the idea with a pencil. As witnesses in behalf of this policy, here are five who could well qualify as experts:

Physiologist R. W. Gerard of the University of Chicago advocated making notes of ideas, whenever and however they come, and cited this case: "Otto Loewi, recently awarded the Nobel Prize for proving that active chemicals are involved in the action of nerves, once told me the story of his discovery. His experiments on the control of a beating frog-heart were giving puzzling results. He worried over these, slept fitfully and, lying wakeful one night, saw a wild possibility and the experiment which would test it. He scribbled some notes and slept peacefully till morning. The next day was agony—he could not read the scrawl nor recall the solution, though remembering that he had had it. That night was even worse until at three in the morning lightning flashed again. He took no chances this time, but went to the laboratory at once and started his experiment."

Dr. Harry Hepner, head of Psychology at Syracuse University, writing of illumination as the appearance of a "good idea seemingly from nowhere," expressed himself as strongly in favor of catching each gleam and caging it as it comes: "Failure to record the flash, or to follow it through, may entail a tragic inability to do so later," was his conclusion. And Yale's Professor of Philosophy, Brand Blanshard, added: "Seize the intimations of the unconscious when they come . . . One should keep a notebook always ready to record them."

Graham Wallas testified that many of his best ideas come to him while in his bathtub, and that he felt there was a great need for new creative tools in the form of waterproofed pencils and waterproofed notebooks.

Ralph Waldo Emerson put the case just as strongly: "Look

sharply after your thoughts. They come unlooked for, like a new bird seen on your trees, and, if you turn to your usual task, disappear."

6.

Illumination comes while coasting, but coasting inescapably implies that *power* has been *previously* applied. A tragic tendency of mental Micawbers is to overrate illumination and underrate effort. The fact is that the ideas we receive while idling are quite often by way of *extra* dividends.

One reason so much is made of brilliant flashes is that they can be dramatized, while the hard truth behind such flashes is usually dull. Charles Goodyear found a new way to make rubber useful, and did so while fooling around the kitchen stove. That's about all the public knows in regard to his discovery. Only a few realize how many years of hard work and sacrifice preceded his moment of triumph.

"Watt invented the steam-engine—he thought it up on a fine Sunday afternoon while taking a walk." That is what most of us believe. How true is it? In the first place, he did not invent the engine—he invented a condenser which made steam-power more widely usable. And what's the truth about Watt's Sunday flash? As a matter of history, he had not only been thinking of the problem, but working on it, for a long time before he took his historic walk.

Anthony Trollope railed against the notion that ideas "just grow" on the tree of illumination. Said he in his autobiography: "There are those who think that a man who works with his imagination should wait till inspiration strikes him. When I have heard this doctrine preached, I have scarcely been able to repress my scorn."

The neatest summary of the cold truth about illumination was written by Henri Poincaré: "This unconscious work . . . is not possible, or in any case not fruitful, unless it is first preceded and then followed by a period of conscious work."

"Butterflies" are likely to come to us willy-nilly, but far more so when we have opened our windows by means of conscious preparation. The more alternatives we have piled up, the more and better butterflies will fly our way during our illuminative periods.

Chapter XXX

LADY LUCK SMILES UPON THOSE
WHO ARE "A-HUNTING"

"*HE* WAS LUCKY—he just *stumbled* on that idea." Quite often there's a grain of truth in such a comment; but nearly always the whole truth is that the inspiration would not have *come* to him if he had not been on the hunt for ideas *at the time*.

Inspiration is quite widely used to cover both illuminative and lucky sources of ideas; but in its strict sense, inspiration implies a supernatural influence or fortuitous factor. The distinction between illumination and inspiration, according to Dr. William Easton, is this: *Illumination* wells up from unknown sources, whereas almost every creative *inspiration* arises from "an accidental stimulus" which can be clearly traced. Another difference is that illumination mostly comes from what the *past* has put into our minds, whereas inspiration usually comes from something that happens in the *present*. Then, too, illumination has to do with ideas which come to us while idling, whereas the luck of inspiration may strike us either while driving hard or while coasting.

But enough for academic difference. The practical questions are: "How and when do these accidents happen?" . . . "What should we do about them?"

Let's first dispose of sheer accidents, as when Charles Dickens wanted to go on the stage but was turned down because of his husky voice due to a head-cold—a happenstance that made him become an author instead of an actor. The discovery of coal in America was likewise an out-and-out accident. A Pennsylvanian hunting in the mountains built his camp-fire on an outcropping ledge of black rocks and was amazed when they caught fire and burned.

The discovery of iron in Minnesota in 1892 was far less of an "accident." The seven Merritt brothers had long tramped the Mesabi Range, convinced by the vagaries of their compasses that worlds of ore lay hidden there. When their wagon mired down in rusty red mud, they found the iron. How "accidental" could we call that? Remember, they had been hunting it for nearly 10 years.

Just "getting around" tends to court Lady Luck. Wagner was always thinking of new ideas for operas; and yet, if he hadn't gone to sea and ridden through a storm, he might never have thought of *The Flying Dutchman*. Mendelssohn stumbled on his theme for *Hebrides Overture* when he heard waves lapping into a cave which he was exploring. If a young lawyer had not gone down the Mississippi in a river-boat, his patent for an attachment to speed up stern-wheelers would not be on file in Washington, D. C. The lucky inventor was Abraham Lincoln.

2.

Luck does most for those bent on a specific search. Sometimes even a chance remark may turn the trick. For example, when telephone engineers were developing Permalloy—which ultimately six-folded the speed of under-ocean cabling—they were stuck for a flux that would weld the ends together. "Let's try salt," said one of them in fun. A salt-cellar happened to be handy, so he shook it; the cap flew off and soon a foam-like flux completely covered the weld. Salt turned out to be the answer.

Frank Clark, a G-E engineer, could have been reading the comics on a certain evening; but his mind was on a certain hunt. So instead of loafing he leafed through a technical publication. A word leaped up and hit him in the eye. "That's it!" he exclaimed. It was "Diphenyl," which turned out to be the missing-link in his search for a way to prevent short circuits in power-line transformers. That was a stroke of luck which keeps communities from being thrown into darkness when transformers are struck by lightning.

Lady Luck gave two Frenchmen a lift toward the discovery of photography. Louis Daguerre and Nicephore Niepce had long been on their hunt and had found a way to sensitize glass-plates so as to "*catch*" images; but how to *keep* those pictures on the plates had the Frenchmen stumped. Nothing would stop the images from fading. One day Daguerre accidentally left some exposed plates next to a flask of mercury. Something startling happened to those plates. "That," said Hendrik van Loon, "was the beginning of a marvelous piece of chemical sleuthing which ended with the invention of the art of photography, 'the art of drawing by means of light.'"

And how about Madame Curie and her husband—how did they "stumble upon" radium? What happened was that Madame Curie's thesis for a doctor's degree dealt with the problem of why uranium seemed to shed light-rays. She tested countless chemical elements, compounds and minerals, but was frustrated at every turn. Her husband then joined her in the search and at long last they "accidentally" got on the trail of a new and mysterious material which they called "radium." After spending four years in a dilapidated shed, processing ton after ton of ore, they finally produced a batch of radium as big as a baby's tooth. Whatever luck the Curies had came from unswerving perseverance.

3.

While active on a certain quest, luck may lead us toward an entirely different objective. "Koroseal," said *Fortune* magazine, "was discovered in 1926 by Dr. Waldo Semon of

B. F. Goodrich *while he was looking for something else."*
The far better light-bulbs which Dr. Langmuir gave us were
filled with argon. Who found this gas? It was Lord Rayleigh,
back in 1894. But he was not on the hunt for argon at the
time; he was determining the density of nitrogen and noticed
some strange discrepancies in his measurements. "He was
led by this accidental observation to the discovery of argon,"
according to Henri Le Chatelier.

In 1876, Robert Koch noticed that spots on a boiled potato were of different colors. This chance observation led to
his discovery of how each species of germ multiplies and
colonizes. A similiar accident led to penicillin. Alexander
Fleming didn't know exactly what he was looking for but
when a culture-plate became contaminated with mold, he
examined it carefully and saw colonies of bacteria that looked
like islands—each surrounded by *clear* spaces. This suggested that the mold might be preventing the spread of the
bacteria. Thus the Goddess of Chance opened the door to
penicillin. But let's not forget that many biologists had often
handled just such molded plates; it was only Dr. Fleming
who saw the meaning of that contamination. How tragic it
was that no penicillin was produced for therapy until 12
years later!

Lady Luck also likes to cross-ruff. Edison was working
on telephone transmission and incandescent lamps at the
same time. He was stumped on both. On his table was a
mixture of tar and lamp-black which he had been testing for
his telephone transmitter. Absent-mindedly he rolled some
of this material between his thumb and forefinger and formed
it into a string. There he had the lamp idea he was hunting
for—a filament of just such a carbon element could solve the
problem of his electric bulb. And it did.

4.

Boners sometimes turn into lucky accidents. One day
when William H. Mason went to lunch, he forgot to turn

off the heat and pressure on an experimental press in which he was trying to create a new form of porous insulation out of exploded wood fiber. He dawdled at lunch, and when he went back to his lab was chagrined to find that heat and pressure were still being applied on his experimental fiber. He assumed that the batch was ruined; but when he released the pressure, there he had a hard, dense, smooth board—the first piece of "hardboard" ever made. Part of his "luck" was that he recognized what he had. On "Masonite Presdwood" he built a fortune—he turned a boner into a bonanza.

There are many stories about the start of Duco and most of them include luck; but here is probably the most authentic of them all, as told to me by a man who ought to know. After the first World War, du Pont had a huge amount of left-over explosives on hand. To salvage this material, chemists thought they might make from it a new kind of paint. They conducted thousands of experiments, and came close to the answer; but no paint worthy of the du Pont name came out of all their research.

One of those chemists happened one day to visit another du Pont chemist and on his way out of the latter's laboratory noticed a can of stuff which he picked up, looked at and smelled. Excitedly he asked, "What is *this?*" The other chemist said it was just one of those mistakes. "I got some of that material you fellows are working on, hoping it might do for something I am trying to make. I put the stuff in an oven, but forgot to take it out when I went home last evening." The paint chemist dashed back to his own lab yelling, "We've got it! We've nearly had it for a long time. We didn't know we had to heat it *all night.*" He was clutching in his arms the first can of "Duco."

Perhaps the luckiest accidents are those which happen when we are not on the hunt for anything special, but are creatively on our toes at the time. Robert Louis Stevenson tells in *Juvenalia* how he hit on the idea for one of his classics. He was entertaining a little boy by drawing a map of an island, serrated with capes and coves, under which Stevenson lettered, *"Treasure Island."* "Immediately," said he, "the characters of the book began to appear in the imaginary trees."

Edna Ferber tells a similar story in her autobiography. After rehearsing an early play, a co-worker said to the cast, "Next time I'll tell you what we'll do . . . we'll all charter a Showboat and we will just drift down the rivers . . . !"

"What's a Showboat?" asked Miss Ferber, for she had never heard of such. "A Showboat is a floating theater. They used to play up and down the Southern rivers, especially the Mississippi and the Missouri. They'd come downstream, calliope tooting, and stop at the town landing to give their show." Miss Ferber, always on the alert, immediately recognized that description as an exciting challenge to her high talent.

The son of Elmer Sperry put to him this question: "Daddy, why does a top stand up when it spins?" That chance remark helped lead Sperry to his invention of the Gyro-compass which revolutionized marine navigation and made modern aviation possible. But wasn't it lucky that Sperry knew enough to recognize and to adapt that accidental suggestion?

5.

Accidents are seldom the *answers.* Good breaks count most in what they lead to—*if* we follow through. A lucky turn may merely speed our way toward the idea we seek and upon which we might have come anyway, only later. Most creative experimentation is done in tiny steps and a bit of luck may bring a long leap.

Luck may likewise switch us from one creative pursuit to another. According to Lorton Stoddard, Sir Walter Scott was looking in a drawer for fish-hooks when he fumbled upon a part of a novel he had written and thrown away. He was losing out as a poet, eclipsed by Lord Byron. "So," wrote

Stoddard, "Walter Scott looked over the forgotten fragment with interest, went to work on it—and began a new and greater literary career. For this chance discovery led to the whole series of the Waverley Novels."

Physical accidents have been known to start a new creative aim. It is said that Charles Kettering once broke his arm cranking a car, and it was that which set him in search of a self-starter. Gene McDonald's car got out of control on Lookout Mountain. He came out of the wreck with a fractured skull and a deaf ear. This started him thinking about a new hearing-aid. About thirty years later, as head of Zenith Radio, he offered his brain-child to the hard-of-hearing at less than half the usual price.

Young George Westinghouse, riding on a railroad, was held up by a collision between two freight-trains. Such smash-ups were then taken for granted, because the brakes on each car had to be set by hand and a long train took a long time to stop. It was that accident which inspired Westinghouse to invent his system of air-brakes which could be applied to the whole train simultaneously.

Music-writers speak of accidents as "tips." A few hits, like *Shoo, Shoo, Baby,* have come largely from a chance remark. But according to Gertrude Samuels, *Shoo Shoos* are the "accidents of the profession" and far from typical. George Gershwin wrote: "Out of my entire annual output of songs, perhaps two—or at the most, three—came as a result of inspiration." In Miss Samuels' judgment, talent plus knowledge plus effort, instead of accident or inspiration, account for nearly all the 50,000 songs which publishers annually audition, "only 2,000 of which see the light of Broadway."

6.

"Time and time again throughout the history of science," wrote Dr. James Conant, "the consequences of following up or not following up accidental discoveries have been very great. There is a real analogy to a general's taking advantage of an enemy's error or a lucky break, like the capture of the Remagen bridge."

A Dutch naturalist named Swammerdam had observed the same frog-leg accident long before Galvani did; but Swammerdam never followed up his observation. On the other hand, that twitching electrified Galvani into action. "Whereupon," wrote Galvani, "I was inflamed with an incredible zeal and eagerness to test the same and to bring to light what was concealed in it."

As in piling up alternatives, we have in accidents the benefit of the law of probabilities which academic logic makes much of, but which seems to boil down to the fact that the more we fish, the more likely we are to get a strike. As Matthew Thompson McClure has told us, the idea that comes "as a flash" usually comes to the man who is experimenting with the problem.

"Some people deliberately hunt for inspiration," said Dr. William Easton, "as one hunts for game. They go where they are likely to find it; they keep constantly on the alert for it. Although inspiration is uncontrollable, the chances that it will occur can be increased by enlarging the stock of ideas in the mind and by multiplying observations."

Yes, in creative effort we can largely make our own lucky breaks; we can help inspire our own inspirations. Here again quantity attracts quality. It's the same in sports. The more we swing for the fence, the more likely we are to homer.

Speaking of the good breaks a hard-hitting batter is alleged to enjoy, Branch Rickey told Arthur Daley: "Luck is the residue of design." And Daley added this comment: "The good hitter forces the breaks. . . . In effect, it's the law of averages working overtime."

In the creative game, it takes driving power to pile up alternative upon alternative. In the main, luck is the by-product of this effort. How rare an accident it is when inspiration comes without perspiration! And how can we ever hit beyond the infield unless we follow through?

Chapter XXXI

MOST IDEAS ARE *STEP-BY-STEP*
CHILDREN OF OTHER IDEAS

WHEN I WAS ABOUT 10, a Mrs. McCabe ran a candy-store around the corner on 178th St. near Third Avenue. One day she bought herself a new gadget so she could make "sundaes" by shaving ice into snow-like balls which she could then douse with flavor. She paid me a nickel to make up a sign announcing her new department. I played up the *price* plenty big—it was *one penny*. This was my first ad and I wonder if I ever wrote a better one.

That incident is cited to introduce a characteristic feature of ideas—the fact that almost every idea stems from another idea and that the best ideas are improvements on previous ideas.

The story of ice cream well illustrates this step-by-step process, for it covers a span of over 1800 years. Mrs. McCabe's flavored snowball was new to her, and yet the same concoction was served by Nero in 62 A.D. To celebrate a gladiatorial contest, he rushed runners from Rome to the mountain-tops and had them bring back snow which Nero's cooks flavored with honey.

History loses track of ice cream until about 12 centuries later, when Marco Polo brought a startling new recipe from Asia to Rome—a kind of dessert just like Nero's ices. Two centuries later, the Medicis made a hit by climaxing their feasts with what Catherine called "fruit-ice."

In the 17th century King Charles I paid 500 pounds to a French chef to make ice cream for the royal table; but the chef kept his recipe a secret.

The idea of ice cream came out in the open about 1707 when the New York *Gazette* ran advertisements announcing our first ice-cream parlors. George Washington is said to have bought ice cream from one of these New York shops around the corner from where he lived when he was President of the United States.

Dolly Madison made ice cream in the White House entirely by hand. The new idea of a crankable ice-cream freezer was the brain-child of Nancy Johnson just about 100 years ago.

And so it went, improvement after improvement, one new idea on top of another—until came Eskimo Pie, and now a ready-prepared sundae in a paper box with the chocolate sirup frozen right over the ice cream! What next?

This history of ice cream not only illustrates the step-by-step process and the long lapses between new ideas on a given subject, but also illustrates how often someone thinks up something "new" without knowing that someone, somewhere else in the world, has thought up almost the same idea.

2.

Ideas come and go in cycles. A friend of mine recently invented a new plumbing gadget, only to find that it had been patented 40 years ago. Such is a frequent occurrence.

While visiting Nela Park, I asked General Electric vice-president M. L. Sloan, "Have you heard about the fellow who has taken advantage of President Truman's popularization of bow-ties and has thought up a new one with a light at each end?"

"Yes," said Mr. Sloan, "and it interests me a lot; because when I came to work here 30 years ago my first assignment was to work with a customer who wanted tiny lamps for stick-pins."

Sometimes a man may have the seed of an idea, but fails to make it grow. Near a southwest hamlet, I saw a group of people in a vacant lot, and, being curious, joined the crowd. The magnet was a photographer who, for 25¢, would take your picture while you sat on a 1,000-lb steer. He pointed his black box at me, clicked a shutter, fumbled around in the box, and in about a minute handed me my finished photo. His name was Russell Chamberlain. He had been taking pictures all over the West for 22 years with that all-inclusive camera which he had made for himself out of an old lunch-box. Although his product was a tin-type, I couldn't help but think: "What if Russell Chamberlain had not stopped with his creation of that one crude device, but had gone on in search of the similar, but far superior, all-in-one camera developed and perfected 16 years later by Polaroid scientists?"

Many patents are on ideas which someone else thought up first, but did nothing about. Many more patents are slight improvements on the ideas of others. Remember the story of the clerk who resigned from the U. S. Patent Office some 50 years ago because there was nothing left to invent? Over 1,000,000 new patents have been granted since then. According to my patent attorney, Dr. Malcolm Buckley, "about 50,000 patents are now issued every year, and about 40,000 of them are for nothing but *improvements* on ideas already patented."

3.

A composite brain like that of Nela Park almost continuously improves upon its own ideas. Here's a high-spot record of what General Electric scientists did with lamps in a span of only 20 years, starting 25 years after Edison created his first incandescent. In 1905 a new filament, electrically treated, lifted the efficiency of lamps by 25 per cent. In 1911 a new rugged metal filament made possible more efficient sources.

In 1912 new chemical "getters" reduced bulb-blackening and made smaller sizes adequate for any given wattage. In 1913 came the gas-filled lamp, with another big jump in efficiency. In 1915 the coiled filament was re-designed and made non-saggable. This meant still more light and longer life. In 1919 the bulb was made tipless. This reduced break-age and improved appearance. In 1925 the glass bulb was frosted on the inside instead of the outside. This gave us smooth bulbs which diffused light, with practically no loss in output.

The early development of the automobile was far from a continuous process of improvement by one man or one staff. Gottlieb Daimler, called "the father of the automo-bile," turned out his gasoline motor in 1884. In 1891, Pan-hard and Levassor used Daimler's engine on the world's first commercially made motorcar.

Reference books give credit to Charles E. Duryea for the first automobile made and sold in the United States; but the fact is that J. *Frank* Duryea, father of a friend of mine, was the man who created and ran America's original gasoline motorcar. He developed his first model in 1892–1893. He won the first American automobile race in Chicago in 1895, the only rivals being Benz cars imported from Germany. In 1896 he made and sold 12 Duryeas, one to Barnum and Bailey.

Henry Ford meanwhile was busy perfecting his car; but he never sold one commercially until 1903. (Incidentally, this was the year when the Wright brothers flew America's first airplane, which was substantially a new version of the automobile, with wings instead of wheels.)

Way back in 1879, George Selden of Rochester, N. Y., had applied for a fundamental patent on a road-vehicle powered by a gasoline motor—12 years before any motorcar was ever offered anywhere in the world. Selden had the *idea;* but he let Henry Ford and others run away with it by their creation of improvement after improvement and by starting production.

Henry Ford in his early years was almost a one-man creative staff. Throughout his active life, part of his wizardry was to pile one improvement on top of another. For instance, before he adopted the final design for his first tractor, he worked up 871 successive models.

4.

An idea can be ahead of its time, like Leon Forcault's Gyroscope. He worked this out in 1852 to demonstrate the rotation of the earth. Thus its only use at that time was to prove something already known. On the other hand, when Elmer Sperry worked out his Gyrocompass, there was an urgent need for it on airplanes, as well as on modern oceanliners.

When Robert Thompson thought up pneumatic tires in 1845 it was a case of "so what?". But when, in 1888, John Boyd Dunlop brought out an improvement on Thompson's creation, Dunlop's new air-filled tire fitted a need that was just starting to snowball—automobiles were on their way.

Ideas by way of improvement sometimes have to wait on other ideas before they count. For example, the medical profession had made great progress in diagnoses, but these new ideas largely depended on new ways to explore the human body. Diagnosis of tuberculosis took a long stride forward as soon as fluorescent X-ray screens were able to reveal the inside of chests in less than a second.

The fluoroscope made it possible for diagnosticians to watch the actual functioning of living organs. This internal camera was another example of improvement upon improvement. The basic idea originated with William Roentgen and was improved by Thomas Edison. It was an unknown by name of Carl Patterson who developed, in his home laboratory, the new material which finally led to fluorescent X-ray screens. Many a new blessing is similarly a "Tinkers-to Evers-to Chance."

5.

The mills of the gods grind slowly, the progress of ideas takes time. For thousands of years after man found out about fire, there was practically nothing new thought up for cooking food until the wood-burning range was invented. Then, in a few short years, came the coal stove, the gas stove, the electric stove; and now we have the Radarange which roasts five pounds of meat in four minutes, cooks a live lobster in 75 seconds, bakes a cake in 35 seconds, and pops corn in 15 seconds.

There were practically no improvements on recipes for generations, until Fanny Farmer added one new and important idea. Before her time all recipes had read "Take a heaping teaspoonful" (how much is heaping?) . . . "Season to taste," etc. Fanny changed that to: "Take *two level* teaspoonfuls." . . . "Season with *seven drops* of vanilla." Women's magazines quickly copied her idea and began printing such recipes by the page.

In 1936, *McCall's* introduced a dramatic improvement by using color to picture how recipes should turn out. Other magazines followed suit. But meanwhile, there had been a big change in American girls. Millions were growing up without ever having spent any time with their mothers in the kitchen; they were going straight from school to business, and getting married without ever peeling a potato or boiling an egg. To them, the recipes in magazines were like Greek; they listed the ingredients and amounts, but failed to tell the *how*.

And then a few years ago, *McCall's* came out with the needed improvement in the form of new recipes which went right into the kitchen with the reader, and guided her head and hands through the minutest parts of the culinary process from raw materials to finished food.

Even an individual project takes time and more time—a fact which we should realize lest discouragement stop us too soon. "Inventions become perfect by slow improvement," said Joseph Jastrow, "and each step is itself an invention."

Take the case of Christopher Sholes, the piano-tuner who invented the typewriter. In 1867, he typed a letter to James Densmore on the machine he had just completed. Densmore agreed to finance the invention; but he found it so full of bugs that Sholes had to make one improvement after another during the next five years. It was not until 1874 that Remington and Sons, gun-makers, sold the first typewriter as designed by Sholes. (Parenthetically and paradoxically, the first *adding machine* was invented by Blaise Pascal 225 years *before* Sholes turned out the first typewriter.)

As fast a worker as was Thomas Edison, he early learned how long it took to carry a crude idea to where it would be good enough. "Many people think of inventions as coming on a man all in one piece," said Edison. "Things don't happen that way, much. The phonograph, for example, was a long time coming, and it came step by step. For my own part, it started way back in the days of the Civil War, when I was a young telegrapher in Indianapolis." That was in 1864. It took him till 1877 to work out his first crude model.

6.

In view of all this, we should not be too quick to reject any of our ideas as too trivial. Above all, we should think up *other uses* we could make of them. Steam was used in Egypt in 120 B.C.—but only to spin a toy. The world might not have gone without benefit of steam for the next 16 centuries if that Alexandrian thinker-upper, instead of being content with its use as a child-entertainer, had asked himself: "To what *other uses* could this steam be put?" . . . "How about using it as a labor-saver?"

The biggest lesson we can learn from the step-by-step nature of ideas is that *we can never stop improving*. One day on the way to the General Motors Research Laboratory I passed a group of abandoned buildings and asked what they were. "There," said my Dayton friend, "is where the great firm of Barney and Smith used to make most of the world's railroad cars. When steel cars started, they stood firm in their belief that wooden cars were better. That's why they went up the flue."

Remember Pierce Arrow? Along about 1910 that was the best-known car and known to be the best car. At one time just those two words "Pierce Arrow" could easily have been sold for at least a million. But while competitors were innovating one idea after another to make cars better and cheaper, Pierce Arrow engineering stood still creatively. Just before the company's end, I was authorized to try to sell the name. I went to Detroit and did my best; but by that time, no other car manufacturer wanted those two words at any price.

One of the most creative leaders I know is James F. Bell, head of General Mills. At the age of 68 he said this: "By resorting to the stimulus of imagination, we can look on daily tasks, machines, or any other thing with interest and a questioning mind. 'Yes, it is *good*,' we say, 'but how can it be made *better*? . . . One of the greatest dangers that any man or corporation faces is coming to believe, after a period of well-being or success, in the infallibility of past methods applied to a new and changing future. If we are to enjoy continuing success—our ideas, methods, goods and services must always be '*better-than*'."

7.

These last 16 chapters have outlined basic procedure. Before we leave this part of our subject, let's take a look at the final and often indispensable step—*back-tracking*.

When stumped in the course of a creative project, we need to stop and review. We should analyze the problem anew, should think up still other alternatives, and then proceed all over again. We may find that we were on the right road, but had taken a wrong detour. As Joseph Jastrow said, imagination can easily "run off the track and wreck the train of thought."

When, at the end of a creative project, we find we have failed, it usually pays to reprocess from start to finish. We should review the relevant data, and even re-check the aim; but, above all else, we should pile up more alternatives. Here again we should seek *quantity*, with wildness wilfully allowed. We should get in step with Edison, who said: "I'll try *anything*—I'll even try limburger cheese!"

If we have met with seeming success in our creative pursuit, we should then replace imagination with judgment and ask ourselves questions like these: "Are these ideas good *enough*? . . . "Could they be *better*?" . . . "Will they *work*?"

At this point, we might well seek the judgment of others. And better yet, we might put our ideas to test either scientifically, or in the next best available way.

Then we might well go further and try creatively to *improve* upon our ideas—*refine* them the way authors do almost endlessly. Edgar Allan Poe wrote well enough in his first drafts, but claimed that his work would have been mediocre without his "painful erasures and interpolations." After the manuscript for the "One-Man Show" was just about good enough for Broadway, the Goetzes rewrote parts of it as many as 25 times: they refined 1500 sheets of paper into 136 final pages.

But let's beware of *perfectionitis*. A fair idea put to use is better than a good idea kept on the polishing-wheel. The best way to help insure quality is to go after quantity. A super-critical attitude toward our ideas tends to paralyze our creative power; whereas the more alternatives we pile up, the more we step up our creative power.

Chapter XXXII

"TWO HEADS ARE BETTER

THAN ONE"—BUT NOT ALWAYS

HOW CAN WE WORK best creatively—singly, in teams, or in groups? Since now, as never before, so many of the best ideas come out of research staffs, let's first glance at this highly organized method of harnessing creative power.

Scientific research started only a few centuries ago. The early investigators, according to Dr. James Conant, were "lone workers." Then some of these amateurs began to collaborate, or rather co-operate, in "scientific societies." In 1651 several Italians banded together and later founded the *Accademia del Cimento*, which outshone the British Royal Society of that day in both brilliance and continuity of effort.

That kind of loose organization was about all there was until about 50 years ago, when organized research, as we now know it, came into being; and in this half-century such research has grown to be the fountain-head of most new ideas.

Modern research laboratories—what creative power-houses they now are! For example, in the new B. F. Goodrich Research Center, 250 workers—most of them chosen for their *imagination* as well as their knowledge—are hard on the hunt for ideas every hour, every day. They are divided into 12 specialized groups—one for each major phase of chemistry, one for each major phase of physics, and so on. A research director quarterbacks each of these teams on which there are about a dozen creative scientists.

That new multi-million-dollar laboratory stems back to 1895 when Charles Cross Goodrich inaugurated the rubber industry's first attempt at creative research.

Despite such advances in organized research, the creative power of the *individual* is what still counts most. This truth is recognized by heads of all the great research departments. Dr. Howard Fritz of B. F. Goodrich has gone so far as to set up a new procedure by which even the youngest researcher can be sure that his own brain-child will be credited to *him*. On other matters he reports to his group-head; but he is authorized to go straight to an executive in charge of patents and register ideas directly with him as custodian.

"In that way," said Dr. Fritz, "we always know who started what and on what date; but even more important, this system encourages each individual to do his best on his own—to keep his creative power turned on not only during working-hours but all the time."

To the far-flung research staffs of Du Pont, Dr. Ernest Benger has spelled out this philosophy: "No idea has ever been generated except in a single human mind . . . No matter how you toss this thought around or how you add to it by consideration of the effect of getting people into a co-ordinated organization, the fact still remains that every idea is the product of a single brain."

2.

Creative history sparkles with names of solitary thinker-uppers. Paul de Kruif rightly called Robert Koch a "lone-wolf searcher" who knew "nothing whatever about the art of doing experiments." A lowly medical practitioner with a high creative urge, he even lacked experimental apparatus. All alone, against his wife's snarling protests, he fought his way from one idea to another until he isolated bacteria by types. "I beg leave," wrote de Kruif, "to remove my hat and make bows of respect to Koch—the man who really proved that microbes are our most deadly enemies."

A. Atwater Kent was a one-man research laboratory. Against the competition of the biggest companies, he won first place in the radio industry with a production of over 1,000,000 sets in one year. Even after his personnel numbered well in the thousands, it was he alone who still designed each new model. I was in sales-conferences with him when he jumped up, locked himself in his laboratory, and tackled a new idea he had just thought up to improve his product.

Just as there are those who temperamentally can do their best creative work by themselves, others have to work on their own through the very nature of their calling. Ministers are among them. Most lawyers are also on their own, especially in the country. In a rural district where my brother has his summer home, a local lawyer showed how solitary creativity can win cases. A woman was being tried for murder. Her lawyer knew about the church opposite the courthouse. He timed his plea to the jury so that he ended at exactly noon—just as the chimes were ringing *Rock of Ages* into the jury's ears. The woman was freed and my lawyer-brother claimed that the hymn had most to do with her acquittal.

3.

Sheer circumstance sometimes forces us to think up by our lonesome. Robinson Crusoe was the peerless exemplar of this.

When I was 24 I got in an international jam. Sir Wilfrid Laurier of Canada and President Taft were trying to get our two countries together on a reciprocity treaty. A powerful daily in Montreal was hot after Sir Wilfrid's political scalp, and ran a series of articles reporting American cities along the Great Lakes to be in such dire straits that they sought Canadian markets into which to dump their surplus wares and thus avert disaster.

As an assistant in the Buffalo Chamber of Commerce, I

resented those false reports, and compiled the true facts. Then, with the faith of youth, I wrote the newspaper and demanded that they retract. On top of that, I thought up a counter-offensive by way of a publicity program; but it seemed unwise to attempt this on *both* sides of the border without Sir Wilfrid's blessing. So I got a date with him and went to Montreal.

At the Premier's headquarters in the Hotel Windsor, I soon realized that something terrible had happened. Sir Wilfrid quickly brushed me off to his secretary, and the latter then told me that an edition had just come on the streets with a blast against me—yes, *me*—for attempted bribery. The front page shouted with an article, a cartoon, and an editorial—all based on deliberate misinterpretation of the letter I had written the editor. I quickly agreed with the secretary that I should disappear. When I insisted on outlining to him my publicity plan, he told me it had to be submitted to Sir George Graham. I asked him where he was; he said he didn't know and pushed me out.

Back in the hotel-lobby I almost laughed to think how silly it was that a $35-a-week youngster, with no expense account except for travel, could be emblazoned as an international scoundrel. But it was no laughing matter. "How can I get in touch with Sir George?" was the problem that posed itself. Of course, I could not ask anybody—my friend the editor would have loved to learn that I was in town and would claim I was there to bribe Sir Wilfred. So I sat there and thought up one alternative after another. The idea I chose was simple, in all meanings of the word. I sent a telegram addressed to Sir George Graham in every important city in Canada. I did not dare use my own name, so I signed the 12 wires with the only alias I have ever used, "Oliver Alexander."

"Mr. Alexander! Mr. Alexander!" A page-boy came through the lobby yelling my first name, and I took the telegram. It was from Sir George Graham in Ottawa, asking me to see him there immediately; so I went. He approved my plan and won my heart. He was one of the most gracious men I have ever met. He convinced me that I was not as criminal as the great daily had painted me.

4.

Many of us can work much better creatively when teamed up with the right partner. Men's doubles are common in comedy-writing. Two congenial fellows working in a spirit of fun can be so mutually contagious that they spark each other. Criticism is likely to be less of a blight, because it is usually so spontaneous—a fair gag will get only a faint smile, but a good gag will get a belly-laugh out of the teammate.

Radio-writers nearly always team up to create scripts. Bob Hope has almost a dozen people turning in ideas each week. From this material, his "head-writer," like a managing editor, selects a joke here and a situation there. He then sits down with the star and the producers, and together they work up the show.

Radio is full of interesting writing pairs—like Robert Tallman and Gil Doud, who do the "Sam Spade" scripts. For years Tallman wrote radio for our New York office all by himself; but he now admits that, with a creative partner, he can write still better. "We tried three kinds of collaboration," said Tallman, "and found one that really works." The chosen method is jointly to prepare an outline—a "beginning-and-end treatment" which enables both to know where they are heading. After mutual discussion of each scene, they then split up the job of writing first drafts of the actual lines.

Most successful radio-writing teams do similar thinking-up together. Ray Singer and Dick Chevillat work that way on the "Sealtest" and "Phil Harris-Alice Faye" shows. Don Quinn and Phil Leslie do likewise for Fibber McGee and Molly. The same basic technique is used by Norman Panama and Melvin Frank, who graduated from radio to movies and wrote most of the stories for the "Road" pictures of Bing Crosby and Bob Hope.

The most famous thinker-uppers among actors are Freeman Gosden and Charles Correll, radio's "Amos and Andy." Heading their writing staff is Bob Ross, who gathers different gag-smiths around him. For some radio shows, the main writer thinks up only the bare plot and others write the dialogue for the characters assigned to them.

David Victor and Herb Little were magazine editors. Their first radio effort was "Her Honor Nancy James." Then came their "O'Neills," "Junior Miss" and "A Date With Judy." They keep regular office-hours and make a business of their writing. My associate Wayne Tiss asked them how they go at it. "We do what we learned in school," replied Herb Little. "We make a complete, detailed outline after we discuss and settle upon a plot."

"We talk as much as we write," Dave Victor chimed in, "and we never argue. When one of us disapproves of a certain line or idea, we drop the matter immediately and make up our minds to think up something better. If we let ourselves argue, we'd both get stubborn and could not collaborate." Thus they deliberately avoid mutual discouragement—the D.D.T. that so often kills ideas in the embryo.

In business, a spark-plug and a brake may make a good team. Such are Hull and Dobbs of Memphis, who built two great food-chains on their Toddle House idea, sell more Ford cars than any other dealer in the world, and supply 14 airlines with daily meals. Here's how Arthur Baum described these two opposites: "Jimmy Dobbs is amiable, persuasive—a salesman. Horace Hull is precise, thorough—an engineer. Dobbs paces the floor, jingles keys, incubates endless ideas. He will fire at any target that moves. Hull sits still, analyzes and censors. He will not fire without a range-finder, double-checked."

John Winthrop Hammond wrote about a famous trio in General Electric: "These three constituted a team whose fame penetrated in 10 years to every corner of the electrical realm. Together they originated a complete line of alternating-current equipment, announced and advertised as the 'SKC' system—Stanley, Kelly, Chesney. They were an aggressive triumvirate, and their work greatly accelerated the development of the alternating current."

5.

A high tribute to man-and-woman relationship is the brilliant list of creative teams made up of married couples. The "who-dun-it" Lockridges, authors of "Mr. and Mrs. North," the Goetz team of playwrights—these and many other such partnerships make me wonder whether mixed pairs can't write better than two-man teams.

Distinguished historians are Dr. Charles A. and Mrs. Mary Ritter Beard. She worked hand-in-hand with him on at least a dozen histories bearing his name, and was co-author of at least five others. My partner, Bruce Barton, has often spoken to me about this couple. "When I discuss history with them," he once told me, "I forget which one I am talking to—their minds seem to merge."

In scientific research, there have been more than one mixed team like Madam Curie and her husband. The David Bruces stood out as creative pioneers. David Bruce could not have thought through to the cause and cure of sleeping sickness without his wife's help. But what a contrast she was to Mrs. Robert Koch! The latter was always badgering her husband, trying to get him to give up his dissection of animals because it made him smell so bad; whereas Mrs. Bruce not only cheered her husband on, but did much of the dirty work.

About 12 years after Dr. Fleming had got track of penicillin mold, the Nazis were sending to their death thousands of British people whom penicillin could have saved. But there was none of it to be had, except a handful in the London laboratory of Dr. Howard Florey. To get it into production fast and on a large scale, he had to prove its efficiency on enough humans. His wife, a doctor, did this almost singlehanded and almost over-night. She used it successfully in 187 cases and that started the flow of penicillin in time for its wartime miracle. So let's add the names of Howard and Ethel Florey to the list of immortal man-and-wife teams.

6.

A physician often teams up with a consultant when a case gets grave. The two medical men go over the symptoms together, jointly study the X-rays, and finally agree on the diagnosis. And this is likely to be more reliable, for one thing because the reading of X-rays requires *judgment* with imagination excluded.

But what about the *treatment*? This usually calls for imagination, and, whereas two minds are always better than one judicially, they may warp each other creatively. It might be better in such a case for our family physician to say to us: "Dr. Specialist and I agree on the diagnosis. As to treatment, we are going to ponder that over-night. Each of us will separately concentrate on the question as to what to do to effect the fastest cure. We will meet in his office tomorrow morning and will each bring a written list of ideas that seem promising. We will compare these and then try to arrive at a still better plan. A combination of the best of our ideas is likely to be the answer. I will be back here at 10 tomorrow to put our treatment into action."

That hypothetical case is offered to point out the danger that, in team-work, one of us may numb the creative power of the other. The more faith one has in his team-mate, the more his instinct is likely to say to him: "What's the use of my trying too hard? He'll think up the answer."

Intensity of effort is the without-which-nothing in thinking up solutions to difficult problems—we must have a feeling of "mustness" to be at our creative best. If we were on a ship and someone asked, "What would you do if we crashed into an iceberg?" most of us would reply: "I have no idea. What would you do?" But if you were alone in your cabin, heard a deafening crash, looked out of the porthole and saw an iceberg, and felt the floor sinking beneath you—you would *have* an idea. Your intensity of interest would drive you so hard and so fast that it would *force* you to think up something to do. On the other hand, if there were two of us in the cabin, wouldn't we be more likely to look at each other blankly and wait for the other to suggest something?

Some of the hazards of team-work can be avoided by simple procedures. For one thing, during certain periods in a creative quest, each member of a team should go off by himself and do some brainstorming on his own. When the partners come together after such solo thinking, they will find that they have piled up more worthwhile alternatives than if they had kept on working as one all the time.

Then, too, it is sometimes well for two team-mates deliberately to change roles. At one time let "A" act as creator and "B" as critic. At another time let "B" be the one who shoots wild, with the other acting as judge. But even in such a change-about we should always beware lest we judge prematurely—we should hold back criticism until the creative current has had every chance to flow.

Chapter XXXIII

HOW TO ORGANIZE A *SQUAD*
TO CREATE IDEAS

EVERY DAY, EVERYWHERE in a democracy, juries are proving that a dozen minds can jointly judge and judge well. But that's judicial thinking; how about creative thinking? Can a squad produce ideas? The answer is yes. Properly organized and run, a group can be a gold-mine of ideas.

It was in 1939 when I first organized such group-thinking in our company. The early participants dubbed our efforts *"Brainstorm Sessions"*; and quite aptly so because, in this case, "brainstorm" means using the *brain* to *storm* a creative problem—and do so in *commando* fashion, with each stormer attacking the same objective.

Judicial thinking must be kept out of such brainstorming. Even discretion is unwanted. As one of our radio-men remarked, "At any brainstorming table the villainess is a gal named *Prudence*." In this operation all present must shoot wild and pile up every possible alternative by way of ideas.

Hundreds of such brainstorm sessions have been held in our 11 offices and nearly all have been worthwhile in terms of ideas produced. The few fiascoes have been due to failure of leadership. If a group-chairman displays his omniscience, he makes his more timid members afraid to open their mouths, and makes the others say to themselves: "All right, *you* know so much about it, *you* think up the ideas." The leader who allows criticism to creep into the proceedings likewise fails to get the best out of his brainstormers.

2.

The conventional conference over-emphasizes judicial thinking, and almost ignores creative thinking. This has always been so. Even at the council-fires of the Mohawks and Senecas, there were too few burning embers by way of ideas and too much cold water by way of judgment. Our forefathers thought of their Town Hall meetings mainly as occasions for debate. Their functions seldom called for any thinking-up of ideas while in session.

Most conferences, as we still know them, are non-creative. Their usual purpose is to consider whether this is better than that; and such juries work well because we all love the role of critic. Truly creative conferences are not only rare, but likely to be abortive. Jim wants to impress, so he talks big and echoes: "In other words . . ." But he springs no ideas of his own. Joe hangs back until someone suggests: "Why not do so-and-so . . .?" And then Joe proceeds to pin his ears back with: "That's interesting, but it won't work. . . . You don't understand the facts, you . . ." Joe then demonstrates his encyclopedic mind, but offers no ideas of his own.

Our nation's Cabinet has to be most judicious and yet, according to James L. Wright, ex-president of the National Press Club, Cabinets have been good or bad according to the degree in which they have encouraged ideas. "A President's Cabinet," he said, "is at its best when all members are encouraged to express ideas on any national problem and when no member is confined to the particular portfolio on which he is working, such as agriculture or interior."

In education, the seminar method is based on participation by all present, but seldom calls for *creative* thinking. However, one high-school principal I knew did put into his "Group Study Plan" one of the features of our brainstorm sessions, the philosophy of mutual encouragement. Principal

Edward R. McGuire stressed this to his teachers, saying: "Try to get the group-members into the habit of bucking each other up. They will not only learn more, but they will *contribute* more. There is no mental stimulation like the social encouragement of one's fellows."

Since group-brainstorming devotes itself *solely* to *creative* thinking, such seminars are hardly parallels. In seeking examples of comparable conferences, I thought the most likely source would be the armed services; so I inquired of LeRoy Whitman, editor of the *Army-Navy Journal.* Here's what he told me: "The only service unit I can think of that is solely an 'idea-thinking' organization is the Advanced Study Group appointed by General Eisenhower.

"Of course, the entire General Staff of the War Department, the Air Staff of the AAF, and much of the Office of Naval Operations, and to a great extent the specialized boards, are largely devoted to studies into the future and the laying of plans to meet any emergencies; but they also handle problems of current administration."

Yes, the only exclusively creative group seems to be the one announced by the War Department in May, 1947. The duty of these young officers is solely to use their imaginations to picture warfare in the future. "The ideas they develop," said General Eisenhower, "will give us a trend which will have an influence upon our war-planning.... This new group is divorced of all the practical and mundane things of today."

3.

How big should a brainstorming group be? The ideal number is between 5 and 10. What sex or sexes? A group of men seems best; but our Vice-President, Mrs. Jean Rindlaub, has had great success with groups of young women. We have also found that mixed groups work well.

What caliber of minds? Strangely enough, the less experienced sometimes spark better; but the ideal group should include both brass and rookies. At least two of the group should be self-starters, and they should begin sparking the moment the problem is stated.

In our business, it is relatively easy to conduct brainstorm sessions. I found it far tougher when I organized a volunteer group of the brightest young executives in our community to brainstorm civic problems. Even after our first 10 sessions, some of them still could not get themselves to shoot wild at our luncheons. One of them was vice-president of a huge corporation, and, after he got into the swing, he told me this:

"You know, it was hard to get through my head what you were trying to do with us. My 15 years of conference after conference in my company have conditioned me against shooting wild. Almost all of us officers rate each other on the basis of *judgment*—we are far more apt to look up to the other fellow if he makes but few mistakes than if he suggests lots of ideas. So I've always kept myself from spouting any suggestions that my associates might sneer at. I wish our people would feel free to shoot ideas the way we have been doing in these brainstorm sessions."

4.

What *subjects* lend themselves best to this kind of brainstorming? The first rule is that the problem should be *specific* rather than general—it should be narrowed down so that the brainstormers can shoot their ideas at a single target.

A client wanted ideas on a name, a package and an introductory plan for a new product. We made the mistake of trying to brainstorm this multiple problem. Soon after our session started, one of us suggested a few names. We were just beginning to click with still more, when someone suggested a packaging idea. Before we built up momentum along that line, someone switched us to marketing ideas. The session was a flop. We decided never again to tackle a complex subject in group-brainstorming.

When a problem calls for the use of a pencil and paper, the session may likewise fall flat. We mistakenly asked a brainstorm group to produce jingles on a certain topic. The chairman was unable to ignite the needed crossfire; the members were too anxious to think in silence and to write. They would have turned out more and better jingles if each had worked by himself.

It is well if a subject is familiar as well as simple and talkable. We sought suggestions for the opening of a new drugstore. In 90 minutes, 10 people produced 87 ideas—many of them useless, some meritorious, and a few downright brilliant.

Leo Nejelski, speaking of the launching of any kind of conference, said this: "Meetings drift aimlessly when a clear statement of the problem is lacking. By stating the goal of the meeting, a framework is established within which all thought can then be directed."

Such initial statements can be much briefer for creative conferences than for judicial conferences. Facts are the brick and mortar out of which judgments are built; but in creative thinking, facts serve mainly as springboards. Too many facts can stifle the spontaneity needed in group-brainstorming.

5.

Group-brainstorming needs a few simple ground-rules, and the leader must make sure that these are understood by all present. So, in addition to outlining the problem, he should explain at the start:

1.) *Judicial judgment is ruled out.* Criticism of ideas will be withheld until the next day.

2.) *"Wildness" is welcomed.* The crazier the idea, the better; it's easier to tone down than to think up.

3.) *Quantity is wanted.* The more ideas we pile up, the more likelihood of winners.

4.) *Combination and improvement are sought.* In addition to contributing ideas of our own, let's suggest how another's idea can be turned into a *better* idea; or how two or more ideas can be joined into still another idea.

Those are the guides. The leader should put them into his

own words because a brainstorm session should always be kept informal. Here's how one leader interpreted the first rule to one of his groups:

"If you try to get hot and cold water out of the same faucet at the same time, you will get only tepid water. And if you try to criticize *and* create at the same time, you can't turn on either *cold* enough criticism or *hot* enough ideas. So let's stick solely to *ideas*—let's cut out *all* criticism during this session."

A few incurable critics will still disregard that rule and will belittle what others suggest. At first, such a transgressor should be gently warned; but if he persists, he should be firmly stopped. In one of our sessions, when one man kept on criticizing, the leader blasted him with: "If I were less vulgar, I might say, 'We *don't want your opinions* at this time.' What I do say is, '*Think* up, or *shut* up!'"

Breaking up into little groups is another hazard; and this, too, may call for a bit of discipline. The leader must make sure that the session is always a single meeting, with all minds working together.

The only strictly formal feature should be a written record of all ideas suggested. This list should be reportorial rather than stenographic. At times, the ideas will tumble out so fast that even a shorthand expert could hardly record them verbatim.

The leader should see to it that all his group-members later receive a copy of that list. He might also arrange that thank-you notes be sent by those who benefit from the suggestions. If and when any of the ideas are adopted, the leader should inform those who took part and thus keep them encouraged.

6.

The *spirit* of a brainstorm session can make or break it. Self-encouragement is needed almost as much as mutual encouragement. A perfectionism complex will throttle effort and abort ideas. One of the ablest members kept mum throughout one of our sessions. I button-holed him afterward and begged him to spill whatever ideas might come to his mind at our next meeting.

"All right, I'll try," he said, "but here's what happened. After our last meeting I jotted down about 15 ideas, with the thought that I would bring them to our next session; but when I looked them over I decided that they were worthless, so I just tore up the list."

It took him quite a while to loosen up to where he realized that one of his "worthless" ideas could be better than most of ours, or could be improved or combined into one which might become the best of all our ideas.

"When I can make my brainstorming team feel they are playing a game, we get somewhere," said one of our most successful leaders. Yes, each session should be a game with plenty of rivalry, but with complete friendliness all around. Paradoxically, we can think up more ideas when trying hard, but in a relaxed frame of mind. A good device is to create the atmosphere of a picnic. Some of our best sessions have been sandwich-luncheons in the office, where our attractive dietitian makes all feel at ease. After coffee and cake we convene, the ground-rules are laid down, the problem is assigned. Suggestions begin to flow. Every idea, crackpot or crackerjack, is written down. Even silly thoughts are helpful—they keep the group relaxed.

The proof of a good brainstorm session is the number of ideas produced and the way the participants feel afterward. If, as they go back to their regular tasks, they tell each other, "Gee, but that was fun!" the session was probably a success. One of our 165 associates who were in the armed forces served on a bomber, and went through so many harrowing experiences that when he came back it was hard for him to feel that any business was important. We were fearful lest he could not rekindle the keen interest that had marked his work before he joined Uncle Sam. He reluctantly accepted an invitation to sit in our brainstorm session. Afterward, on his way back to his desk, I noted the old sparkle in his eye. "That was the best fun I have had since I got back into business," he told me.

7.

Why is group-brainstorming productive? The main reason is that it concentrates solely on creative thinking and excludes the discouragement and criticism which so often cramp imagination. Another reason is contagion. As Fred Sharp of our Cleveland office has said, "When you really get going in a brainstorm session, a spark from one mind will light up a lot of bang-up ideas in the others just like a string of firecrackers." Another man called this same phenomenon "chain reaction."

Association is a two-way power in brainstorming. When Frank spouts an idea, he almost automatically stirs his own imagination toward another idea. At the same time, Frank's ideas stimulate the associative power of all the others.

A psychological factor in group-thinking is academically known as *social-facilitation,* a principle that has been proved by many scientific experiments. Tests have demonstrated that students could do better while working together than as individuals. Other experiments have proved that "free associations" on the part of adults are from 65 to 93 per cent more numerous in group-activity than when working alone. This same fact was recently confirmed by the Human Engineering Laboratory of Stevens Institute. According to its director, Johnson O'Connor, both men and women show greater creative imagination in groups than individually.

Then, too, there is the stimulus of rivalry. As early as 1897, psychological experiments indicated the power of pace-making. Later psychologists have proved that rivalry will increase accomplishment in mental work by adults or children by 50 per cent or more. Such motivation counts most in creative thinking because this depends so largely on the urge-to-try.

8.

Our Minneapolis office recently held seven brainstorm sessions within a single month. One meeting developed 45 suggestions for a home-appliance client, another turned up 56 ideas for a money-raising campaign, another produced 124 ideas on how to sell more blankets.

For a New York client we organized 150 of our people into 15 separate groups to brainstorm one and the same subject. This multiple activity turned out over 800 ideas, 177 of which were chosen for submission in the form of concrete suggestions.

In addition to producing rafts of ideas, such joint ventures in thinking-up do something for those who take part. They gain in creative power. They see proof that they can spark if they will. They get baptized into a habit which can help them in private life as well as in business.

One of our brainstorm leaders lives with his folks and five unmarried brothers. They are quite an explosive family, susceptible to squabbles. It took courage on his part, but our lad organized a creative group consisting of his parents, his brothers and himself. They hold regular meetings and brainstorm one family problem at a time. "Some of our ideas worked and improved the harmony of our home," he told me. "Much to my surprise, we all have a lot of fun in these sessions."

If I were a minister, I would pick out a good leader to organize a brainstorm group. I would give her six problems on which I needed helpful ideas, and ask her to conduct six weekly sessions, one session on each subject. In between, I would coach the leader. And in between, as well as at the end, I would go out of my way to express my thanks for the effort and for the lists of helpful ideas which, in all probability, would come to me from this activity each week.

If I were Ambassador to Canada, I would organize a brainstorm group of five Canadians and five Americans to meet with me once a month to produce ideas as to how

Canada and the United States can be made to feel more and more friendly to each other. There are hundreds of opportunities for concentrated creative thinking in our public affairs.

General Eisenhower set up a brainstorm group for *war*. Why couldn't the U.N. use more of this same technique for *peace*?

Chapter XXXIV

IDEA-THINKING ON LARGER SCALE—
SUGGESTION SYSTEMS

WHEN IT COMES TO organizing idea-hunting on a large scale, the usual setup is the *suggestion system*. Under such a plan, employers induce employees to think up ideas by themselves, rather than in groups. Large-scale brainstorming by *groups* has not been attempted, as far as I know, except by Jean Rindlaub, who has organized and conducted such sessions in our New York office with as many as 150 of our young women taking part. In such mass brainstorming, as ably led by Mrs. Rindlaub, there is a reassuring anonymity about voicing suggestions, a free and easy informality, a speed and pace that make ideas fly fast. As in small brainstorm groups, the leader must boil down the problem. The ground rules must be strictly observed, especially the ban on criticism. Every idea must go down on the record.

The leader's job is to grab ideas as they pop and rapidly translate them into practical suggestions. If someone says, "But that won't work," the leader must act fast with something like, "Okay, let's leave that to the legal department. But it's an idea. It sounds worth trying. Who has *another*?"

In mass-brainstorming, it is well for the leader to spring a few ideas to start the ball rolling. Mrs. Rindlaub began one session with this: "It's a simple problem today—we have a little character, Chiquita Banana. You've heard her on the

275

air, in singing commercials. You've seen her, perhaps, in minute movies. What can we do to get Chiquita still better known? Should we have an animated Chiquita in electric lights on Times Square? Or put her on dining-car menus? Or what would you suggest?"

On that one subject, Mrs. Rindlaub's large group produced over 100 suggestions in 40 minutes.

2.

About 6000 American companies now conduct suggestion systems by which Tom, Dick and Nelly are coaxed and coached to think up ideas on their own. This movement looms larger and larger as a creative leaven for our nation.

In 1880, in Scotland, shipbuilder William Denny originated the idea of asking employees for ideas. His plan consisted of a wooden box into which his workers were invited to drop suggestions for building better ships at less cost. That box was the great-grandaddy of the many thousands of similar boxes now found in American factories and offices.

The first full-fledged suggestion system in the United States was installed by the Navy in 1918. There followed many others; but of all the suggestion plans installed in American industries prior to 1940, only about one out of 10 kept going. The mortality rate was high mainly because top management had not yet learned how to run idea-systems. Too many executives merely put up suggestion-boxes and then sat back and hoped for some million-dollar ideas. No wonder their "plans" petered out.

3.

It took World War II to put new life into the suggestion-system movement, with Donald Nelson applying the hypodermic. And what a resuscitation! One authority estimates that ideas from such systems saved Uncle Sam nearly five billion dollars during the war—*billions* of dollars' worth of ideas from rank-and-file employees who, if called "creative" would blush and protest: "Who, *me?*"

Starting in 1942, thousands of war-plants set up suggestion systems and buckled down to make them work. Patriotism spurred employees to think up and turn in more and more ideas. Before the war ended, such systems were going strong in 6000 industries. General Motors, for instance, in one 30-month period paid out over $2,000,000 in awards for ideas which substantially increased the output of war-implements.

A suggestion system in the War Department stimulated civilian employees to think up 20,069 new ideas which saved $43,793,000 in 18 months. Navy's Secretary, Frank Knox, set up the Beneficial Suggestions System through which new ideas were reaped right and left and disseminated to all naval yards and plants. In addition, each of the 48 largest shore establishments had a similar program. In one of these, over 900 suggestions were received and processed within one fortnight.

At war-end, suggestion systems suffered a letdown; but there soon came another revival. To a large extent this was inspired by the National Association of Suggestion Systems. Then, too, industrial engineers had seen how well such programs had worked and sold their clients on the peacetime value of full-fledged systems.

Smaller businesses then started to install such plans—even local enterprises. One soft-drink bottler in Boston established a program almost as complete as those used in a great industry. Charles Diefendorf, president of the Marine Trust Company of Buffalo, recently announced a completely organized plan for securing ideas from the 820 men and women on his staff.

In the last year or so, about 1,000 new full-fledged suggestion systems have come into being. According to Fred Denz, president of the National Association of Suggestion Systems, "one reason for this increase is that such systems are more and more recognized as highly profitable."

John A. Barkmeier of Marshall Field recently told 800 leading executives that, to cope with the critical period which business may have to face before long, "creative thinking of every worker from the bottom to the top of each organization is needed." That's the basic reason why suggestion systems are now more numerous and more solid than ever before.

4.

The success of such plans largely depends on the personal factor. The enthusiastic support of top-management is indispensable. The vital key is the man who heads up the program. The main cause of most failures has been the inadequacy of those directly in charge. "You can't get big league results from minor league talent," said I. D. Chamberlain of Lever Brothers.

In many instances the right man can direct the idea-system as a part-time task and do so successfully. In some cases, the boss himself personally handles this portfolio. In about 100 of the biggest industries, an expert devotes himself exclusively to this function. Such specialization seems likely to achieve the stature of a profession in the near future.

The attitude of the supervisory force can make or break a suggestion system. When a worker fails to volunteer ideas, it is often because he is afraid to "go over the head" of his foreman. Some supervisors, against their own good, have actually discouraged participation. Many companies find that the most and best suggestions come from those departments which are headed by men who not only encourage but actually help their people to submit ideas.

Too many employers seek suggestions without assigning specific subjects. In a few cases employees have been asked for ideas under general headings such as: selling, advertising, material-handling and so on. But such targets are too vague and too wide. Why not ask more *pointed* questions? When creative thinking is thus focused, the quality as well as the quantity of suggestions is likely to increase. After all, our imaginations must have bones to gnaw upon.

It might even be well to plan a *series* of *drives* for ideas on specific subjects. For example, in February the subject might be safety; in May there might be a drive for ideas on product-improvement; in September there might be a drive for ideas on Christmas merchandising; in November there might be a drive for ideas for new products. There might even be an intensive campaign for ideas on the question, "How can we make our suggestion system work better?"

With a series of stepped-up projects like these, we could harvest more and better ideas and also inspire and maintain a wider and keener interest in our idea-systems.

5.

Richard Borden, nationally known advisor, urges his clients thus: "To get suggestions from your people, you need primarily a front office that is genuinely *eager* to get suggestions, and *determined* to get a lot of them. But the success of a suggestion plan also depends on how you *handle* suggestions once they come in. They must be treated in a way that will make each contributor feel richly rewarded for the effort, even though his suggestion is impractical, or too trivial."

For one thing, the suggestor should *quickly* know what has happened to his idea. For, as psychologists have demonstrated, "the knowledge of results" does much to inspire "intent for accomplishment."

There should be a well-thought-out device for rejections. When an employee's idea is turned down, he wants to know why *in detail*. He's less apt to try again if curtly brushed off by a form letter that fails to explain *why* his suggestion was unacceptable. In addition to written communication, personal interviews should also be made available. B. F. Goodrich prints on all suggestion blanks: "If you prefer to discuss the idea verbally, you can do so by calling at the office in Room Nine, Bldg. 24-B."

In peacetime, the biggest incentive for the flow of ideas is *money*. Most of the successful systems offer a minimum award of $5 and *no* maximum. Each adopted suggestion is paid for in relation to its merit. Where savings can be figured, the suggestor usually receives 10 per cent of the gross savings during the first year his idea is used. In large companies contributors can dream in terms of checks for over $1,000. Such awards are not uncommon; a lowly employee in the Pullman Company received $2,325 for just one simple idea.

Even if an employee fails to land a large award, he can pile up plenty by winning often. One young veteran I know came out of the war with a greatly enhanced ability, but went back to his old job at the same salary as when he joined up. He threw himself wholeheartedly into the company's suggestion plan. Month after month his cash-awards exceeded his regular pay. Management noticed his success in this, and he soon found himself in another department at double the salary.

6.

But generous cash awards are not enough to keep a suggestion system humming. It must be continually "sold" to employees. One way to do this is to dramatize the presentation of awards. Some companies hold rallies now and then to honor major winners. There should also be plenty of publicity about each large award—not only in company publications, and on the loud-speaker system, if any, but also in the local newspapers. Editors like to play up this kind of success story.

The basic promotional tool should be an attractive booklet which tells employees what the suggestion system is, how it works, what they've got to gain, and so on. This booklet should be something more than a few drab pages. It should be lively and compelling like the one published by B. F.

Goodrich, which increased the volume of suggestions by nearly 85 per cent after it first appeared.

Interest must be kept alive by sustained promotion. Plant posters are important. One new design after another should be displayed on bulletins and on suggestion boxes. Armstrong Cork advertises its suggestion plan on employees' time-cards which are seen 15 or 20 times every week. Some companies include suggestion blanks with pay-checks. Some change the colors of their suggestion-boxes every now and then to keep them from becoming just part of the scenery.

The Illinois Central Railroad promotes its idea-system with talkies in color, especially produced at great expense for this one purpose. This reel runs for 30 minutes and shows employees how to come up with prize-winning ideas. United Air Lines publish a special magazine, called *The Suggestor*, which features all ideas adopted during the previous month.

If properly run and adequately promoted, suggestion systems can do much to keep American business going strong. Uncle Sam has recognized their value; 28 government departments have already installed full-fledged idea-plans. According to Fred Denz, Russia, too, now has suggestion systems which offer huge awards to Soviet citizens for their ideas.

Americans are supposed to excel in ingenuity. The environmental influences which made us creative are fast vanishing. This loss is being partly offset by the suggestion systems which are now stimulating the creative power of some 5,000,000 individuals in the companies where idea plans are now on the march.

Chapter XXXV

CREATIVE EFFORT CAN MAKE
LIFE *BRIGHTER*

HAVING COVERED WAYS TO ORGANIZE creative thinking, let's now look into a few of life's phases in which more and better ideas are vitally needed. Let's first spend a few minutes on how imagination can brighten personal existence. This point has been repeatedly brought out on previous pages, but it well deserves a chapter of its own.

Talk about the "sweet mystery of life"—what a *bitter* mystery it is that most of us so miserably fail to use our heads to avoid head-on collisions with those about us. Instead of just *worrying* about our personal relationships, *waiting* for things to take a better turn, *dillydallying* in hope of hunches —why don't we *deliberately use our creative minds?*

We must know by now that all of us *can* think up good ideas if we but try. If any further proof were needed, the evidence of the suggestion systems should suffice. And yet, of those multitudes who are pouring ideas into suggestion boxes in thousands of workshops—how many of these people ever try to think up ideas for their *home* problems?

Why this paradox? A likely answer is that those who run suggestion systems actively persuade their people that they *can* create ideas, and continually *urge* them to *try*—but who ever even hints to them that they could and should call on their creative minds to help solve their *personal* problems?

282

Another partial explanation is that suggestion systems dangle *prizes* in front of their people, and that these prizes are what make them jump through their creative hoops. But how tawdry are those dollar-awards compared to what we can gain by putting our creative power to work on our personal problems!

"Resourceful people," said Dr. James F. Bender, "always get more out of life than those who do not develop this invaluable trait." Can anyone doubt that those who *consciously* put this trait to *work* will live brighter lives than those who let it loaf?

2.

Modern aptitude-tests have confirmed the findings of psychologists to the effect that the female of the species is more creative than the male—at least potentially. Women certainly do more than men to smooth the way of life; but couldn't they do still more if they tried harder to use their creative power? If married, a wife's ideas can do most to keep her home-life happy. If single, she needs to use her creative head to make her life a pleasant journey.

Although, in America, the privileges of both sexes are now fairly equal, there is still inequity in the fact that a woman has so little say as to whether or whom she can marry. Spinsterhood, whether voluntary or involuntary, is a creative challenge; but many women are well up to it—in fact some of the most consistently happy women I know are unmarried. The top secretaries in New York have a club called the Seraphics in which my partner's assistant, Louise MacLeod, is a leading spirit. Over the years I have admired the way she and her friends think up so many ideas to brighten their days and keep their outlook upward

These unmarried women think up ideas for others as well as themselves. One of our young women has a married sister with two babies and no help. The sister's cross is that she and her husband can never step out. Last Christmas this young mother received plenty of presents; but the one which made her rush to hug the giver was this document:

"To My Married and Harried Sister: The services of housekeeper, nurse, baby-tender, handy-man, errand-boy or cook will be gladly rendered by the undersigned for one solid week (or by the day or half-day, depending on the needs of the recipient). Merry Christmas!"

3.

A lone man needs to hunt ideas to brighten his life, as did Captain Stringer of the Army who found himself dismally stranded in Washington during the war years. His nights-off in his tiny hospital-room were so drear that he finally thought up the idea of offering himself as a "sitter."

"When Captain Stringer first came to my home," said Dorothy Mallinson, "my first reaction was, 'Are you kidding?' But he quickly pointed out the advantages of sitting in my living room instead of in his gloomy bedroom. He liked our man's-size easy chair. He could play our radio and phonograph combination. Our library was more to his liking than the medical books at the hospital. Far from being annoyed when my two-year-old decided not to retire on schedule, Captain Stringer said he liked the mental gymnastics of 'fighting him off to bed.' "

Captain Stringer thought up a way to make himself happier during a transitional period. Other men reach a point where there seems to be no brightness ahead as long as they live. Such a man was an old friend who knew my hobby was imagination and appealed to me for help, saying: "Ever since my wife died, I have been at wits' end. I don't know what to do with my future. Have you any suggestions?"

"You've got to solve that for yourself," I said. "But how about starting by deciding on your *aim*? Why don't you write your son a letter and define your goal? You will probably have to tear up the first two, or three, or five attempts.

But ultimately, in this way you can set your aim on exactly what you're after.

"Then," I continued, "write down every item you can think of which might advance you toward your objective; maybe dancing lessons, maybe learning to play bridge, maybe joining a certain club, maybe going to church, maybe marrying again, maybe moving to another city, maybe. . . . Well, anyway, there would probably be over 100 alternative ways to help yourself achieve the kind of life you seek.

"Put those ideas down on paper, and then forget them for a spell. After a few days, or a few weeks, your *sub*conscious mind, having been *consciously* put to work, will probably suggest still other things you might do. Okay. Go back to your list. Cross off the items which, by then, seem less promising. Add the new alternatives you have meanwhile thought up. Then lay off for another spell and let the problem simmer. Again study the alternatives. Talk them over with your closest friend, and crystallize a program; then put it into action step-by-step with all your might. If you do all that, you may not be as happy as you were while your wife was alive; but I'll bet that you'll come lots closer to it than if you just moped and hoped."

Six months later, he wrote me: "I think I'm now as happy as any widower my age. Many thanks for making me work my bean."

4.

Stevens College is famous for preparing women for married careers and Dr. Henry A. Bowman, its president, is an authority on marital problems. "Successful marriage," said Dr. Bowman to his students, "is a *creative* achievement."

What a need there is for education to make brides and grooms realize the need of conscious creative effort to make the most of their lives together! There is too much propaganda to the effect that *minds* have naught to do with married happiness. Thinkless romance is poured into our young people at every turn. Novels, movies, society pages—all make it seem almost sinful to use one's head in affairs of the heart.

But isn't it sinful *not* to? When a marital wreck ruins little children—and failure to avert that disaster is due to lack of conscious use of creative power—isn't that criminal negligence?

Arnold W. Green, sociologist of the University of Pennsylvania, said that romantic love "is good for getting people married but not for keeping them married." How can we teach our newlyweds that the "highly styled drama," the wedding, should be only the curtain-raiser to down-to-earth creative thinking?

Should we *brief* brides and grooms for their marital flights? A minister I know does this, but mainly by way of coaching the young couple to expect ants in their nectar. He points out to them the inevitable jams of the first year. He prepares their minds for the emotional strains they may face when babies begin to arrive.

It is well thus to warn, and to urge patience and understanding. But why not suggest a *positive* course—why not show the boy and girl how conscious use of their creative minds can even overcome "inevitables"? What a job Kathleen Norris could do as such a coach! Her works are full of examples of how ideas can help keep bright the early years of marriage.

5.

Romance makes for smooth sailing during early years; in later years, a couple needs more and more creative thinking to keep marriage off the rocks. Divorces have doubled in 10 years. In how many cases have the man and woman *consciously* tried to chart ways to reach reconciliation before too late?

Sometimes they seek aid from outsiders. Psychiatrists and family lawyers often give helpful diagnoses; but too seldom do they suggest *treatment*—the *ideas* that might bring the couple together again. An exception was what a family physician did when a husband sought his advice, saying: "My wife whines all the time. She thinks she's sick. If she is, I'll stick to her. If she isn't, I am going after a divorce."

The doctor examined the woman and found no real physical ailment. But he hit upon an idea. He told her she must take a month's rest in bed, that her nerves needed absolute solitude, and that, therefore, even her nurse would have to stay out of her room as much as possible. He forbade the husband to visit her sick-bed; instead, he directed him to play cards with the nurse each evening outside the patient's room.

The nurse was pretty and vivacious. The patient could not help but hear her husband's happy chatter while he and she played gin-rummy. A few days passed. The wife could stand it no longer. She insisted she was completely well. Thus, an idea robbed Reno of another case.

A man wanted a divorce to marry another woman. The wife appealed to her lawyer for help. She was attractive and so were her children. The lawyer suggested a trial separation. "Ask him to go away for a month all by himself," he advised. "I'll bet he'll be back in two weeks." That's exactly what happened. The other woman had lost her lure.

Many couples run no risk of divorce and yet acquire the habit of quarreling. The man and wife would laugh at two other people indulging in similar spats. They should look at themselves the same way. "In such cases," says Dorothea Brande, "imagination can help us to stand back and see that relationship in perspective."

6.

If we parents could only nudge instead of nag! Nagging takes only a tongue; but nudging calls for creative thinking. Oh, how we need ideas for leading our children through the wilderness of infancy, through the jungles of adolescence, to the land of maturity!

Take the ever-pressing problem of obedience. A mother who had been a tennis-champion coached her 11-year-old so well that she won her way into the finals of a juvenile tournament at a seaside resort. The little girl balked at taking her usual after-lunch rest before the decisive match. The mother did not nag. Instead she said, "Hanna Ray, you don't seem to think a rest-hour is good training for a tennis player. So why not take a walk along the beach before you play?"

Hanna Ray did just that. Then she went into the tournament and lost. Afterward her mother added: "Maybe a rest-hour does make sense after all. If you *had* done as you should, you might have won that silver cup."

To stop bickering about practicing the piano, a Westchester mother bought a little notebook and a box of colored stars. Now each of her children sets the timer on the kitchen stove, and practices for 15 minutes. At the end of that period, the mother pastes a star in the child's practice book. On Sunday, the child with the most stars for the week wins a prize. "Their music improved," she told me, "and each child developed a personal sense of responsibility about her practicing." What a simple little idea! Yet how many parents would rather nag than try to think up new ways of any kind!

Why shouldn't parents try to use some of the principles set forth so far in this book? If a man and wife would put their heads together and pile up alternatives, wouldn't they be more likely to find solutions to child-training problems? After the first few attempts at such team-brainstorming, they would at least find it to be fun.

7.

Ideas can likewise be diamonds in our relationships with neighbors, with household helpers and with relatives.

A year before war ended a new liquor store opened in our neighborhood. Dropping in one evening, I was a little shocked to see that the proprietors were two white-haired ladies of gentle mien. A few months after war's end, a young man took their places. This made me curious. Here's the story he told me:

"My two maiden aunts were worried about me while I was overseas, and thought they might be happier if they had something to do. They considered this idea and that, and then one of them wondered what kind of a job I might land when I got back. So, out of all that, came the plan of their opening up this liquor store. When I arrived home, they turned it over to me, all set and going strong."

That was a two-way idea—a new way for two spinsters to keep happy during wartime, and then to make their nephew's life brighter when he took off his sergeant's uniform.

Business employers give lots of thought to keeping their staffs happy in their work, and housewives lucky enough to have employees at home need likewise to do creative thinking. At times when it seems well-nigh impossible to engage domestic help, an idea may do wonders. A family in the country was desperate for a housemaid. The housewife tried employment agencies and ran the usual ads in vain. She had once led one of our brainstorming groups. "In despair," she told me, "I finally sat down and did some creative thinking. Out of that one-woman brainstorm session grew a thoroughly unconventional ad which said:

" 'Can you clean a house and keep it clean—not spotless. just clean? Can you do a little wash (not laundry—we send that out)? Can you do all this in three full days or six half-days? (We'd like that better.) The food is good, the family is friendly. Telephone——.' "

She got 20 responses—plus a friendly, intelligent woman who never worked as a maid before, but who fitted into her household like a charm.

The usual neighborhood problem likewise lends itself to creative thinking. An unusual problem may call for an unusual measure such as group-brainstorming. A Pennsylvania friend of mine found his neighborhood in a snarl over race relations. He was tempted to move his family away, but decided to think it through. He organized a forum at his own local church, to which he invited old neighbors, personnel directors from nearby industries, and also some Negro pastors. They had a healthy, sane, free-for-all discussion and produced several ideas of immediate and practical benefit to both races in that neighborhood.

When it comes to human relations, either with ourselves or with others, we may not be able to make ourselves the captains of our fate; but we *can* think up ideas to make our lives a bit brighter—*if we try.*

Chapter XXXVI

IDEAS ARE THE KEYS TO BETTER
EMPLOYEE RELATIONS

WHETHER FREE UNIONS, free enterprise and a free society will live or die together will largely depend on the mutual attitudes of employers and employees; and these attitudes, in turn, largely depend upon ideas.

Strong influences are at work to poison the worker against his boss and against his job. Employers are up against great odds to offset this poison. Our own attitudes toward our employees will largely determine our ability to improve their attitudes. One secret of the successful program of human relations at the Hawthorne Works of Western Electric was described by F. J. Roethlisberger as follows: "Only when the people at the top really understand the feelings and sentiments of the people at the bottom, can they make the needs of management understood by the workers."

To think creatively on employee relations, management must go to heroic measures to steel itself against discouragement. There are too many cases where *good* employers are treated by labor as badly as *bad* employers.

No companies have tried harder to do right by their people than the telephone companies. Nearly all their bosses came up from the ranks—each pushed up by his fellows because they liked his character and recognized his ability. And yet one telephone girl blurted to the New York *Times* during a recent strike, "We're telling the company we're not

part of the switchboard any more. We are people and we've
got to be treated like people." I asked a telephone executive
for his reaction to this complaint. "We don't let ourselves be
disheartened by blasts like that," he said. "We have to keep
in mind that nine out of ten of our people *know* and *feel*
that our companies do go out of their way to treat their
people like people."

Managements are using more and more surveys and polls
to find how their people think and feel. But such analyses
provide no solutions—they merely point up the facts out of
which ideas must be wrought.

Most surveys aim to find out what's *wrong,* and this is
helpful because such knowledge can lead to corrective ideas.
But how about surveys to bring out what's *good*? A broad
study along this line was suggested by Charles Luckman,
head of Lever Brothers:

"In America," said Mr. Luckman, "we have hundreds on
hundreds of case-histories of peaceful and successful labor-
management relationships. Why are they peaceful? Why are
they successful? I suggest we find the answers! I urge that
Congress establish a tripartite commission representing the
public, labor and management. The sole function of the commission would be to study the causes of industrial *peace* . . .
to formulate a *positive* program for industrial harmony."

2.

Management has thought up many ways to make their
people like the places where they work. Brighter painting,
better ventilation, and improved safety are common practice.
Cleaner rest-rooms and low-cost cafeterias give workers welcome breaks during the day. In many plants, pension and
insurance plans have reduced the off-job worries of the
worker.

In recent years the idea of music-while-you-work has
gone far. Many a plant now has a loud-speaker system on
which happy tunes are played. In still more plants, music

is wired in from outside services such as Muzak. One company I work for installed such a system. The workers were enthusiastic and so was the management. But then Muzak started to play *Deep in The Heart of Texas* several times a day. Whenever the time for clapping hands came around, the production-lines came to a halt—the workers could not help but stop and clap. A frantic call to Muzak brought the promise that pieces requiring audience-participation would no longer be played.

These extras not only help make workers like their jobs, but tend to reduce turnover. The lessened expense of hiring and training new people helps offset the costs. And the boss sometimes gets an extra compensation from these benefactions. An old employee stopped Harry Lehman of Wildroot and said, "I'll tell you something. With all the things that you have done around here to make things more pleasant, a lot of us are happier *at work* than we are *at home*." When Harry told me about this he added: "You know, that one remark made me feel better than a trip to Florida."

3.

"If we could only make our people understand that we are all in the same boat, even though only a few of us can be in the pilot-house. This task is *the* key to better relations," one industrialist told me. Another executive put the same thought this way: "We have to teach 'togetherness.'"

We certainly need ideas to induce a sense of personal participation on the part of our people. During the war, the "E" awards were an effective device to that end. Suggestion systems likewise tend to make plant workers feel that they "belong."

Polls can mar or improve employee relations, depending upon how they are conducted and what is done about the findings. Above all, they must be kept free from fear of reprisal. Said B. F. McClancy, "Only after a management has conducted enough polls to prove to employees that they may talk frankly without retaliatory action, do the workers begin to express their candid opinions."

How to inform employees is a challenge to creative thinking. Every company should have an adequate system of communication. Said Joseph Moody of the York Corporation, "When we contact an employee on the job we are contacting an individual, but when we reach the man in his home, we are in contact with the employee's friends and family. It is much better to establish a sound relationship in the kitchen than to try to mend the mistake on the picket line."

To communicate the truth to employees is a tough enough creative job, but it is even tougher to remove untruths from their minds. When the Taft-Hartley act started, workers were led to believe that it was wholly adverse to their interests; and yet the truth was that most of its provisions were in line with what they wanted.

Employers who tried to meet that issue head-on found that their efforts boomeranged. Whatever they said was smeared with the accusation that they were buttering their own cake.

Several big companies hit upon a better idea. They circulated reprints of a magazine article which outlined the findings of Claude Robinson's nationwide survey of workers. This showed that only 31 per cent favored the Taft-Hartley law as a whole. But it also showed how workers felt about the separate planks in the act. When they were asked, "If you were in Congress would you be *for* or *against* laws to do the following things?" . . . 70 per cent of them favored a law to require 60-day notice before striking, 77 per cent favored outlawing communists from labor leadership, 85 per cent favored the publication of financial reports by unions.

Thus, through a strategy made up of factual analysis by a third party, management was able to show workers that their hatred of the Taft-Hartley act was largely based on misunderstanding.

Another misunderstanding which calls for strategic thinking is that of corporate profits. Surveys of employees show that the average worker thinks his company makes at least *three times* as much on each dollar of sales as it *actually* does, even in good years. The percentage of profit which the average worker thinks his company *should* make is likewise far higher than the actual.

Such educational problems baffle the best of our industrial leaders. Anybody who can think up how to teach employees the *truths* of business can turn his ideas into gold.

4.

Emotional understanding counts even more than intellectual understanding in employee relations. Every boss might well adorn his office-wall with this quotation from Abraham Lincoln: "If you would win a man to your cause, first you convince him that you are his friend."

Unless an employer *likes* people in all walks of life, he will fall down in employee relations. His spirit of friendliness cannot be faked; employees soon get the number of the insincere back-slapper.

"But if you like them you should show them that you like them," said the old head of a business to the young manager of one of his branches. The latter had come to the home office to discuss the problem of how to keep his girls from leaving for other employment—for no more and sometimes for less pay. That noon the two men were at lunch in the head-office cafeteria when a girl stopped at their table and said: "Mother thinks maybe you're right." The old man smiled and said, "Thanks."

"That's what I mean," he exclaimed to his young associate. "The other morning I noticed that she had on green shoes and when I told her they looked pretty, I found that her mother had scolded her for wearing them to work. Evidently she told her mother about my compliment, and now they both seem to be happy about the whole thing . . . I wonder if you show enough personal interest in your employees? If you like your people, you should constantly 'make love' to them in nice simple, human ways like that." This little idea helped make the young man a far better manager.

A courageous idea to put the emotional equation on the highest plane is credited to Maurice C. Smith, Jr., president of the Bristol Manufacturing Corporation of Bristol, R. I. He created a department of Christian Relations, hired a young minister to head it, and made him vice-president of the corporation. In announcing this startling new idea, Mr. Smith said: "Our instructions to the Reverend Dale D. Dutton are simply these, 'Go about doing all the good you can find to do in this world, and look to God for His leadership, not to the directors or officers of our company.'

"This idea," explained Mr. Smith, "started with my brother. One night while tossing in a Pullman berth he reviewed the many steps our plant had taken to improve working and living conditions of our 800 employees and their families." But he felt all these steps fell short. From one alternative to another he came to the idea of a new department "which would operate as did Jesus Christ 1900 years ago when 'He went about doing good.'"

By the end of his first year, the Reverend Dutton and his seven assistants were handling requests for help at the rate of over 150 a week.

Another evidence of the power of a spiritual touch was in Milwaukee, where the long strike against Allis-Chalmers seemed hopelessly endless. A minister named Ensworth Reisner, who used to preach in my neighborhood, brought together in his own home the company-heads and union-officials, including Walter Reuther. They all sat down to supper cooked by Mrs. Reisner, who later said: "When they first arrived they got into an awful fight. It wasn't long after that before they were giggling and laughing. I thought they were all just as cute as they could be. Toward the end of the meeting they were telling jokes and having lots of fun."

By arranging these negotiations in the shadow of his church, the 37-year-old minister succeeded in inspiring attitudes which soon led to the end of the long strike—an illustration of how one good idea can change men's moods and cause emotion to give way to reason.

5.

The tyranny of words is such that terminology is another employee-relations problem which calls for creative thinking.

The smear technique of agitators is based on hate-stirring words. "Scab" was a master stroke worthy of a Shakespeare. The term "slave labor" applied to the Taft-Hartley act closed many minds which otherwise might have welcomed its provisions.

No decent employer wants to meet such fire with fire; but too many employers seem to go out of their way to use the wrong words. For example, by and large they have accepted the term "*Grievance* Committee," despite the fact that its connotation carries an emotional chip on its shoulder. G. A. Nairn, head of Lever Brothers in Canada, realized this and chose the name "*Negotiation* Committee." "This simple change of wording," he told me, "did much to change the spirit of our meetings between management and employees."

Creative thinking is likewise indicated for better *clarity* of expression, as was recently brought out by Dr. Henry C. Link. "Many publications are written far above the educational level of the people addressed," he said. "In a recent labor dispute the president of a company wrote his employees a letter which we analyzed and found to be written in words that only 20 per cent of his people could grasp. The letter was rewritten so that it would be readable by at least 90 per cent of the employees."

Fortunately, more and more managements are putting their cases in words and pictures that workers can understand. One example is what Allegheny-Ludlum did with its story, allegedly written by "Al," a personification of all "the 12,639 workers" . . . and "the 13,009 shareholders."

"Al" admitted he had had a good year, but he also told in simple words just what happened when the bill-collectors got at his income. He broke the company's dollar down to the scale of one week's work by one man. On this basis, the company paid an average weekly wage of $57.28. For the same one-man work-week, it paid $75.73 for materials and overhead, $10.46 for taxes, $.98 to officers and $4.20 "in dividends to our 13,000 owners whose buildings, machinery and money we are using." Reserves on the same basis were $6.55 —which "Al" said was "left in the company so it can grow and prosper, buy new equipment, provide new jobs, and carry on in hard times."

Simplicity like that can take some of the suspicion out of profits, depreciation and reserves. Employee relations could be bettered if managements borrowed more of the ideas used by P.A.C. in selling its political wares to voters.

6.

Johnson O'Connor's exhaustive aptitude-testing indicates that creative imagination is relatively stronger in labor men than management men. He tested a factory-worker who "scored high in every aptitude for his own job and then equally high in creative imagination."

"How do you use it?" he was asked.

"Organizing strikes," was his matter-of-fact answer.

To that narrative, Johnson O'Connor added this comment: "While an unsympathetic public often views the resistant trouble-maker as a bungling craftsmen reaching for any excuse not to work, the cause is occasionally *too much ability*, rather than its lack. For idle aptitudes lie at the root of many industrial strikes."

The *resourcefulness* of the Reuthers is probably the key to their power. Beyond imagination, they have other advantages over their opposite numbers in management. The latter have to deal in *judicial* judgment almost all of the time, and thus tend to let their *creative* power lag. Then, too, labor leaders have but one job—the job of employee relations. Although this same subject should be at the top of every chief executive's list of duties, he has at least 10 other functions to which he must put his mind.

In 60,000 union locals there are 110,000 paid executives. All of these 110,000 people have risen from their own ranks largely because of their creative power. Their daily challenge is, "What *strategy* can I think up?" . . . "What *tactic* can I create?" Far more than men in management, union leaders are dealers in *ideas*.

But management is learning. More and more industrialists are realizing that, in addition to lawyers to handle legalities, they need topnotch creative people to think up the ideas which will reduce the likelihood of labor-snarls and make it easier to straighten them out when they turn into Gordian knots.

Many managers will admit that many of their labor-pains have come through their own bungling. But a new day is coming, according to Paul Garrett, vice-president of General Motors: "Business executives will be on as familiar ground in the realm of human relations, as yesterday they were expert in the arts of production. The leaders in industry who are blazing new trails are precisely men of this type; and 10 years from now American industrial leaders, as a group, will have become experts in the field of human relations, just as they always have learned to become experts in every field on which industrial progress depends."

Higher education will help too. Both management-men and labor-men are already being trained in industrial relations at M.I.T., Pennsylvania, Dartmouth, Cornell, Princeton and other institutions. But such education may fall short unless imagination's place in this field is understood and stressed.

"Progressive management," said Edward L. Bernays, "has already demonstrated in action a number of ideas that represent the beginning of an attack on the industrial-relations problem; but these methods are only a first step. Additional ways and methods must be found."

Yes, Mr. Bernays, the big need is for new and better ideas. Employee relations could possibly be the cancer which might put an end to the American way. The safest preventive is large and continued doses of creative thinking—especially on the part of *management*.

Chapter XXXVII

CREATIVE POWER'S PLACE IN LEADERSHIP

"CREATIVE THINKING UNDERLIES resourceful leadership," said Elliott Dunlap Smith, and countless others attest to the same truth. The logic of it is that a leader must be versatile. Although he must possess judicial judgment to a marked degree, he cannot be solely a judge—he must at least know his way around creatively. If he has creative lieutenants, he may not need to be a sparkling thinker-upper on his own; but he will at least need to recognize the value of creativity, and to know how to tap and encourage the creative power of his associates.

"The ability to approach each problem with cold objective analysis is essential for success as an executive," said Richard Fear of The Psychological Corporation. Yes, but even decisions—especially if difficult—call for creative power.

What do we do to decide? First we get all the facts, and list the pros and cons; but to do this well we also have to reach for the unknown—we have to guide our creative minds through the maze of *what-would-happen-if?* More often than not, a remote contingency, foreseen by imagination, turns out to be the determining factor.

Executives of long ago purred with pride over their ability to make decisions, single-handed and fast. When Brand Whitlock first became mayor of Toledo at the age of 36, he asked the advice of old Tom Johnson, who had been mayor of Cleveland for six years. "Decide quick," said Johnson, "and be right 51 per cent of the time."

A score of 51 per cent is not good enough today. That's why a business leader, to stay on top, has to combine creative thinking with judicial thinking in arriving at decisions. To get surer answers than his own one-man judgment could reach, he tries to think up how to pull in the experience of others; he tries to think up how to get *composite* judgment through conference-groups, or through surveys; he tries to think up ways to put the problem to actual test.

For example, suppose your company were about to put out a new pill and that you as manager were asked to decide whether it should be white or pink. Your grandfather would have probably said, "White!" or "Pink!"—according to his own prejudice. But today the good executive would send out interviewers to show housewives a pill in each color and get consumer votes. Through such tests, the decision would be almost automatic.

Decisions which have to do with selling naturally call for creative thinking; but even buying—yes, even accounting—can do with ingenuity. Carl C. Colbert came from the bottom to the top of the Nehi Corporation via the bookkeeping route. At the depth of the depression his life-and-death problem was whether he could collect funds fast enough to keep the business going. Mr. Colbert solved that by thinking up the idea of offering prepayment of freight as an inducement for cash with orders.

Recently, as president of his now prosperous company, he busied himself with buying. With prices sky-rocketing after the war, he took on the task of keeping costs down so as to avoid raising his company's prices to its enfranchised bottlers. By doing this he could make it possible for the bottlers still to charge the public only 5¢ for twice the quantity of highest-quality cola as his biggest competitor. Night after night at his home in Columbus, Georgia, Mr. Colbert pored over that problem, filling page after page with figures; but nothing from the science of accountancy gave him the answer. He got it, he later told me, through the use of his own ingenuity and by tapping the ingenuity of his associates.

2.

The advertising world gasped when the news broke that Ben Duffy, president of our company, had secured the Lucky Strike account in an hour flat. It was Ben's *anticipative imagination* that did most to make this possible. Said American Tobacco president Vincent Riggio to a group of friends: "I had made a long list of questions to ask Mr. Duffy in our first interview. He had no idea, of course, what was on that list. Without any priming on my part, he answered every one of those questions and also others which I should have thought of asking him. Before the hour was over I knew that here was a man with his feet on the ground—a man who knew advertising from the bottom up. So I gave him the business."

To keep his feet on the ground a leader needs *precautionary judgment,* and this likewise calls for *anticipative imagination.* One of the ablest executives I know recently said to his board of directors: "We're sailing along fine but we ought to be on the lookout for rocks ahead. I made up a list of 20 things that might wreck us. Here they are." Later, he enlisted the help of five creative men with business experience and worked out a check-list of 179 such hazards.

Such vision must likewise be applied to positive questions of policy. More than one business has gone on the rocks through too much reliance on slide-rule judgment and too little use of anticipative imagination. Almost in the center of Canton, Ohio, an impressive group of factory buildings sprawls over a plot of 20 acres. That idle plant is the tombstone of an industry which died mainly because of failure to think forward. According to a friend of mine, here's what happened:

"People used to walk into jewelry stores and ask for

Dueber-Hampden watches. They were fine watches—the best in the world at that time—and they had a world-wide reputation for quality. Then one year the business felt the effects of a mild depression, and the management looked for ways to reduce expenses. A big item was advertising. 'Why not do away with it?' they asked. 'Everybody knows what a fine watch we make. Why spend money on advertising?' "

American business bounded back on its feet again, but Dueber-Hampden sales continued to slump. Jobbers and retailers supplied the reason. "There's not much demand for your watches any more," they told the company. "People aren't asking for them."

The company failed; and here's an interesting side-light. The Soviet later bought the machinery, and about 50 Dueber-Hampden foremen went with the machines to Russia to run the plants there. These American supervisors found that with the same machinery, but without the enterprise and ingenuity of American craftsmen, they were unable to turn out watches which would keep time.

3.

When you go into business for yourself, the first thing you need is an *idea*. Little businesses that have grown big under the leadership of their founders are monuments to creative power. Ford is a shining example.

Imagination has likewise been an outstanding trait of some of the leaders who merged several companies into one. Such was W. C. Durant, who formed General Motors. But he used imagination almost to excess. His failure to turn his merger into an operating success under his own leadership is said to have been largely due to his unwillingness to allow his associates to judge and temper his ideas.

Walter Chrysler, on the other hand, not only took over a going business but personally led it to greatness. It was because of his outstanding ingenuity that, while still in his twenties, he had commanded the then sensational salary of

$12,000 a year while working for a locomotive company. Foreseeing the future of the automobile, he quit that job and started to make motorcars at half the pay. As president of his corporation from 1925 to 1935, he so stressed the part played by imagination in engineering that his successor, K. T. Keller, inherited the same creed. Ideas are still regarded as diamonds in the Chrysler organization—so much so that its battle-cry is *"Creative Imagination."*

Too many big-business executives tend to peter out creatively. They are not driven by sink-or-swim goads as in a little business; the sense of security in a large company tends to induce a "play-safe" policy. "Why should I try to think up ideas? Some of them would look screwy and might give me a black eye. In an organization as big as this, nobody will notice if I don't offer any suggestions, so to hell with ingenuity!"

Big business also offers so many *props* by way of analyses, surveys, and other studies; and props, whether for arches or for brains, weaken us when we lean on them too much. With fewer props, a small business is more likely to force each executive to keep up his creative power.

Every business, big or little, needs spark-plugs—leaders who have ideas and know how to make them click. In large concerns, the ideal top executive doubles in brass as a creative pace-setter and a creative coach. He cultivates the creativity of those around him and makes it bloom despite the stunting climate of magnitude. Above all else, he must feel a real regard for the power of ideas. He cannot be like a man I know who made a name for himself in the war despite his habit of looking down his nose and saying, "Ideas are a dime a dozen." Instead, he must be like John Collyer, who, according to his Research Director, Dr. Fritz, "not only welcomes every possible idea but makes us all feel that what he most wants from us is utmost use of our creative imagination."

Like trees, businesses tend to die from the top down, for the reason that the founders, as they grow older, sometimes tend to keep younger associates from trying their creative wings. An outstanding exception is Clare Francis of General Foods. "Younger executives come to me with what they think are new ideas," said Mr. Francis. "Out of my experience I could tell them why their ideas will not succeed. Instead of talking them out of their ideas, I have suggested that they be tried out in test areas in order to minimize losses. The joke of it is that half the time these youthful ideas, which I might have nipped in the bud, turn out either to be successful or to lead to other ideas that are successful. The point I had overlooked was that while the idea was not new, the conditions under which the idea was to be carried out were materially different."

4.

One of the needs of big business is to bring up the creative power of second-line executives. They sit in plenty of conferences, but these too often tend to cripple rather than to strengthen creative power. The younger conferees too often use their imaginations merely to anticipate how their associates will react; then, too, the conference-subjects usually call for judicial rather than creative thinking.

Although many businesses now have suggestion systems to gather creative contributions from the rank-and-file, far less is done to stimulate ideas from associate executives. More of this might be achieved through group-brainstorming, as set forth in a previous chapter. Or how about a special suggestion system for second-layer executives? Why not designate one of these men as a custodian for ideas, and ask other executives to file with him, in confidence, suggestions along *any* line. The custodian could then transmit these ideas to top management without revealing their authors. If an idea looked good to the big boss, the custodian could then divulge the identity of the originator. In some such way we might overcome the stifling effect of the self-protective instinct which cripples the creative effort of so many junior executives.

Not only in business but in every line, the quality of leadership depends on creative power. This is certainly true in science, as another chapter will show. In medicine, the Cushings and the Mayos have stood out mainly through heroic use of their imaginations. Even in law—surely it was the creative power of Justice Oliver Wendell Holmes that made him stand out.

In public affairs, our nation was wrought out of creative minds like that of Thomas Jefferson. And in recent years, the creative thinking of citizens like Bernard Paruch has done much for America.

And military leadership? How could any soldier be a great General without driving his imagination to the utmost? "How much in military matters depends on one master mind!" said Abraham Lincoln. Master mind? Of course this includes a mastery of knowledge. But isn't knowledge only part of it? Isn't it mastery of imagination that makes leadership magnificent on the field of battle as well as in every other field?

Chapter XXXVIII

THE NEED OF MORE CREATIVE
THINKING IN *PUBLIC AFFAIRS*

"WE'LL EXPLORE AND DEPLORE, only that and nothing
more," said a cynical senator concerning our national habit
of going all-out in fact-finding, and then petering out when
it comes to applying creative thinking to the facts as found.
In discussing this with David Lawrence, he remarked:

"In Washington in 1933, I had the opportunity of seeing
thousands of letters received by congressmen, government
officials, editors and columnists, all discussing the country's
difficulties. The interesting fact was this. All the writers devoted some time to analyzing the causes of the situation and
very intelligently, too, although all did not agree. However,
once they had made such an analysis, they seemed to have ex-
pended their energy. The creative spark so badly needed was
sadly lacking."

"The fundamental issue of our time," said Raymond Fosdick, "is whether we can develop understanding and wisdom
reliable enough to serve as a chart in working out the problems of human relations." He recommended more research;
and, undoubtedly, there should be more scientific study to
clarify our public problems. But investigations cannot find
solutions unless implemented with *ideas*. We would have
failed in our atomic research if our scientists had not thought
beyond the facts and beyond the known techniques. It was

308

the *new* techniques they thought up, and the countless hypotheses they dreamed up, which solved the atom.

2.

Community pride was one of the strengths of America; then cynicism set in, and those of us who spoke well of our towns came to be looked down upon as Babbitts. This trend hurt our country; we need new ideas to make more people appreciate their communities. The old-time flag-waving methods of our forefathers will no longer do—our people are now too sophisticated to be exhorted into civic pride. Nor will Hollywood stunts fill the bill. When the redcaps in the Omaha station grew beards to commemorate an event in local history, how could those beards make Omahans think any better of their city?

Boston recently set an example of what can be done when the Hub's civic leaders invited 1000 taxi-drivers to dinner. They even sang parodies written by a Harvard conservative, Francis W. Hatch. To the tune of *Hit The Line For Harvard,* one of his songs began: "Beat the drum for Boston. Plug the Hub each day." One talk at the banquet was partly as follows: "If Boston simply sat back, in 20 years it could easily live in a glass case, it could become the historical museum of the nation; and you fellows would make a good living taking American sightseers to dead places. Is that the way you want it? The other way is to believe in the blood-streams which still pulse in the arteries of this old town . . . If you can look about and still believe that Boston's future is as great as her past, why then you are going to have a good many envious out-of-towners in your cabs year in, year out. Stay with it!"

Does that sound like a Chamber of Commerce professional imported from California? The man who made that speech was Edward A. Weeks, Jr., the proper editor of the staid, old *Atlantic Monthly.*

The taximen even took an oath that night: "I pledge myself to acquaint myself thoroughly with all that is fine in Boston's past and present, to interest myself actively in Boston's future, to praise, not knock, to build, not belittle, and always to conduct myself so that I am a worthy 'Bostoneer,' an asset to my city."

The proper Bostonians also put on a prize-contest for suggestions to improve the city. Wouldn't our nation be better off if more communities used ideas like these to revive civic pride?

3.

The need, however, goes far beyond the kindling of civic spirit. Scores of municipal problems are begging for ideas— city-planning and traffic-safety, for instance.

In New York, Robert Moses has shown what imagination can do. If, technically, he were the world's greatest engineer, he could not have done half as much for the metropolitan area as he has done through the creative power he has put into his planning

William Zeckendorf has likewise endowed New York City with ideas. As one of my landlords, I know him well. He is a master of the real estate business in all its technical phases; but the one thing that has brought him so quickly from obscurity to well-nigh the top among realtors is the continuous use of his creative power.

Some of his ideas may never work out, such as the city within itself in downtown Manhattan with a roof so large that it would serve as another La Guardia Field. He also dreamed up the new dream-town which is now being erected on the lower East-Side to house the vast population of the United Nations Organization. John D. Rockefeller, Jr., thought well enough of this idea of Zeckendorf's to put up $26,000,000 with which to buy the land and hand it to the U.N.

In traffic problems, ideas can save lives. My home town of Buffalo has been constantly rated by the National Safety Council as at, or near, the top of all large cities in prevention of traffic deaths. This record is mainly due to the creative thinking of the volunteer head of the local safety setup, a manufacturer named Wade Stevenson.

The newest ideas are by way of switcheroo. Instead of dramatizing the danger of bad driving, the Buffalo safety authorities have dramatized the virtue of good driving. Instead of handing out summonses, the police have been handing out flowers. On one evening, Patrolmen William Collins and James Kelly ordered 25 women drivers to the curb, then complimented them on their careful driving and handed them fresh orchids.

To make democracy work as it should, it is vital to get out the vote. Pontiac, Michigan has adopted a new idea to that end. All the churches of that city ring their bells simultaneously once an hour while the polls are open on election day.

4.

With so many now set on exaggerating America's faults, we need more than ever to dramatize the good things about the U. S. A., so that more Americans will believe more strongly in America.

Our enemies from within turned May Day into an occasion for defaming Uncle Sam. This poison is now being antidoted by an idea which substitutes love of God and country for hatred of both. I saw a demonstration of this in a public square last May Day when 5,000 men, women and children gathered to offer up prayers for America—and also for the people of Communist Russia. There was no cheering, no applause. Instead there was reverent silence as the crowd listened to speakers like former police-chief Austin Roche, who struck the keynote:

"We believe we have the weapon that is more powerful than the atom-bomb, and that weapon is prayer. But we must use this weapon, just as our soldiers did back in the days when George Washington was saving our country. It's well known that he was once found in a forest, on his knees with eyes and hands raised, praying to God for guidance."

Similar observances were held all over Western New York with some 250,000 all-told in attendance. In many other cities, too, loyalty was thus substituted for the treason of the usual May Day. Hats off to the originator of that idea, whoever he or she may be!

We had long been in need of ideas to make us appreciate our inheritance, and then came the Freedom Train. In every city visited, the reaction has been thrilling. One famous editor summed up this whole project as "a big and fundamental idea," and congratulated the creators of the Freedom Train on having thought up a way "to 'sell' what centuries of struggle and rivers of blood had brought us, and what we so carelessly have accepted as indelible."

It is even harder to sell America on America's way of doing business. Those who understand it believe in our competitive system. Others just don't comprehend, and can be easily duped by those who would impose on us some other system in which *they* could hold the reins. Even in our colleges, instead of teaching how our economic methods have made it possible for almost everyone to fare better than anywhere else in the world, our free enterprise is either damned with faint praise or openly smeared.

Oh, how sadly we need ideas as to how to enlighten the average American on the simple arithmetic of the American way! And how sadly we have fallen down on this in the past! As Raymond Rubicam said, "The forms in which economic information is usually presented to the small groups it now reaches will never be effective with average people. Simpler and less dull techniques must be applied."

5.

As good as our country is, there is hardly a phase of national life which does not cry for improvement; and in nearly every case, the key is more and better creative thinking. Take the baffling problem of labor and capital, for instance. Irving Ives discussed this with me just after he was elected to the U. S. Senate. "The solution is not yet in sight," said the Senator, "but if we would put half the effort into thinking up *ideas* for straightening out our labor snarl as we put into finding *facts*, we could save years in bringing order out of our industrial chaos."

If you were Secretary of Labor wouldn't you like to have a creative group of your own, with absolutely nothing else to do but think up ideas—new ideas for you to judge, to adopt, to modify or combine for your use?

Some enemies of America hope that her downfall will come through collapse of the nation's finances. The problem of taxation is therefore vital. Why is it that we have so long stumbled from one expedient to another instead of creating a long-term plan of sound taxation? Our hats should be off to Paul Hoffman and Raymond Rubicam, who, as private citizens, tackled this problem. After four years of earnest analysis, *and* creative thinking, they drew up a plan for stabilizing tax-rates in a way which would balance the budget and provide a surplus for debt-reduction whenever employment and national income reach high levels. Their plan may never be adopted, but the ideas they put into it are sure to be helpful in charting the nation's course in taxation.

In our national problems, we need the best thinking of our most creative people. Some of them are occasionally invited by Washington to lend a hand, especially in wartime. During the first World War, Thomas Edison was called in, not to contribute his scientific knowledge, but to think up how to save the farmers. It was he who suggested the plan which, in substance, became the "ever-normal granary."

Why does Washington make so little use of our creative citizens in peacetime? One reason is that, in addition to their creative power, a power of judgment is asked of them—a judicial ability which is impossible without a deeper knowledge of the subject than can be quickly acquired. Why not ask such creative minds to perform a creative function only?

Why not divide each problem so that one set of experienced experts will take care of the fact-finding and judicial judgment, while the creative consultants will concentrate solely on suggesting idea upon idea?

One obstacle to new ideas in national problems is lack of opportunity to test. Many of industry's greatest advances would never have seen the light of day had it not been for experimentation. Instead of the big boss saying, "That's an interesting idea, but I don't think it will work, so forget about it," he has been able to say, "Well, it sounds screwy, but let's try it out."

If it were only feasible to take some part of our country and turn it into a test *state!* To be a scientific testing ground such an area would have to be made cross-sectionally typical of the whole country. There would need to be just the right proportions of income, education, size of family, and all that. At best, such a laboratory could not be truly scientific; but it still might be worthwhile as a test-tube in which social ideas could be tried out.

From time to time, there have been laboratories something like that. The outstanding one was in Central New York where the Oneida community carried on a long experiment in communal living on the highest plane. As a laboratory, the community was too small and too unrepresentative; but it was big enough to prove that the idea would not work.

It is probably foolish to hope that some day we might find a way to test ideas for possible adoption by the nation. But, surely, it is sensible to try to get more creative thinking into our national problems. Surely, with better use of our nation's creative power, we can make America better.

6.

No matter how many good ideas we may think up to solve our problems on the local and national levels, we may still be lost unless we are creatively sharp enough to cut our international knot. One great challenge is how to sell America to the rest of the world. American ingenuity did much to win our last fighting war, but, in the cold war since then, Russia's ideas have been hot enough to drive our country back on the European front, step by step. "Ideas will have to be fought with ideas," said Ernest Hauser . . . "In our attempt to hold the line against Russia in Europe, we have not even begun to use ideological weapons."

Some businessmen have recognized that need. William Benton, who made his start in the creative ranks of our advertising agency, felt so strongly in the matter that he went to work in Washington to try to get more creative thinking into our foreign affairs. He did much, including helping to establish the "Voice of America" by which some truths about our country are now put into some ears in Europe. But Mr. Benton had to fight so hard to make our lawmakers and bureaucrats see the need for such new ideas, that he reached the point where his creativity was so crippled by discouragement that he withdrew.

If Drew Pearson had relied upon those same legislators and bureaucrats to bless the Friendship Train, he could not have so successfully promoted that idea. But he went ahead on his own and, almost singlehanded, showed how America can shower gifts in a way that can make foreign recipients recognize our generosity and appreciate our donations.

The Dunkirk idea is another hopeful example. "This latter-day miracle," wrote Meyer Berger, "originated in this smoke-blackened city on stormy Lake Erie. It has spread with astonishing swiftness to cities all over the United States. Dunkirk, N. Y., took Dunkerque, France, to be a kind of sister city. Her little people established warm kinship with the little people of the North Sea Dunkerque. Americans in other states looked upon this sisterhood and found it somehow heart-filling and genuine. They moved toward similar adoptions."

The Dunkirk idea was a project which our Federal Government might well have done something about—not by way of taking it over, but by way of sponsorship. While at war,

Washington rightly helps to organize local volunteer bond-selling campaigns throughout the country. Just so, our government might well put its weight behind a movement like this, which, if multiplied nationally, could build more friendships in Europe than billions of dollars shoveled out of our treasury in cold-blooded routine.

The Friendship Train, the Miracle of Dunkirk—these are but models of what we need, and there is hope that more and more will come. For example, why not have naturalized Americans write home to their families in Europe and tell them the truth about America? This idea *was* put into action by millions of our citizens to help keep Italy from bowing to Moscow in the 1948 election.

"The most effective inspirer of letters," according to Drew Pearson, "was Generoso Pope, the Italian-American newspaper publisher in New York, who organized letter-writing clubs and committees among Italian-Americans throughout the United States. He estimates that over 2,000,000 letters were written to Italy alone. . . . Equally effective can be letters written to the countries just inside the Iron Curtain . . . Individual Americans can automatically enlist in the people's army for peace by getting busy in all sorts of ways to build up American friendship."

Another man has suggested that the best way to sell America to Russians is to let them drool over the pages of Sears, Roebuck catalogs. He is trying to figure a way to drop ten million copies from the sky, each with its own parachute. "This last one sounds crazy," you say? Yes, but how often a wild idea has been tamed into a *great* idea!

Why not seek suggestions from amateurs for our cold war just as we sought them for our last World War? The National Inventors' Council brought in 200,000 ideas between 1942 and 1945—many of them looked "crazy" at first—but in the net they helped speed our armed forces to victory.

Or why not set up a group of creative people in the State Department with just one function—to suggest new ways and more ways to win the friendship of the rest of the world?

All week long this group could sit and pile up alternatives. A committee of trained diplomats could then pick out from that week's crop the few ideas which they deemed most promising.

Maybe such a brainstorming group is a bit far-fetched; but, surely, we need somehow to put more creative power into our international salesmanship. We need more boldness. We need to look *up* to, not *down* on, *audacity* in ideas— *just as we look up to audacity in armed conflict.*

7.

So much for the problem of propaganda. Even *more creative* thinking is needed in our international *statesmanship* than in our international *salesmanship*. We will spend billions of dollars and mountains of imagination preparing for war. And yet to ward off war, what will we do? Will we let ourselves be the victims of events, or will we think up the moves which may "*make* circumstances"? If the armed forces need a General Staff to create our military strategies, don't we need a creative group to plan our peace strategies?

"Admittedly," remarked David Lawrence, "lots of research is applied to our international problems, but mainly in the form of finding facts and making diagnoses. There is but little by way of conscious *creative* effort to arrive at new and good ideas to guide our international policies—relatively *nothing* compared to the efforts that industrialists put into bettering the things they make."

In his letter to the Corinthians, Paul spoke of "the things that are *not*" as the keys "to bring to nought the things that *are*." The frictions among nations are "the things that *are*," while "the things that are *not*" are the ideas which are still to be born—the *new* ideas we need by way of major moves which might make for international co-operation. Such ideas call for unconventional thinking—the right idea is often the opposite of the obvious. Such was a suggestion advanced by France to help solve the problem of Germany. Her obvious move was to ban all Germans; but instead, she invited former Nazis in great numbers to come and live under the tri-color.

If you were Secretary of State and about to go to Moscow, wouldn't you like to have a highly intelligent group of strategists spend 100 hours doing nothing but thinking up 100 ideas as to the moves you might suggest while there?

Such men—with no need to *judge* their ideas, with no need to watch their step *politically*, with *no ax to grind* whatsoever—surely such men could think up more and better ideas than could men with so much *else* on their minds that they could not help but be creatively cramped.

Suppose you, as Secretary of State, with the judicial help of your associates, were then to weigh those 100 ideas. You might throw out 50 in the first sieving. On further thought you might throw out 30 more; but you would still have 20 left. You might combine some of these—or even some of the discards—into five still better ideas. You could then go to Moscow armed with 25 promising alternatives—25 constructive suggestions—to present to Europe's statesmen.

Such a board of strategy should, of course, be made up of men both highly creative and also well versed in international affairs. Wouldn't you, Mr. Secretary, like to have on tap the creative power of five Dave Lawrences—five great Americans who *would do nothing else but think creatively on our nation's international strategies?* If only *one* worthwhile suggestion came out of a whole year's work by such a group, its cost could be one peanut compared to the cost of one atom bomb.

Chapter XXXIX

THE PART PLAYED BY CREATIVE POWER IN *SCIENCE*

ON A JUNE AFTERNOON at Hamilton College, where Dr. James B. Conant was about to receive an honorary degree, I told him I had just read his new book, *On Understanding Science*, and added: "What impressed me most was how you stressed the part played by *creative imagination* in science."

"It's the *whole* of it," he replied without hesitation. Of course he did not mean that literally; but his book does recognize creative power to be far more vital to science than most of us have realized.

When I later told a young scientist of Dr. Conant's remark, he stated: "I'm just beginning to realize how true that is. Throughout my undergraduate and post-graduate years only one professor ever talked to us about the creative side of science, and he did that outside our curriculum."

What is science? The accepted definition is "classified knowledge." But where has this knowledge come from? Where else but from men's hunches—from their thinking up countless alternatives—from their dreaming up new ways and new devices by which to test their guesses? The basis of such testing is still trial-and-error; but this is now known as scientific experimentation and rightly so, because of its orderliness and its controllability.

T. Percy Nunn urged that the "*static* conception of

319

science as a body of truths" be changed into a "*dynamic* conception of science as a definite pursuit." For, said he, "science is a *creative* process." And Dr. Conant said: "Science is that portion of accumulative knowledge in which new concepts are continuously developing from experiment and observation and lead to further experimentation and observation." From this you can see why he has so highly rated creative power in scientific activity.

Before the dawn of science, imagination in the form of superstition conceived and maintained beliefs which were not true. The exploding of these fallacies was the first triumph of Galileo and the other early scientists along about 1600. As science strode forward in the 17th, 18th, and 19th centuries, and even more swiftly in our century, scientists naturally glorified its technical side. Only recently have they recognized the part played by creative power. Kettering of General Motors has done much to stimulate this recognition, and so have Dr. Suits of General Electric and many of the younger leaders. The American Society of Mechanical Engineers recently conducted a series of sessions solely "to emphasize the importance of creative ability in engineering." The American Chemical Society's Committee on Professional Training recently reported: "It is lack of ability in *original thinking* that makes far too many men of doctoral training unsuitable for industrial research."

2.

"Many have insisted that the imaginative process is different in art and in science," said Dr. R. W. Gerard. "On the contrary, the creative act of the mind is alike in both cases. . . . Imagination enters into the devising of experiments or of apparatus or of mathematical manipulations and into the interpretation of the results so obtained. But these are likely to be minor miracles compared with the major insight achieved in the initial working hypothesis."

"It's generally a hunch that starts the inventor on his

quest," said Dr. Suits of General Electric. . . . "Later on, perhaps after weeks of fruitless searching, another inspiration, arriving when he least expects it, drops the answer in his lap. I've seen this happen over and over. But I've yet to meet that 'coldly calculating man of science' whom the novelists extol. Candidly, I doubt that he exists; and if he did exist, I fear that he would never make a startling discovery or invention."

More often than not, it is the more imaginative scientist who rises to the post of research director. Of course, he must be of sound technical background; but, to be the real spark-plug of his group, he has to shoot wild himself, at times, and to encourage ideas from those about him, with the sky the limit.

A research-head also needs the ability to create cooperation. This is particularly stressed in the Du Pont organization, where teamwork is zealously sought "not only on the part of men in a particular laboratory, but also as regards inter-departmental co-operation." So said Dr. E. K. Bolton of Du-Pont, and Dr. Ernest Benger, also of Du Pont, stressed the fact that their researchers actively seek ideas from *throughout* the organization. "I do not know what percentage of our ideas come from other sources," remarked Dr. Benger, "but certainly a great many do. Some of our best thoughts have come from managers, from production people and from salespeople."

3.

Although the 17th century shone with illustrious discoveries, it created almost nothing really useful to mankind, except by way of navigation. "It is not until the 19th century," said Dr. Conant, "that we begin to see anything like the *practical* influence of scientific progress to which the first scientists so confidently looked forward." According to A. N. Whitehead, "the greatest invention of the 19th century was the invention of the *method* of invention. . . . A new method entered into life. . . . That is the real novelty, which has broken up the foundations of the old civilization."

Organized research, as we know it today, really began in this country. It was in 1902 when Du Pont's first formal research laboratory was started. The great upsweep came from 1920 on. In 1920 there were about 300 industrial research laboratories in America. In 1946 there were 2,500 such laboratories, staffed with about 150,000 people and costing over $500,000,000 a year. Du Pont has just started another research center which will cost over $30,000,000.

Substantially there are two kinds of scientific research: one the *specific*, and the other the *fundamental*. "The aim of *specific* research programs," said James Bell of General Mills, "is the continual improvement of existing goods and services, and the creation of new goods and services at constantly diminishing costs." Perhaps the outstanding record in research for creation of new products is that of Du Pont. Over half of this company's present line was not even thought of 20 years ago.

Du Pont is also doing more and more in *fundamental* research, which was started by Dr. Stine in 1927. Its purpose, according to Dr. Bolton, is "to establish or discover new scientific facts without regard to immediate commercial use." Specific or practical research calls for imagination; but scientists in fundamental research need even more creative power. To quote Alexis Carrel, their minds "must pursue the impossible and the unknowable."

The entrance to any scientific project must be paved with ideas. There must be an "imaginative, new approach," said Research Director W. B. Wiegand . . . plenty of "tentative stabs" at the problem must be made at the start.

Much of the most brilliant research has started from an idea that seemed wild at the time. Pasteur soared high in thinking up his projects. According to de Kruif, Pasteur's assistant learned to listen "bright-eyed" to Pasteur's "fantastic imaginings." . . . "Another man than Roux might have thought Pasteur completely crazy." In our century, trail-blazers like

Stine and Kettering have likewise been noted for their startling ideas for starting scientific studies.

Dr. Edward Goodrich Acheson reached for the sky and started a great industry. Francis Bowman, a friend of mine in cub-reporter days, has often told the story of Dr. Acheson's original idea to hunt for "diamond" dust: "Dr. Acheson had a hunch that an abrasive material could be created which would be harder, sharper, faster-cutting than abrasives made by Nature, such as emery, corundum, and garnet. He knew that carbon was used as the hardening agent in making steel and that, in its crystalline form, it was the hardest known substance. He, therefore, started experimenting by impregnating clay with carbon under a high temperature produced electrically.

"In his first examination of the fused mass, Dr. Acheson was painfully disappointed. However, his trained eye suddenly detected a few tiny sparkling crystals—crystals that man had never seen before. He collected the crystals on the end of his pencil and drew them across the surface of a pane of glass. They scratched the glass as sharply as a diamond. The first few handfuls of the new substance were readily purchased by cutters of precious stones at the rate of $880 per pound. They found it worked as well as diamond dust which cost $1,500 per pound."

What created Carborundum? Didn't it stem from Dr. Acheson's imaginative approach? Yes, but scientific advances usually depend, not on one idea, but on many new ideas from which to choose at the start. "Hundreds of new ideas will flow from preliminary conferences," said W. B. Wiegand. "From these, one, or perhaps two new approaches may emerge. Upon the soundness and fundamental originality of these new approaches much will depend."

But always the right idea at the start is more than half the battle. Surely here, at least, it is *creative power* which must supply the springboard for scientific *knowledge*. Without imagination, even the Solomons of science would fall flat.

4.

From the imaginative approach, the aim is set. Then comes the shooting in the form of experimentation; and, here again, imagination is called for at every turn. For one thing, there are scores of different ways in which experiments might be made, and an unheard-of method often has to be thought up.

To stimulate the kind of creative thinking needed in experimentation, Dr. Paul Eaton, professor of mechanical engineering at Lafayette, has recommended that teachers of science "arrange the problems to be determined through test in the laboratory in such a manner that 'cut-and-dried' technique through mere formula substitution is eliminated. The student should be set free to pick and choose his path."

The early scientists not only had to think up methods, but also their own devices. After Galvani got the first inklings of electricity from the twitching of a dead frog, Volta, in 1790, invented a new instrument for better detection of small charges of electricity. With this he found that he could experiment with almost any moist material instead of with frogs' legs. Thus, solely for the purpose of conducting his experiments, Volta had to invent the electric battery.

Experimentation is far more scientific today because new devices have eliminated guesses—especially by way of *measurement*. "And," said Dr. James B. Conant, "new degrees of accuracy in measurement often, but not always, *bring to light unsuspected facts*." Mainly through these new devices, research can now carry on *controlled* experiments. "And this means in essence," said Dr. Conant, "the control of the relevant variables such as temperature, pressure, light, and presence of other materials, particularly small amounts of air and water."

With the creative researcher the power of association must come into play at every step. "This" suggests "that," and "that" leads to something else. "New concepts," said Dr. Conant, "arise from experiments and observations; and these new concepts in turn lead to further experiments and observations." It is along this winding trail that our scientists finally find the *new* for which they search.

Experimentation can never be a machine into which you slip a coin and get the answer on a neatly printed card. Any slavishness to a notion like that is a handicap to any scientist, according to Elliott Dunlap Smith. He carefully traced the steps that led to typical inventions and concluded: "The act of inventiveness which achieved the solution was not logical scientific thought at all. Unless the inventor is willing to relax the meticulous step-by-step procedure of logical science, he will get nowhere."

Optics is the one of the most rigid of sciences. In creating the 200-inch mirror for Mt. Palomar, the researchers of Corning could, through calculations, arrive unerringly at the composition of the glass needed for that unprecedented product; but the first attempts failed because the huge discs cracked while cooling. A simple idea solved the problem. The mirror was cast with deep indentations in the back. By thus omitting much of the thickness, the white-hot molten glass could, and did, solidify without cracking.

The solution of that problem was not so "scientific," was it? It was just plain ingenious. And years later, when the mirror was about ready to pry into the heavens, the scientists were stumped as to how to clean the disc. They solved it by trying a lanolized hair preparation, Wildroot Cream Oil, and found that it *worked*—as *Time* magazine fun-pokingly reported.

5.

Creative research is packed with questions like "How about?" . . . "What if?" . . . "What else?" At the end come the questions *"Will it work?"* . . . "Can it be made commercially?" Technology has created ways to answer this last question through pilot-plants and semi-works techniques. For example, each and every step of the nylon process, together with the equipment for it, were worked out on a semi-works scale, and so thoroughly that except for size, the first commercial plant which went into full blast in 1940 practically duplicated the pilot-plant in all details.

Automobile companies have created vast proving-grounds on which to verify the findings of their research laboratories. Chrysler goes beyond this, and by means of huge guinea-pig fleets, road-tests the products of the minds of the Chrysler engineers. "These cars," says the Chrysler Corporation, "cover high, cold mountains, big-city traffic and open highways, back-country dirt roads and winding tourist routes. And every day—by phone or wire or mail—detailed reports on the day's performance of each car go back to Detroit. Facts reported today may set designers and engineers to work tomorrow, and lead to another improvement on our cars. Thus we apply *creative imagination* even in such a practical thing as road-testing."

General Electric operates a huge flight-test laboratory with a fleet of experimental planes to try out the ideas developed for better aviation by G-E researchers.

And yet, beyond all such scientific testing, it is still advisable sometimes to "try it on the dog." B. F. Goodrich pioneered with a tubeless tire about 50 years ago. About 17 years ago the company tried out a tubeless tire cured directly to the rims. The tubeless tire stayed on the shelf until World War II when the Army asked for a tire which, even when deflated, could carry a load at least 75 miles. The combat tire developed by B. F. Goodrich to answer that call was the first successful tubeless tire. Improvements went on until, finally, scientific tests and scientifically controlled road-tests had proved the tire worthy. But even that was not enough. Before offering the tire nationally, the new tubeless tires were put to actual *user*-tests on many private cars, taxi-fleets and police-cars.

It takes creative imagination to think up the best ways to test. The scientists in charge of the proving have to do more than just answer the question, "Will it work?" Of course, their judicial judgment does come into play, together with their power of analysis. But they cannot stop with "This won't do," even if they add, "Here's why." Their challenge is to help think up the *what-if?* and the *how-else?* and thus answer the *so-what?* of the facts which their tests reveal.

Thus from prelude to the payoff, in any scientific project creative imagination may not be the "*whole* of it," but surely it is a *without-which-nothing*.

6.

When the new is found and it is found to work, imagination is again called on to think up *how it can be used*. The man-made diamond powder which Dr. Acheson first created to polish precious stones was the acorn from which came a mammoth tree. Dr. Acheson himself thought up many other uses; but it was Dr. Frank Jerome Tone, father of Franchot Tone, whose creative imagination made the great oak grow. As head of the Carborundum Company from 1916 to 1944, Dr. Tone multiplied the uses of Carborundum. Its application to the working of marble and granite revolutionized the stone industry. Its application to precision-grinding made it possible to cut and to shape harder steels than the usual lathe could handle.

Dr. Tone modified the same substance to make refractories, and again to make filters for clarification of water and for treatment of sewage. Still other applications included heating elements, lightning arresters, radio transmitters and other electronic devices.

Instead of diversity of use, new applications sometime result in evolution, as illustrated by the history of jet-propulsion. In ancient days, a man named Hero demonstrated his "Aelophile," a rotating ball operated by jets of steam. Sir Isaac Newton planned a jet-propelled carriage in 1680. About 100 years ago, Charles Golightly worked on a jet-propelled plane which he described as "a steam-horse on which one may ride through the air from Paris to St. Petersburg in one hour."

In September, 1941, General H. H. Arnold summoned General Electric engineers to Washington and asked them to produce a jet plane. Almost overnight the G-E engineers, under the leadership of R. C. Muir, designed a jet-propulsion engine. Within 11 months of the day on which General Arnold had held his historic conference, the first jet plane ever to fly in America left the ground at Muroc, California.

That miracle is explained by the fact that General Electric had been experimenting on gas-turbines since 1895. The turbo-supercharger which did so much to speed our planes in the last war, came out of that long developmental work. Jet propulsion was a natural step from there. It was the evolutionary outcome of over 45 years of creative effort by two generations of G-E engineers.

7.

Fact-finding is a new form of research which has gone far in recent years. It stems from the straw votes of yesteryear, but is more precise. It copies the principles of scientific research in that it is orderly and so arranged as to reduce inaccuracy due to variables. Its test-tube is usually a true cross-section of people, so that the facts found in regard to a relatively small group will be fairly representative of the whole. Surveys of this sort usually deal only with facts; but Dr. Henry Link and Dr. George Gallup have gone beyond that and have developed ways to research *opinion*.

Arthur Nielsen of Chicago created new methods of commercial research which reveal to manufacturers what they never knew before about their markets. Manufacturers of foods and drugs are paying Nielsen upwards of $6,000,000 a year for facts about *consumer* purchase of their goods and the goods of their competitors. Art Nielsen has also created a new way to measure radio-audiences, having developed a machine which is attached to receiving sets in homes and which records on tape exactly what station is tuned in by each family at each minute of the day and night.

These new forms of research have helped make selling and advertising somewhat more scientific—to the extent that creative minds in sales departments and in advertising agencies have far more facts to guide them; but, here again, we are in danger of overrating technique and underrating imagination. An outstanding analyst, Elmo Roper, warns us that too great a reliance on research can hurt creativity. Movie-producers who have tried to tailor-make pictures to the expressed desires of audiences have fallen down through over-formulization.

"The public," Mr. Roper adds, "can't tell you what it wants when the thing under discussion doesn't exist. As an example, a pre-publication attempt to determine whether anyone would buy *Life* showed that 'no one' wanted the magazine."

Even in the doing of that kind of research, creative power is everything. Undoubtedly, Arthur Nielsen is a splendid engineer; but without his creative power, he could never have built so huge a business in fact-finding. The planning of and the execution of such research calls for imagination galore. It takes plenty of creative thinking merely to work up questions to be asked.

Dr. Robert Elder, as a former member of the faculty of M.I.T., knows his science. As director of research at Lever Brothers, he knows first-hand all the commercial techniques of investigation. When I asked him what part he thought imagination played in research, his answer was practically the same as Dr. Conant's: "Apart from thoroughness and accuracy, the essense of research of any kind is *imagination*."

Chapter XL

DOES AMERICA'S CREATIVE POWER FACE A *DECLINE?*

WHAT ABOUT THE CREATIVE power of our people as a whole? The future looks far from promising. We have been losing that spirit of effort which led us to make the most of our creative talent. The influences which built that effort are on the wane; to take their place, few if any new influences are in sight.

Our philosophy of effort was due partly to environment and partly to heredity. Our basic inheritance, according to Edna Lonigan, came from "the English seafarers who, venturing out from their sunless island in search of a livelihood . . . learned how to manage new and strange employments, in which the penalty of failure was death. By trial and error they learned how to plan their enterprises—and how to carry out their plans. They learned how to work with their fellows, how to organize private 'ventures' with only their own resources. 'It couldn't be done, but they, poor fools, didn't know, and they went ahead and done it.' "

Forebears like those from England poured the first buckets of effort and ingenuity into our national bloodstream. As time went on, almost every country added to our inheritance. The call of the new America fell on the deaf ears of the lazy and the unimaginative, whereas the same call was a clarion to those of greater gumption—the softies stayed in their fatherlands while their braver brothers and sisters came here in hordes.

The harder their lots had been in Ireland, Italy, Germany, Poland and other countries, the stronger was their urge to use their minds and muscles to the utmost in order to make good in their new America. The Jews, conditioned by tough going through the ages, brought with them an even stronger urge and, by and large, an even greater creative power.

Some of those who came had been known as "crackpots" back in their native villages; but America served as a melting-pot even for the crackpots, and thus absorbed new blood profusely rich in imagination.

From all those sources, there came into our nation what Paul Hoffman has described as "the discontented, youthful, and pioneering spirit which forever quests for that which is better." The essence of this spirit was hard work. The result was a climate which cultivated creative imagination as never before, anywhere in the world.

With no intake of fresh blood, how long can that inheritance carry on? Millions of Americans are still living on the religion of their parents; but unless their children actively build up their religious carryover, their children's children will be churchless. Isn't this likewise true of creative power? We cannot count on inherited momentum. Unless we can find ways to activate creative effort, America may soon lose her leadership in ingenuity.

2.

W. L. Merrill of General Electric put environment ahead of heredity in explaining America's creative power. "The environment of our early settlers," said he, "forced them to exercise a tremendous amount of Yankee ingenuity or starve."

America's ingenuity is called "Yankee" for good reason. New Englanders creatively contributed by far the most to the early development of our nation. "The home of the New

Englanders," said Arnold Toynbee, "was the hardest country of all." Their outstanding creative power was proof that "the greater the difficulty, the greater the stimulus."

The early Yankees had to hew their way or starve. They ultimately succeeded in raising a surplus of food and raw materials to sell to Europe, thus gaining the funds to import manufactured goods. Had this economy continued, their creative power might have run down; but, among other things, the Stamp Act precipitated a determination to *make* more things in New England.

Thus came a great impetus to New England ingenuity, typical of which was the enterprise of Francis Cabot Lowell. In 1810 he went to England to look over cotton-mills, and to copy the machines and methods. On his way home, he was captured by a British frigate and was thoroughly searched. Therefore he could bring back no sketches whatsoever. It was in his "brilliant and tenacious brain," said Ferris Greenslet, that Francis Cabot Lowell brought back the manufacturing secrets out of which the huge factories of Lowell and Lawrence were created.

During the colonial period, all manufacture had been practically forbidden by the English Parliament. Therefore New England had virtually no production experience to go on. Every little detail of making goods had to be thought up—almost as if no goods had ever been manufactured anywhere. One idea followed another, one enterprise after another got started. Before long, Yankee ingenuity had made such headway that when England sent fleets laden with manufactured goods to recapture her United States market, many of these cargoes were "dumped" in our ports and auctioned off to the highest bidder.

That need to start American industry from scratch spurred creative power not only in Yankeeland, but throughout the Union. We think of this as centuries ago, and yet it is almost within our time—a fact that comes home to me with personal force because, when my great-grandfather died, an obituary in a New York paper stated that he had been "the first to use steam to produce window-sash and blinds in his mill on east Broadway."

After the conquest of the wilderness, and the industrialization of our country, the opening of our West served as the third great impetus to our creative effort. Again the brothers and sisters strong in imagination and gumption left their cozy homes and took the same westward direction as their forefathers from Europe. Like their forebears, they had to force their muscles and minds to the utmost or fail; they had to think up new ways to solve new problems. Their creative instincts were sharpened on the stones of adversity.

Meanwhile, our forebears had become "jacks-of-all-trades," and out of this fact came an ever greater inventiveness, as typified in the case of Thomas Davenport, the young blacksmith from Vermont who changed the world through his invention of the electromagnet, out of which came the electric motor. He had no training in electricity or any other science. He started doing the work of a grown man when he was only 10, and as apprentice to a blacksmith served without pay until he was 21. He read a lot, but above all else, he did this and that and the other thing with his hands, guided by his imagination and his will.

It was from men like Davenport that came our fourth great impetus in creative power—our industrial revolution which took the form of mass production. Our national ingenuity never reached such heights as in thinking up ways to produce so much so fast—with so few man-hours and at so low a cost to the consumer.

A trickle of new creative blood continued to flow from abroad, encouraged by the opportunities created by mass production. Steinmetz came from Germany, Baekeland from Denmark, Alexander Graham Bell from Canada, and Sikorsky from Russia. "But," said Lawrence Langner of the National Inventors Council, "it is probable that these men, in their native environment, would never have achieved the inventions which America brought forth from them."

Our scientific laboratories will still attract the Sikorskys and the Steinmetzes, and will bring out their creative best. But where will be the environment to produce more Thomas Davenports? Where will be the environment to bring out the creative power of America's rank-and-file?

3.

Urbanitis, as well as anemia, tends to enfeeble our creative health. Said Oswald Spengler, "The country bore the country-town and nourished it with her best blood. Now the giant city sucks the country dry, insatiably and incessantly demanding and devouring fresh streams of men. . . ." Whereas 50 years ago two-thirds of us lived on farms or in villages, nearly two-thirds of us now crowd our metropolitan areas.

As a native of New York, I have been impressed by the way country boys made good in that city. One reason for this is that the brother with the greater gumption and imagination was the one who left home to conquer the big town. Then, too, he had been brought up on chores and challenges. Even his hunting and fishing back home had called for the kind of effort which makes for creativity. In the big city, spectatorship tends to supplant participation in sports. Television now aggravates this tendency to sit supinely and watch paid players perform their resourceful feats.

The metropolitan dweller has had no need to be a jack-of-all-trades. "Around the corner" there have been men to fix the plumbing, paper the walls, paint the house, and all that.

Specialism tends to breed a "let-George-do-it" attitude among men engaged in mass-production. I walked through a big machine-shop with the proprietor who, 20 years before, had been a machinist himself. Men were standing or sitting here and there. I pointed to one of them and asked:

"What are his duties supposed to be?"

"Oh, he just watches those two machines. He could just as well watch six."

"Does he fix the machine if it gets out of whack?" I asked.

"Why, no; at the first sign of trouble, he just stops the machine and calls for one of our maintenance men."

With such a combination of effortlessness and specialism, how can the rank-and-file be expected to keep up their creative power the way the previous generation did?

Specialism drains creative power even in the country. A generation ago I knew a farmer toward whom I felt a real inferiority complex. I then knew how to report a murder trial; but in most ways he was far more ingenious than I. When one of his machines broke down, his creative energy and skill had it working again before sundown. His son now operates the same farm. When one of his machines goes hay-wire, he 'phones a specialist 15 miles away to motor over and fix it up.

The very speed of the telephone and motor-car have spread specialism and have thus contributed to a widespread slump in ingenuity. In the early days of the automobile, motorists simply had to "get out and get under;" but now, when stalled, we just 'phone the nearest garage for a tow. Even professional drivers no longer whet their resourcefulness on their motor-troubles. A fouled spark-plug is enough to stump most of today's taxi-drivers.

Radio, on the farm as well as in the city, does away with effort on the part of the listener and thus undermines creativity. Nor do the movies furnish any mental exercise except to those who create them. Comics and batting averages tend to take the place of conversation. Our fathers spent much of their leisure in discussion, even debate, which helped sharpen their minds. Most of us now get our opinions second-hand from commentators and columnists.

Where are the home games of our boyhood—like the charades which used to do so much to develop creative imagination? "We've lost our talent for fun," said Philip Wylie, "it's too organized, too second-hand. Family games at home are all gone. We sit around the radio and listen to Oscar Levant playing games for us. . . ."

"Modern civilization," said Dr. Carrel, "seems to be in-

capable of producing people endowed with imagination. . . ."
And, if Spengler is right, a most destructive phase of American civilization is our exodus from country to city—with the
resultant debilitation of creative power through urbanitis.

4.

Compared to the past, and compared to the rest of the
world, nearly all of us are relatively prosperous. Such prosperity tends to weaken creative power, mainly because, with
no wolf at the door, most men lose their power of effort. Easy
living not only numbs creativity, but tends to make us over-
critical—to feel puffed up, to feel like sneering at those who
stick out their necks with ideas. This attitude in turn tends
to cramp our own creative power.

In the long run, the have-nots will be more ingenious
than the haves. This is true as between individuals and between families in our own country. And, among the nations,
there is an alarming likelihood that those who envy our
prosperity may be spurred by their adversity to creative
heights which may eclipse the ingenuity of prosperous
America.

Our world wars have had a mixed effect. In some ways
they contributed to a possible decline in our nation's creative
power; in other ways they served as a spur.

Both wars stimulated our creative scientists. America entirely depended upon Germany for scientific laboratory
glassware until World War I forced American ingenuity to
lick that problem. The same was true of dyestuffs.

World War II precipitated one creative achievement after
another almost overnight. Nylon was perfected to take the
place of silk, for which America formerly had to pay Japan
over $100,000,000 a year. Spearheaded by the B. F. Goodrich
Company, America was forced to create general-purpose
synthetic rubber. Those are only two of scores of examples.

War, however, has a crippling effect on artists and writers.
"The decline of creative imagination in the fields of litera-

ture and the theatre during war," said Leslie Pearl, "is one of those phenomena so frequently observed and so widely discussed that it has become almost a truism."

Women have more imaginative talent than men, and war tends to widen this superiority by enforcing the effort which turns talent into creative power. During the last war, housewives had to make old things do for new things they could not buy; they had to meet a three-time-a-day creative challenge to get the best for their tables out of so few ration-stamps.

What did war do to their husbands and brothers in uniform? Over 11,000,000 Americans spent an average of one and a half years in the services—largely taking orders, seldom thinking up. Thus over 50 billion man-hours were spent between 1940 and 1945. Undoubtedly the training aimed to teach both officers and men self-reliance and resourcefulness. But, by and large, only those who were in combat were called upon for all-out initiative. And they amply measured up. Said Colonel James Wood, who commanded artillery which spearheaded the Normandy invasion: "Our boys had the guts and ingenuity to act on their own instead of waiting for orders."

Those who were on their own by nature of their duties especially gained in creative power. One combat flier came to us out of the war with practically no business background. We took him on and, within two years, he rose faster than almost any other man we had ever hired. His resourcefulness was what did it for him.

In most cases, however, military training cannot help but regiment men's minds. The initiative so vital to creative effort cannot be courted except for combat purposes. Even junior officers have to learn *not* to stick out their necks. "During the war," said W. W. Lyman, Jr., "reserve officers experienced untold frustration . . . the man with the hot idea invariably failed to reach first base because of fear or jealousy on the part of the officers over him. In too many cases initiative was discouraged rather than encouraged."

5.

Recent polls reveal that fewer than 50 per cent of our people believe that hard work pays.

There's enough in such reports to make any American wake up at night and worry about the future of his country's creative power. For belief in the rewards of hard work is what made America ingenious; and the loss of that belief can tear down our ingenuity.

Our new "why-try" philosophy is the rotten apple in our barrel. Whereas "work-hard-and-be-happy" used to be a religion with most of us, it's now: "Take it easy and don't worry." This new sophistry, more than anything else, endangers America's creative power.

Justifiable fear used to be a healthy tonic. Before the war, many a worker was glad to work hard to keep his job; but now many of us go through the motions with the comforting thought: "They can't fire me." In my father's time, fear of the poorhouse was a prod. Now we lull our sense of effort with the assurance that the taxpayers will take care of our old age or our own hard luck.

The opportunity for wealth used to activate almost every young American. Now almost every poll taken among high-school seniors as to what employment they would choose puts civil service at the top of the list. During the past decade or so, the number of employees on public payrolls has more than doubled. This fact alone is a manifestation of our new "don't-take-a-chance" philosophy. A similar mania for safe and easy berths was one of the causes of the decline of France, according to Henri Le Chatelier.

War contributed to America's passion for lessened effort; but war also pushed taxes up so high that our sons feel far less financial incentive to extend themselves than we, their fathers, felt.

Oh, how we need ideas as to how to teach the sons of America that the god of indolence is a false idol! Oh, how we need to make them understand that, in the words of Dr.

Hardin Craig, "with intelligent effort, greater achievement in this world is still possible." If they only knew what we employers know—how much harder it is to hire a creatively powerful man at $25,000 a year than another man at $3,000.

Some day America may re-awaken to the truth that old-fashioned effort makes us feel better—not only physically, but in our sense of well-being. If and when our people put this true god back on its pedestal, America's creative power will be assured. But as things stand today, we cannot be complacent—we need to think hard on how to counteract the influences which are undermining the future of America's creative power.

Chapter XLI

CREATIVE POWER NEEDS MORE
HELP FROM *EDUCATION*

OUR INHERITANCE IS SUCH that for generations ahead, much of our native *talent* will stay with us. The question is: "Will that talent be static or dynamic?" The answer will depend on how well we *understand*, how steadily we *exercise*, how consciously we *empower* that talent.

Our new environment tends to sap the creative power of all of us except the few who use ingenuity in their daily work, as in the arts and in the creative phases of science and business. What about the nine-out-of-ten of our people whose duties call for little or no imagination? What could be substituted for the forces which formerly kept their creative muscles in shape?

The growth of suggestion systems throughout our factories is one new help toward that end. How about education? Although "education can never be a panacea," as Dr. Robert Hutchins remarked, education could at least act as a leaven—and, importantly so, because in the long run, what education does for youth does much to determine our nation's future.

Many have looked upon recent trends in education as hostile to creative effort. Some go so far as to think Elbert Hubbard was right in railing against all forms of higher education, save one—"The University of Hard Knocks." When Al

Smith was asked if he was sorry he had not gone to college, the great Governor declared: "I probably learned more while working in the Fulton Fish Market than I would have learned in any university."

There have been exceptions like Elbert Hubbard and Al Smith, "but," as Donald Cowling and Carter Davidson have said, "the experience of mankind shows that those with the complete and thorough background of general and liberal education and professional training will eventually pull ahead of their rivals."

"*Passivity* is the most dangerous pitfall in contemporary education," was the conclusion of a group of college professors. "The student is kept happy and satisfied with himself because he is never given anything that might strain his ability," said the same educators. If this is true, isn't the net effect to weaken the effort so essential to creative power?

Some students still swim against that tide, especially those who have to work their way through college. A mid-western university recently made a survey which showed that these earners, with less time to spend on their studies, rank far higher than those who do no gainful work.

There are also exceptions among the veterans now in our colleges. "These are the cream of the student population —in strength of character, personality, intellectual interest and industriousness," said a professor friend of mine. "Their eager upturned faces would dispel any person's pessimism concerning the quality of thinking and effort in our current classrooms." But the G.I.s will soon graduate, and then Dr. Hardin Craig's criticism may be truer than ever: "If we could only find out why college men are so lazy. . . . There is no other group of men that I know . . . who are so indolent."

One reason is that most of our sons deliberately spend their college years just "getting by." The passivity of the college program encourages this lack of exertion. If our future leaders are thus subjected to four years of training in *not trying*, whence will come the effort indispensable to creative power?

2.

To offset that blight, couldn't we do more to give our students a new *concept of effort*? For example, a professor of English might well go out of his way to explode the popular notion that writers are "born," and that what they write just writes itself. He might discuss with students the *lives* of authors as evidence to the contrary. Nearly all their autobiographies rate effort above talent. A professor of music might do likewise. He could discuss Stravinsky's *Poetics of Music*, which stresses how little part inspiration plays in creating compositions.

Shouldn't our educators also try harder to make students understand that the development of conscious effort is a fundamental *purpose* of their education? It certainly *should* be, if there is any truth in Thomas Huxley's statement that "*the most valuable* result of all education is the ability to make yourself do the thing you have to do, when it ought to be done, whether you like it or not."

It might also be well to present to students the "try-again" philosophy as spelled out by Charles Kettering: "If a student flunks once, he is out; but an inventor is almost always failing—he tries and fails maybe a thousand times. These two things are diametrically opposite. Our biggest job is to teach how to fail intelligently . . . to keep on trying and failing and trying." Surely, no man can make the most of his creative power until he has learned that lesson.

And shouldn't the student's mind be disabused of the fallacy that indolence is *healthful*? In classes in hygiene, in physiology and wherever possible, shouldn't he be taught the truth that exertion and health go hand-in-hand—that, according to Dr. Carrel, even "*ceaseless*" work makes us strong? To his students, a professor might say: "Why is it that, on the average, you can expect to live 17 years longer than your grandfathers could expect to live at your age? Is it because you are taking it easier? No! It is because of the life-lengthening therapies like penicillin which scientists have produced.

How did they create them? By *driving* their creative minds hard, and often around the clock."

Most students look at professors and think, "What soft berths they have!" The truth is that good professors put in plenty of hard effort. One whom I know, who *seemingly* works only the 14 hours a week in which he conducts classes, *actually* puts in a good 52 hours a week. And these other hours are just as hard as classwork, for they consist of concentrated preparation, tough personal conferences with students, and creative criticism of work handed in.

Professor Hardin Craig went from Stanford to the University of North Carolina and chose to make himself an Evangelist of Effort on Chapel Hill. Even a one-man campaign such as his could do much to give a student-body a new concept of the indispensability and the satisfaction of trying and trying *hard*. Any educator who might undertake such a drive might find himself unexpectedly popular as a result. American students may be hungry for such a doctrine, as Dr. Craig seemed to find out. In his first address to the student-body, he pulled no punches, and yet, "the students, as well as the faculty, gave him an *ovation*." So reported R. B. House, his president.

3.

Let's leave effort for a moment and discuss education's influence on talent. According to Stanley Czurles, Director of Art Education at New York State College for Teachers, "a child is highly creative until he starts at school. Then, under traditional procedures, almost all our teaching tends to cramp his imagination."

"For instance," said Dr. Czurles, "when in the traditional manner all pupils are given pieces of paper, all of the same color; are told just how to fold and mark them, all in the same way; are shown just how and where to cut, all in the same pattern; the result is that every child comes out with exactly the same design. There is no stimulation of the imagination, no incentive for creativeness. Individual ideas are submerged by concern for a poorly justified conformity.

"How much better it would be to stimulate them to select color, to cut and fold so as to explore various possibilities, according to individual initiative. In this way we would fan the creative spark, whereas, through standardization, we tend to stifle it."

Although memorizing does induce effort, memory-stuffing is another threat to talent. Said Alonzo G. Grace, Connecticut's Commissioner of Education, "We cannot develop creativeness by causing the individual to memorize." Our memories serve best as fuel-bins for our imaginations. Education and experience tend to stock them with good coals; but, oh, the clinkers that come in with much of our formal instruction —clinkers in the form of dead data! "Nothing in education is so astonishing as the amount of ignorance it accumulates in the form of inert facts," said Henry Adams.

Those are a few of education's negative effects on creative talent. What by way of positive influence is being attempted? Trade-schools are the outstanding exponents of creative exercise. The need for more of this has been stressed by Education Commissioner Grace of Connecticut: "The opportunities to do creative work must be present not only in the laboratories and classrooms, but in the procedure of the instructor himself. Recently, I visited cne of our trade schools. Its laboratory was built from the junk-yards, from the cast-off materials of industry, and from whatever could be picked up here and there around the community. Boys designed the instruments and the appliances; the laboratory is their creation. We need more of this. The opportunity to create should be provided in every school and class."

4.

There is an even greater dearth of creative exercise in higher education. Said A. R. Stevenson, Jr., General Electric executive: "When we are selecting college graduates for employment, we like to ask the dean of students: 'Does this young man have ingenuity or creative ability?' Too often the answer is: 'I don't know, there is nothing in the college course which gave him a chance to show it.'" It is a hopeful sign that more and more educational leaders are recognizing this lack. Strangely enough, technical educators, rather than liberal educators, seem to be taking the lead. For instance, A. R. Cullimore, President of the Newark College of Engineering, stressed the need of more education in creative power as of "exclusive importance." He said that this means that "we must set up machinery to stimulate it. . . . It means, certainly, setting up an environment, a place in which this process can go on unhampered and under conditions which will allow the formation of as many images, as many hypotheses, as many suggestions as possible."

If education were to adopt a new concept of the importance of creative power, our colleges would need more clearly to distinguish between planting knowledge and training the mind. Tradition has tended to over-emphasize knowledge. We should recognize that knowledge is not power if made up merely of "inert facts" instead of active fuel for the mind. We should put *understanding* above *knowledge* in every field of study. Any such emphasis cannot help but play up principles and ideas rather than inert content. And this meets the specification laid down by Anatole France: "Let our teaching be full of *ideas*. Hitherto it has been stuffed only with facts."

Our newer concept of knowledge should go further—it should give greater emphasis to *action*. "The failures of modern American education may be due to a tendency to emphasize 'knowing' at the expense of 'doing'," said a leading professor just recently. He thus echoed the words spoken 85 years ago by Herbert Spencer: "The great aim of education is not knowledge, but *action*. Wisdom is the right use of knowledge. To know is not to be wise. Many men know a great deal and are the greater fools for it. There is no fool so great a fool as a knowing fool. But to know how to *use* knowledge is to have wisdom."

And a similar sentiment was expressed 40 years ago by A. Lawrence Lowell when inaugurated as president of Harvard: "Education is not knowledge. It is an attitude of mind, an ability to use information rather than a memory stocked with facts."

Another phase of the needed new concept calls for more emphasis on *mind-training*. "The whole object of education is, or should be, to develop the mind," said Sherwood Anderson. "The mind should be a thing that *works*." In what way should education train minds to work? Critically and judicially? Present-day teaching does that well—perhaps too well when, by over-training our logical reasoning, we tend to make *reason* crowd out *imagination*. This hazard was pointed out by Professor R. W. Gerard of the University of Chicago: "There is the danger of reason stifling imagination, that 'enterprises of great pith and moment' will be 'sicklied o'er with the pale cast of thought.'" Shakespeare practiced what he quoth.

Surely education should give elbow-room to imagination. Perhaps it might well go so far as to glorify imagination. A new and more dynamic concept might well recognize that only creative imagination can give wings to a man's education.

5.

Psychologists are stressing more and more the need to "motivate" the student—to focus his mind on the goal he should expect to attain. Shouldn't we try to make the student think more *about* his mind, and more *of* his mind? To that end, we might motivate through inspiration, and lead him to look up to the mind with the reverence it warrants. In *Human Destiny*, du Noüy concluded that the human brain took 1600 million years to evolve. Wouldn't this awe-inspiring fact be worth stressing? And also the fact that nearly all great thinkers have agreed that *creative imagination* is *the* gift which sets man apart from animals? Even our pride might be appealed to on this point.

College presidents Donald Cowling and Carter Davidson recently clarified "the more essential capacities of the human mind" in their book, *Colleges for Freedom*. Here are five of the seven keys they listed:

"The ability to concentrate attention . . . recognizing the problem to be solved. . . ."

"Accuracies in observation—the ability to see similarities and differences. . . ."

"A retentive memory—the power of 'recovery' or selective recall. . . ."

"Logical reasoning, both deductive and inductive, including analysis and synthesis. . . ."

"Judgment, which remains suspended until all the evidence is in, weighs it critically, recognizes absurdities and inadequacies, then finally evaluates fairly, without prejudice. . . ."

Those five capacities, more or less *incidental* to creative thinking, have most to do with the *judicial* mind which analyzes, compares and chooses. Most college courses do much to train the *judicial* mind.

Two other capacities have to do mainly with our *creative* mind and its power to visualize, foresee and generate ideas. These capacities are described partly as follows in the Cowling-Davidson list:

"Sensitivity of association—A student who is able to concentrate, observe, and memorize may be severely handicapped by insensitivity. Tests indicate that this is a quality which can be improved by training. In the arts it is what Shakespeare and his contemporaries called 'fancy.' It has resulted in figures of speech. . . . In science it may take the form of perceiving new combinations and relationships which lead to the invention of new machines, processes, and products. . . .

"Creative imagination, which takes many diverse parts

and molds them into a new unity. Modern education calls this integration, the attempt to perceive unity in the midst of diversity, to create order and beauty out of chaos. It is the ability to suggest new hypotheses which open up vast new avenues of thought. . . ."

One would expect these latter two *creative* capacities to be covered well in the literature of psychology; but, for some reason, nearly all textbooks seem to slight them. Just as strangely, the *Encyclopaedia Britannica* devotes about 65,000 words to the subject of psychology with not much more than a mention of imagination.

Admittedly, all too little is known about the creative mind. But, surely, this is no reason why students should not be exposed to the much that *is* known. Shouldn't we at least make them *conscious* of their creative capacities? Shouldn't we impart to them the *importance* of their creative mind? Shouldn't we convince them that their creative power does not depend entirely upon talent alone, but also on *will-power?*

6.

"You don't really *know* until you *do,*" said Dr. Edgar Dale, Ohio State's professor of education. By the same token, you learn better when you *take part,* and this is a fact of great force in developing creative power.

"In dealing with children," said Alexander Graham Bell, "the main essential is not to *tell* them things, but to encourage them to find out things for themselves. . . . For example, suppose you wanted to teach a child about moisture and condensation. . . . Ask him to breathe into a glass tumbler. He sees the moisture on the glass. Ask him where it came from. Have him breathe aganst the outside of the tumbler. Have him try the experiment with a glass that is hot and with one that is ice-cold. Have him try it with other surfaces. Don't do his thinking for him."

If it did not cost too much, almost every educator would

prefer to teach *small* groups through seminars rather than *large* groups through lectures and recitations, and mainly for the reason that seminars compel students to *participate*. Seminars could include more projects which demand imaginative thinking. A seminar could do much more to step up creative power if, from time to time, it should become a *brainstorming* group—to think up the *what-if* and the *what-else,* instead of to debate the what-is and the what-isn't.

Elliott Dunlap Smith of Carnegie Tech has also proposed more creative projects *outside* the curriculum: "Students should be assigned creative problems outside of their customary field of work. Such an alien approach, as it so often has with great inventions, may provide a suggestive setting."

No man has been a greater apostle of creative power than Charles Kettering, or a more outspoken critic of higher education. He is strong for the *cooperative* system. He has not only been one of the spark-plugs of Antioch, but also worked with Dean Schneider at Cincinnati for many years and, just before Dean Schneider died, helped him set up a *cooperative* system at Northwestern. But even cooperative education could be pointed up to accentuate *creative* effort. For instance, when a student leaves the campus for a between-term job, why not assign to him the problem of thinking up an idea each day while away?

Many of us got most of our creative training from extracurricular activities while in college. My own creative effort was stepped up by editing the college newspaper, by writing short stories and "poetry" for the literary magazine edited by my classmate, Alexander Woollcott—and by working with Woollcott in organizing a dramatic group, still known as the "Charlatans." Surely such activities should be encouraged by educators. And every effort should be made to expand them.

Even pranks can help develop creativity. It might not be too well to encourage mischief like carrying a live cow into the chapel belfry, but the invention of clean fun should be encouraged. For instance, instead of an inter-fraternity bridge tournament, why not an inter-fraternity gag-writing contest?

Education might well also call for more outside reading. Yale is about to do this by requiring students to read six books during summer vacation, chosen from a list specified by the college. But why shouldn't such books be selected mainly on the basis of their value as creative stimulants—such as the life of Benvenuto Cellini?

To induce creativity, educators should do their best to arouse enthusiasm for imaginative thinking, to encourage every creative effort on the part of their pupils, to act as creative *coaches*. It should be natural for most teachers to do this because, as a class, they rate well up in creative aptitudes. Scientific tests show them to be *twice* as rich in creative imagination as in the power of observation. And, the more imagination they pack into their work, the more effective they are. O. C. Carmichael, head of the Carnegie Foundation for the Advancement of Teaching, has concluded that "the imaginative teacher is the ablest teacher."

By devoting more time and effort to the student's *creative* mind, the good teacher can also get more out of life. For, as Cowling and Davidson put it, *"in the cultivation of creative power lies the greatest joy of the teacher, and the greatest hope for a better world."*

7.

Why not make a conscious effort to weave more of the creative into subjects taught in college? For one thing, by high-lighting the creative, we can put more *life* into a subject and thus teach it better. "The more one vitalizes a presentation," said Professor Paul Eaton, "the sharper will be the rise in the learning curve."

Psychology should, of course, play up creativity more than it usually does. The teaching of English stresses imaginative effort, but could do so more fully. The enforced writing of original compositions is the kind of exercise that is needed. St. John's College made a name for itself by using "The Great Books" as the backbone of its education. What else but creative thought made those books great? Why not high-light the *creative* in them at every turn? In all literature courses, why not lead the student to *look* for, to *take* in, and to be *inspired* by the *creative* thinking in each classic?

We now recognize that history is essentially a serial of *ideas*. History demonstrates how, as in all creative thinking, one idea leads to another—and how big ideas form from many little ideas. If we were to play up the creative thinking that has *made* history, we could teach it better and, at the same time, help stimulate the student's creative mind. We might even use history for creative exercise, as Arnold Hahn has suggested, and ask such questions as: "What would have happened if America had not been discovered by Columbus until the nineteenth century?" . . . "What would have happened if Hitler had made a fair truce with Britain before too late?"

Creative thinking could also be woven into the sciences— even into mathematics. By delving into the lives of the great mathematicians, we could inspire students with the part played by their creative power. The testimony of Sir William Hamilton, Poincaré, and others might well be quoted.

Sciences lend themselves readily to creative indoctrination of the student, as Dr. Conant of Harvard pointed out when he proposed "the establishment of one or more courses at the college level on the Tactics and Strategy of Science. The objective would be to give a greater degree of understanding of sciences by the close study of a relatively few historical examples of the *development* of science." Thus Dr. Conant recommended that science be taught to liberal arts students in terms of case-histories, with emphasis on *creativity*.

Might it not be well, too, to put far greater emphasis on imagination in almost every subject taught in scientific schools? Likewise in law school and in medical school? Yes, even in the theological seminary! For no minister can live up to his calling unless he is truly creative.

8.

Is creative power important enough to justify a separate course? Maybe there should be such in upper classes. The workings of man's creative mind could well be as worthy of a course as is abnormal psychology or the psychology of animals.

There is justifiable skepticism as to the practicability of a course in creativity. One educator agreed that "men can be inspired, even tutored, in creative work," but he doubted the feasibility of creating a "formal course of study." On the other hand, there *are* a few precedents. The University of Nebraska, for instance, inaugurated a course in creative thinking in 1931 and, under the able leadership of Professor Robert Crawford, made it work well. He carried on with this until he was pulled into the war. Writing from Japan where he is just completing a vital job for General MacArthur, he recently informed me: "I expect to return to active teaching at the University this fall and I shall again conduct the course in person. There is no question of the successful nature of the course. Students write and tell me so years after and complimentary letters come in from distant parts of the world."

Here is one testimonial Professor Crawford received a few months ago: "Very shortly after I began the course I hit upon a good business idea that resulted in establishing a new business in Cleveland which has provided steady employment for several persons and over $17,000 surplus for the stockholders." And a girl who studied creative thinking under Crawford wrote this: "I think a course in Creative Thinking should be required in college. Perhaps our world would develop more rapidly if college students were required to take such a course."

Then, too, the General Electric Company has long conducted a course in creative engineering. The purpose is to "teach inventors to invent." College graduates are shifted from laboratory to laboratory "to get the stimulus of rubbing up against the company's most creative minds." Brainstorm sessions are conducted almost every day. The classwork consists mainly of challenges to ingenuity. A typical problem is: "How would you go about inventing a machine to typewrite music?" "The results have been amazing," said Dr. Suits. "One young man who had never invented anything before was inspired during his two years with the class to produce 13 patentable ideas. Others doubled their output."

In that case, creative effort comprised the whole curriculum. The Army conducted a far-flung course for supervisory employees during the war which was known as "Job Methods Training." This was taught in five lessons of two hours each, to groups of ten. It dwelt on both analytical and creative thinking. Even so brief a course, straddling two vast subjects, worked wonders, in the opinion of the Army's administrative officers.

If educators thought that a special course in creative thinking could and should be added to the regular college program, one problem would be that of a textbook. Isn't it a bit strange that publishers have not seen fit to put out adequate textbooks on this subject, and yet have seen fit to put out textbooks on *Wasps and Their Ways* and on *The Irritability of the Flea*? (These, by the way, are *actual* titles of *actual* textbooks.) But a course would need more than a textbook. It would need a program of seminars and, as in the General Electric course, these group-conferences might well take the form of brainstorm sessions as described in a previous chapter. Such a course would also call for outside assignments of creative projects of various types.

A special course in creative thinking might present an especial opportunity for liberal-arts colleges. The cry might arise that this would mean going "vocational," and, in a way, this would be true—for, to learn how to work one's creative mind *is* a definite step toward learning how to make a living in *any* vocation or profession. Alumni and students of liberal-arts colleges might welcome such a course with open arms.

"One of the weakest spots in all college curricula," said Lee H. Bristol, speaking as a liberal-arts alumnus, "is the area of realistically preparing a student for the world and the career that follows graduation. . . . I believe that colleges can do a real job, as time goes on, in this neglected field of preparing our undergraduates for meeting the world that awaits them." As to the attitude of students, Oscar W. Kuolt said: "They will welcome whatever they consider as *practical* aspects of a liberal arts education."

Concentration of education on the creative mind might radically re-make education, according to Professor H. A. Overstreet: "Let us suppose that we should become convinced that creative power is possessed by everybody; and that there are ways of stimulating and of training it which are capable of increasing it far beyond its latent condition. . . . Education would be revolutionized. . . . Its major energies would be directed towards the arousing and training of the inventive powers. . . . A society alive with inventive power would, on the whole, be the most powerfully progressive society."

9.

"Civilization is a race between education and catastrophe." America's future may involve a similar race between education and our ability to keep ahead creatively. "The challenge confronts us as educators," said Professor Eaton, "to develop ingenuity, initiative, and resourcefulness. . . . This challenge becomes the more important when we are brought to the stern realization that the economic supremacy of our country may soon rest upon the creative ability of our citizens rather than upon the rich natural resources we once possessed."

Our fate may be in the hands of other nations. For a time Japan was our worst threat; but Japan lacked what it would take. One shortage was in imagination. Lafcadio Hearn was prophetic when, years ago, he said: "Imagination, the Japs lack it. Unless they acquire it, they will vanish off the face of the earth."

For a time, Germany was an even greater threat. She had a scientific élite of well-nigh unbeatable creative power; but her people had suffered their imaginations to be cramped by rigid regimentation.

And now Russia. Russia has created and organized her scientific élite. The big question is whether the Soviet people, like the Germans, will find their minds too fettered to be creative enough.

It *has* been true that ingenuity has flourished best in democracies, where the urge-to-try has gone hand-in-hand with freedom. Our basic danger is that liberty will breed laxity and that apathy will sap the creative power of our people.

What can be done to offset that danger? This question is a challenge, not only to educators, but to *every* American.

Index

Abercrombie and Fitch, 123
Ability, creative, 31
Absorbine Jr., 152
Accademia del Cimento, 256
Accidents, creative, 239–245
Acheson, Dr. Edward Goodrich, 323, 327
Action, as aim of education, 345
Adams, Henry, 344
Adams, Stanley, "There Are Such Things," 85
Adaptation:
  in humor, 161
  in music, 162
  of a process, 165
  in writing, 161
Adler shoes, 178
Adrian, 163
Advanced Study Group, 267
Advertising Agency Association, 221
Aiken, Daymond, 69
Aims:
  to assay, 131
  basic, 131
  specific, 131
Aladdin's lamp, 6, 23, 49–52, 56
Albright Art Gallery, 217
Alcoholics Anonymous, 202
Alexanderson, Dr. E. F. W., 38
Allegheny-Ludlum Company, 297
Allegories, *see* Similarity
Allen, Fred, 169
Allis-Chalmers Company, strike, 296
Alternatives, 92, 143–155
Altrock, Nick, 180
Aluminum Company of America, 5

American, The, 112
American Chemical Society's Committee on Professional Training, The, 320
American Society of Mechanical Engineers, The, 320
American Sugar Company, 172
American Tobacco Company, 179
"Amos and Andy" (Freeman Gosden and Charles Correll), 261
Analysis:
  aid to imagination, 133
  medical, 137
  over-emphasis of, 308
And Now To Live Again by Betsey Barton, 14
"Andantino in D Flat," *See* "Moonlight and Roses"
Anderson, Sherwood, 346
Angle Tooth Brush, 10
Anthony, John, 182
Antithesis, 65, 212
Antu, 153
"Anxious fear," 45
Appel, Joseph, 219
Arabian Nights, The, 6
Archimedes, "eureka" story, 195
Armstrong Cork Company, 281
Arnold, General H. H., 328
Arrow shirts, 194
Association:
  action of, 71
  in creative research, 324
  power of, 222
  sensitivity of, 347
Association, three laws of, 64, 140
Associationism, 62
"At Sunset" by Julia Ward Howe, 30

357

358

374